D1131347

Apocalypse 1692

Apocalypse

1692

EMPIRE, SLAVERY, and the
GREAT PORT ROYAL EARTHQUAKE

BEN HUGHES

WESTHOLME
Yardley

Westholme Publishing, LLC
904 Edgewood Road
Yardley, Pennsylvania 19067
Visit our Web site at www.westholmepublishing.com

ISBN: 978-1-59416-287-9
Also available as an eBook.

Printed in the United States of America.

Contents

Illustrations

MAPS

ILLUSTRATIONS

Chronology

1502	The first African slaves arrive in the Americas.
1509	The Spanish settle Jamaica.
1642–46	The English Civil War.
1649	Charles I is executed.
1652–54	The First Anglo-Dutch War.
1653	Oliver Cromwell is appointed Lord Protector.
1655	An English expeditionary force under General Venables and Admiral Penn captures Jamaica from Spain as part of Cromwell's Western Design.
1658	Oliver Cromwell dies.
1660	Charles II ascends to the throne thus restoring the line of the Stuarts.
1662	The growing English settlement on Point Cagway, Jamaica, is first referred to as Port Royal.
1664	The English capture the fort of Carolusburg (later renamed Cape Coast Castle) on the Gold Coast of West Africa in the prelude to the Second Anglo-Dutch War.
1665–67	The Second Anglo-Dutch War.
1670	With the Treaty of Madrid Spain recognizes the English right of possession to Jamaica.
1672–74	The Third Anglo-Dutch War.
1673	A major revolt of Coromantee slaves breaks out on Lobby's estate, St. Ann's Parish, Jamaica.
1678	A slave revolt breaks out on Duck's estate, St. Catherine's Parish, Jamaica.
1680	Spanish agents begin purchasing slaves in Jamaica for transshipment to the Spanish colonies of the Americas.

1688	The Glorious Revolution sees James II flee to France and William and Mary crowned joint monarchs of England.
1688-97	The Nine Years' War. France fights the English, Spanish, and Dutch in Europe and the New World.
1689	Aphra Behn writes *Oroonoko, or the Royal Slave, a True History*. September: The Earl of Inchiquin is commissioned governor of Jamaica.
1690	July: Jamaica's largest slave revolt to date, believed to have been led by an Akan slave named Cudjoe, breaks out on Sutton's estate, Clarendon Parish.
1691	March to May: Inchiquin launches a raid against the privateers of Hispaniola.
1692	January: Governor Inchiquin dies and is replaced as temporary head of the island council by Councillor John White. June: A massive earthquake destroys Port Royal.
1693	March: William Beeston, Inchiquin's permanent replacement, arrives at Jamaica.
1694	June to July: A major French invasion is repulsed.
1730-40	The First Maroon War breaks out in Jamaica.
1738	March: Cudjoe signs a peace treaty with the governor of Jamaica giving the Leeward Maroons the right to live unmolested in the Cockpit Country.
1807	The trade in slaves is abolished throughout the British Empire, although slavery continues in the colonies.
1962	Jamaica gains its independence from Britain.

Maps

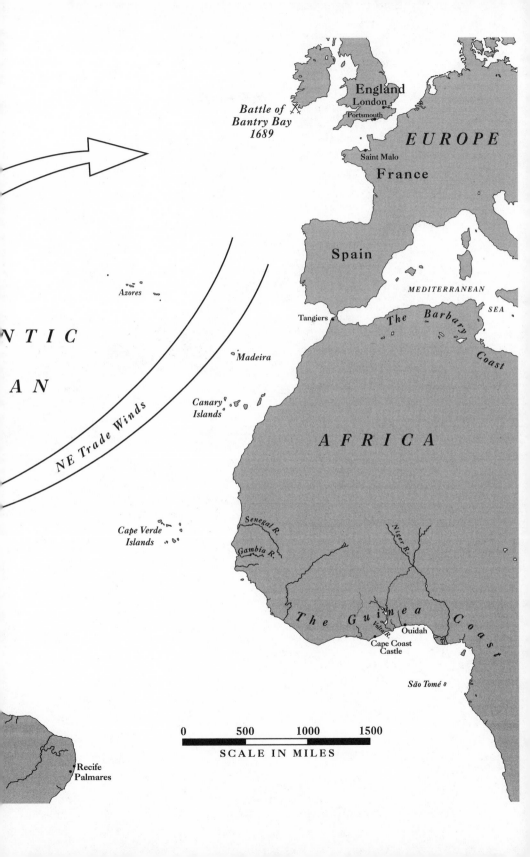

England
London
Portsmouth

Battle of
Bantry Bay
1689

EUROPE

Saint Malo

France

Spain

MEDITERRANEAN

SEA

Azores

Tangiers

The Barbary Coast

NTIC

AN

Madeira

Canary
Islands

AFRICA

NE Trade Winds

Cape Verde
Islands

Senegal R.

Niger R.

Gambia R.

The Guinea Coast

Volta R.

Ouidah

Cape Coast
Castle

São Tomé

0   500   1000   1500

SCALE IN MILES

Recife
Palmares

DISCARDED

0   100   200   300   400   500

SCALE IN MILES

ATLANTIC

OCEAN

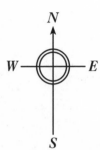

N

W — E

S

Cape
rançois

ispaniola

Puerto Rico

St. Martin

Guavos

Santo
Domingo

Mona

St. Croix

St. Bartholomew

Barbuda

St. Eustatius

Antigua

Cape Altevel

St. Kitts
and Nevis

Montserrat

Guadeloupe

Marie Galante

Dominica

n S e a

Martinique

St. Lucia

L e w a r d   I s l a n d s

W i n d w a r d   I s l a n d s

Barbados

Curaçao

Tobago

Margarita

Trinidad

bo

Caracas

S p a n i s h   M a i n

Orinoco R.

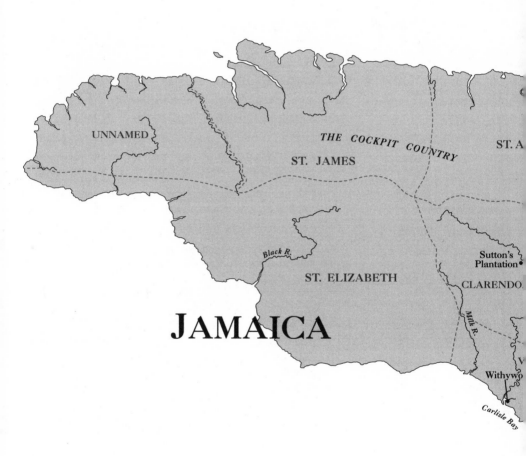

Caribbean S

UNNAMED

THE COCKPIT COUNTRY

ST. A

ST. JAMES

Black R.

Sutton's
Plantation •

ST. ELIZABETH

CLARENDO

JAMAICA

Milk R.

V

Withywo

Carlisle Bay

0   10   20   30   40   50

SCALE IN MILES

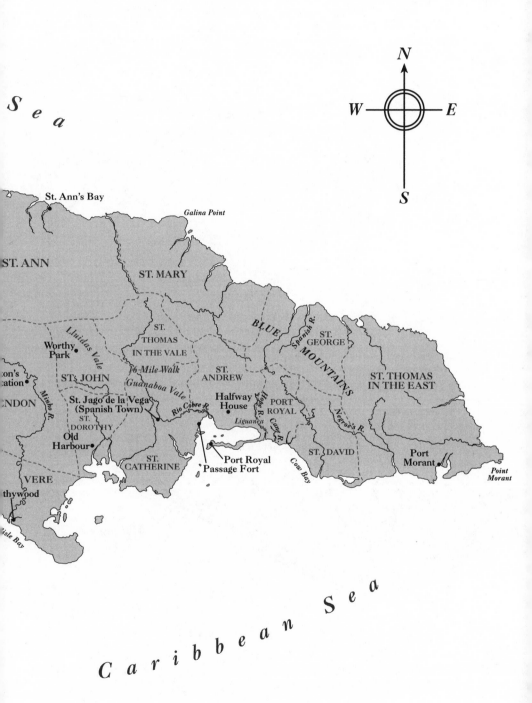

N

W   E

S

Sea

St. Ann's Bay

Galina Point

ST. ANN

ST. MARY

Lluidas Vale

BLUE

Spanish R.

ST.
GEORGE

Worthy
Park

ST.
THOMAS
IN THE VALE

MOUNTAINS

ST. THOMAS
IN THE EAST

:on's
:ation

ST. JOHN

16-Mile Walk

ST.
ANDREW

Minho R.

Guanaboa Vale

:NDON

St. Jago de la Vega
(Spanish Town)

Rio Cobre R.

Halfway
House

PORT
ROYAL

Hope R.

Negro's R.

ST.
DOROTHY

Liguanea

Cane R.

Old
Harbour

ST.
CATHERINE

Port Royal
Passage Fort

ST. DAVID

Port
Morant

Cow Bay

*Point
Morant*

VERE

:thywood

:isle Bay

C a r i b b e a n   S e a

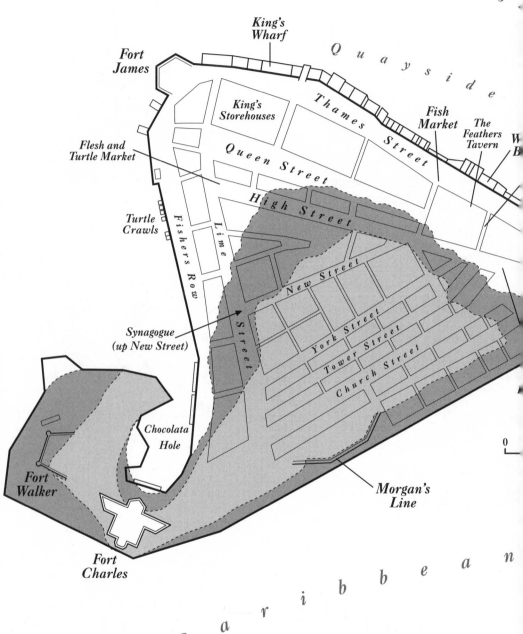

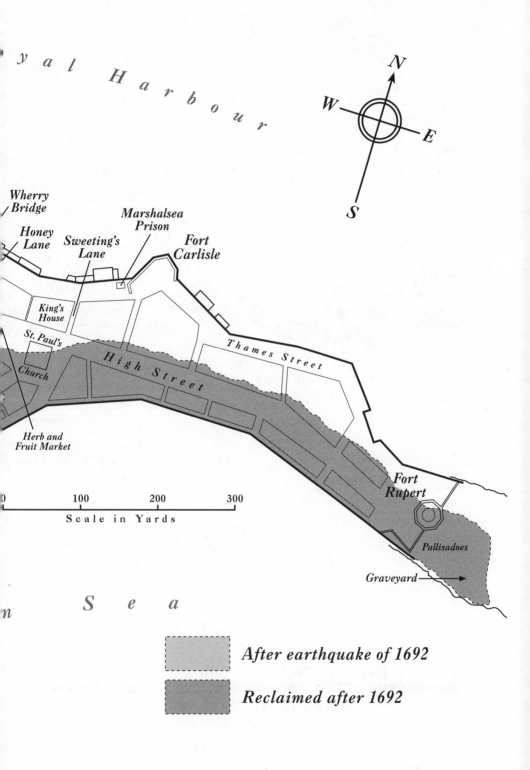

y a l H a r b o u r

N
W — E
S

Wherry
Bridge

Honey
Lane

Sweeting's
Lane

Marshalsea
Prison

Fort
Carlisle

King's
House

St. Paul's

Church

High Street

Thames Street

Herb and
Fruit Market

Fort
Rupert

Pallisadoes

Graveyard

0   100   200   300
Scale in Yards

n S e a

After earthquake of 1692

Reclaimed after 1692

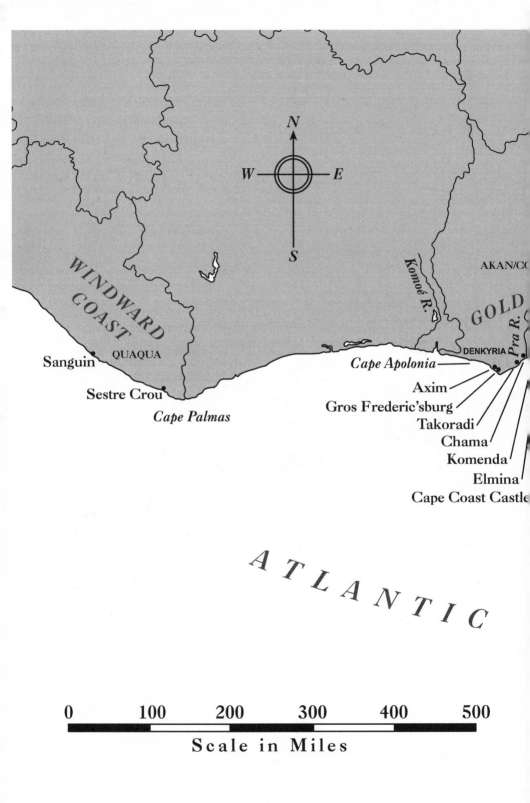

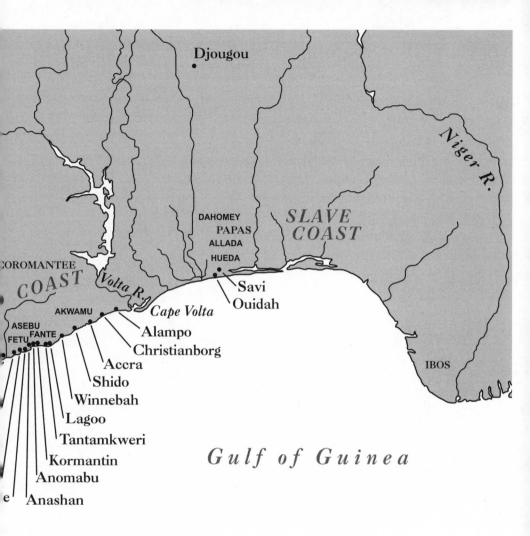

Djougou

Niger R.

DAHOMEY
PAPAS
ALLADA
HUEDA

SLAVE
COAST

COROMANTEE

COAST

Volta R.

AKWAMU

Cape Volta

Savi
Ouidah

Alampo

Christianborg

ASEBU
FETU FANTE

Accra

Shido

Winnebah

Lagoo

Tantamkweri

Kormantin

Anomabu

e Anashan

IBOS

Gulf of Guinea

OCEAN

São Tomé

Prologue

PERCHED ON A SAND SPIT jutting into the muddy waters of Kingston Bay, Port Royal is a sleepy fishing village of 1,600 souls. It is an unassuming place. The sound of the waves slapping the seashore is interrupted only by the fast patrol boats of the Jamaica Defence Force. The locals get by on the profits hooked by a handful of marlin fishermen and a few dollars brought in by occasional tourists seeking an insight into Jamaica's murky past. Those who venture out from the resorts to the north and east of the island and make their way via Michael Manley International Airport and the scrub and sand dunes of the Pallisadoes are rewarded by the sight of a handful of relics which pay tribute to Port Royal's former prominence. Half a mile to the east of town, as the spit narrows, is the eighteenth-century naval cemetery. Crooked gravestones adorned by weather-worn inscriptions bear witness to the toll yellow fever took on the Royal Navy seamen whose base once dominated town. Beyond is the ruin of an octagonal tower, part of the seventeenth-century Fort Rupert. The rest lies under a shallow lagoon whose waters also conceal a large fragment of a brick battery wall. Further on visitors pass Morgan's Harbour, a hotel named after the most famous of Port Royal's former inhabitants: a Welsh farmer turned Caribbean privateer who terrorized the Spanish colonies and rose to the post of lieutenant-general of Jamaica. Beyond Morgan's is St. Peter's Church. Built in 1725–26, the present building lies atop the ruins of its predecessor destroyed on June 7, 1692. An inscription on a gravestone illuminates the events of that day: "Here layes the body of Lewes Galdy. . . . He was swallowed up in the Great Earthquake . . . & by the Providence of God was by another Shock thrown into the Sea & Miraculously saved by swimming until a Boat took him up." Galdy was fortunate indeed: a third of Port Royal sank beneath the sea that day and a third of its 6,500 inhabitants were killed. Buried in the mud and murk of Kingston Bay are the remains of Port Royal's drowned streets. An array of seventeenth-century artifacts have been found: silver pieces of eight and gold doubloons imported by merchants who once traded with the cities of Portobelo and Cartagena; finely crafted pocket watches; gold rings; fragile Chinese porcelain; cannon balls, rusty pistols, and swords; a vast array of broken rum, porter, beer, and wine bottles; iron balances and lead weights; thousands of fragments of clay pipes; and coral-encrusted chains, collars, and manacles once used to constrain the slaves on whose labors the island's legendary former wealth was built.[1]

IN ENGLAND, the second half of the seventeenth century was a period of great change. Where issues of religion, family and clan ties, and the struggle between Parliament and the crown had dominated the early Stuart era, trade, the generation of wealth, and the rise of science and the arts grew in importance after the Restoration in 1660. Three Anglo-Dutch Wars and a series of Navigation Acts prohibiting foreign ships from trading with England's colonies saw the country eclipse the United Netherlands as the leading European player in global trade. This growth was mirrored by an interest in colonial possessions. England's economic and political influence spread along the shores of West Africa, among the islands of the West Indies, the Eastern Seaboard of North America, and the subcontinent of India. In 1688 the Glorious Revolution saw James II, England's last Catholic monarch and would-be emulator of Louis XIV's absolutist France, usurped by the Dutch Stadtholder, William of Orange. The Bill of Rights, passed in 1690, sealed the government's primacy over the crown: the new constitutional monarchs, William and Mary, were unable to suspend laws, levy taxes, make royal appointments, or maintain a standing army without Parliament's permission. The rise of the Whigs saw a shift away from agrarianism and a state-managed mercantilism of cloying tariffs, jealously guarded monopolies, and the belief that global wealth was finite, toward a commercial society built on the potential of free trade.

The Glorious Revolution also gave rise to the Nine Years' War. The conflict pitted France against the League of Augsburg, an alliance of the English, Dutch, Spanish and Swedish, the Duchy of Savoy, and several German principalities of the Holy Roman Empire. While the war's principal theatre, northwestern Europe, played host to a series of bloody stalemates and tactical victories which did little to alter the status quo, the Catholic hinterlands of the British Isles saw ferocious fighting, and a series of engagements in the Channel gradually established England's naval superiority. In the colonies, skirmishes were fought by naval vessels, privateers, and militia on land and sea.[2]

All these changes were evident in Jamaica. In the final decades of the seventeenth century the island emerged from its piratical past into a future of vast wealth and terrible suffering fueled by its sugar monoculture. In the 1690s, the elite deposed the absolutism foisted upon them by a despotic, populist, and self-appointed governor; free traders fought monopolists in the courts, the Council, and Assembly chambers; and the merchants of Port Royal struggled with the plantocracy for control of the island's economy. On the plantations, the subjugation of African slaves caused bloody revolt. Scientists traveled to the colony to study the island's flora and fauna, while the Nine Years' War saw Jamaica raided by French privateers, and the island's militia, naval forces, and privateers launched counterattacks against enemy bases on Hispaniola. *Apocalypse 1692* ties all these threads together in a narrative which explores the personalities and motivations of the individuals involved, from the departure of the colony's newly appointed governor from London in 1689 via the brutalities of the transatlantic slave trade to the cataclysmic events of June 7, 1692.[3]

CHAPTER I

The West Indies Fleet

On the 15th [March] we met a violent storm, which on the 17th increased so much that we were near foundering. The upper deck was full of water up to the gunwales, and the tarpauling not being good the water in the hold was above the ballast. . . . Our foremast was dangerously sprung, and as we ran before the wind a great sea pooped us, filled the cabin so full that it set me and the other gentlemen swimming, and did much damage.
—Governor Kendall to the Earl of Shrewsbury, April 4, 1690

ON A FRIGID DAY in late November 1689, beneath a choking blanket of smog, a forest of two thousand ships' masts was spread across the Thames in London's thriving commercial district. Cursing as they slipped on the cobblestones, scores of laborers manhandled puncheons, casks, crates, bags, and boxes from the riverside warehouses to the cranes at the quayside. Horses and carts, peddlers and hawkers, their breath frosting in the gelid air, added to the confusion. On the river, a turgid, stinking, brown effluent, watermen directed a myriad of wherries, hoys, prams, lighters, and barges ferrying the goods out to mid-river. The ships at anchor in the Pool ranged from 40-ton pinks, sloops, brigs, schooners, and brigantines to mighty broad sterns of over 500 tons bristling with cannon. On board, skeleton crews rigged hoists to the spars and lowered the goods into the ships' cavernous holds. On the north bank stood the Custom House built in the aftermath of the Great Fire of 1666 for a little over £9,000 to Sir

Christopher Wren's design. Illuminated by the wan winter light seeping in through its tall riverside windows, the Long Room on the second floor was busy with merchants and their liveried servants, paying bonds to bewigged clerks for passes to clear their goods. Nearby was the Excise Office, whose police force of several thousand battled hosts of smugglers to enforce the trading laws. In the warren of streets and alleys beyond, merchant sailors loitered in gin shops and dockside inns. Amidst a fug of tobacco, they drank, smoked from communal clay pipes, and played cards, dice, or ten-bones while merchant captains competed for their attention with whores intent on parting the tars from their pay. Alongside the taverns, their signs lit by gas lamps, were several coffee shops. Among the most popular was the Jamaica, in St. Michael's Alley, whose patrons perused the news sheets for updates on the war against France and the situation in the colonies while taking stock of the commodity prices quoted in *Whitson's Merchants Weekly Remembrancer*.[1]

Several blocks to the north was Leadenhall Street, the commercial district's principal thoroughfare. Among the main buildings was the Royal Exchange, an imposing building with an ornate clock tower which stood midway between Cornhill and Threadneedle Street. The upper floor of the exchange housed two hundred shops "full of choice commodities, especially for men's and women's apparel." Downstairs were a series of piazzas surrounding an interior courtyard where merchants traded their goods. Jewish merchants were segregated to the covered colonnades to the southeast. Nearby were Englishmen dealing in Spanish, Portuguese, and Italian products, while those selling Jamaican produce gathered in the southwest corner. A few blocks east were the offices of England's largest joint stock companies, state-backed giants whose royally decreed monopolies had ensured their rise to commercial prominence. The headquarters of the East India Company, a "corporation of men with long heads and deep purses," stood near those of the Royal African Company, an enterprise which had been granted a thousand-year monopoly in West African trade by Charles II in 1670.[2]

An economic revolution was taking place in England in the second half of the seventeenth century. Since the Restoration of 1660, when Charles II had returned to the throne after a decade of Cromwell's

Commonwealth, there had been a boom in ship building and manufacture, and the country's rising merchant class had begun to exploit the emerging markets of the New World. By the end of the century, English merchant shipping was frequenting the ports of North America, the Caribbean, and West Africa, exchanging manufactured goods for lumber, agricultural and animal produce, mineral wealth, and slaves while vessels of the East India Company brought tea, spices, silk, textiles, and porcelain from India and China. In an attempt to secure a global trading hegemony, the English had fought three wars against the Dutch since mid-century. Although frequently bested in the naval battles that characterized these conflicts, the English had eventually ground down their opponents. Backed by Parliament's Navigation Acts of 1651, 1662, 1663, 1670, and 1673, which forbade foreign ships from trading with England's colonies, by the last decade of the seventeenth century London was beginning to outstrip Amsterdam as the principal hub of international trade. Imports and exports had grown by a third since the Restoration, while the lucrative reexport trade, which saw English ships serving the ports of Europe, would rise from a turnover of £700,000 per annum in the 1660s to £1,677,000 by 1699.[3]

FIFTY OF THE merchant vessels at anchor off Custom House Quay that November were bound for the West Indies. After rendezvousing with fourteen warships of the Royal Navy, the fleet was to sail across the Channel, heading south through the Bay of Biscay before calling in at Madeira to gather wood and water and load up with wine. The fleet would then brave the open Atlantic before gathering at Bridgetown, Barbados, from whence eleven merchant vessels, with a single frigate acting as escort, were due to sail on to Port Royal, Jamaica, the commercial hub of the English Caribbean, while the rest of the warships would be sent against the French. As the majority of their cargo would be picked up en route at Funchal, Madeira, most of the merchant vessels were lightly loaded, their gunwales riding high above the brown waters of the Thames. The largest, at two hundred-tons displacement, were the 28-gun *George* and the 24-gun *Antilope*, both London-built broad sterns designed to cope with the treacherous conditions of the North Atlantic. The *George*, whose thirty-six "English Saylors" were commanded by Master John Robinson, was loaded with twelve casks of French brandy, two hundredweight of bottled claret, ninety-eight puncheons of English beer, and one hundred and fifty tons of dry goods. The latter could include such diverse items as silk scarves and woolen bays, fans, gloves, hats and wigs, locks and keys, books, tanned leather, whips, pipes, saddles, coaches, parrot cages, and tombstones. The *Antilope*'s master, Jonathan Harle, had loaded a similar cargo alongside sixty tons of arms and ammunition "for their majesties service." Nine other vessels were also bound for Jamaica. Five were broad sterns of between one hundred and one hundred and eighty tons. All carried similar cargoes to those stowed by Harle and Robinson. There were also five pinks, small, narrow-stern vessels with shallow drafts built in the Dutch style. The smallest was the forty-ton *Robert*. Having no cannon on board, her master, James Coates, and the seven sailors under his command would have to rely on their consorts' firepower if they encountered French men of war or privateers or the much-dreaded pirates of the Barbary Coast. Coates would pick up all his merchandise in Madeira. Like several of his fellows, he would set sail from London without a single barrel, puncheon, or bag of cargo on board.[4]

In December 1689, the West Indian fleet departed from Custom House Quay. The first leg of the voyage saw the ships sail past the impoverished districts of London's East End. The narrow-fronted, two-story wooden houses of Stepney, Whitechapel, Aldgate, Spitalfields, Shadwell, and Ratcliff were home to many of the sailors on board. At Wapping, the fleet passed the scaffold at Execution Dock, where pirates and mutineers were launched into oblivion on the orders of men such as "Hanging Judge Jeffries." Alongside the scaffolds, blackened, decaying corpses hung in gibbets, slowly turning in the breeze. Later, the ships passed Gravesend, "the last town of the River of Thames," before passing on to the Nore, a vast anchorage in the estuary to the north of Sheppey Island. There they would remain for the next two months while several of the men of war due to escort them across the Atlantic joined them.[5]

By December 1689 the Nine Years' War had reached an impasse. After several initial successes earlier that summer, notably the siege and capture of the fortress town of Mainz, by autumn Louis XIV's invasion of the Rhineland had ground to a halt. As several German principalities, including Brandenburg, Saxony, and Hanover, had mobilized against them, the French had withdrawn, laying waste to the borderlands to deny their enemies the supplies they would need to launch a counterattack. In Ireland, James II and his deputy, the Duke of Tyrconnell, had been struggling to pacify several Protestant strongholds ever since the ousted king had landed in Kinsale in March 1689. The siege of Derry, opened in April, proved particularly grueling. After one hundred days without a breakthrough, the Jacobites withdrew. At sea, the only fleet engagement of note had taken place at Bantry Bay off the south coast of Ireland on May 11, 1689. A French force of twenty-four third and fourth rates, two frigates, and a number of fireships had landed reinforcements for James's army before turning on a numerically smaller English fleet. A four-hour engagement resulted in an inconclusive victory for the French. While neither fleet lost a ship, the English suffered four hundred casualties and were forced to retreat to the open sea. Wary of French invasion, the English made their way back to the Channel. The French admiral, François Louis de Rousselet, Marquis de Châteaurenault, failed to follow up his advantage. In August 1689, the commander of William's land forces, the Duke of Schomberg, arrived in the north of Ireland with fifteen thousand Danish, Dutch, Huguenot, and English troops. The capture of Carrickfergus proved Schomberg's sole success. His offensive stalled at the siege of Dundalk and, as the winter set in, fevers and scurvy killed six thousand of his troops. Many others deserted. Thus, with stalemate in Ireland, on the high seas, and in the Rhineland, were the battle lines drawn at the end of 1689.[6]

Among the twelve Royal Navy ships that would gather at the Nore to convoy the West Indian fleet that winter was HMS *Swan*, a 32-gun fifth rate destined for Jamaica. Originally built by the Dutch, the frigate measured seventy-four feet along its keel, had a breadth of twenty-five feet, and a burden of two hundred and forty-six tons.

After being captured in the English Channel in 1673 during the Third Anglo-Dutch War, it had been commissioned into the Royal Navy's Irish Squadron. Over the next fourteen years the *Swan* had seen service in the English Channel, the Mediterranean, and the Caribbean, as well as off the coasts of Newfoundland and Virginia. In 1688, considered well past its prime, it had been converted into a fireship and sent to the Baltic only to be recommissioned as a fifth rate the following January on the outbreak of war. On March 10, 1689, the *Swan* took on a skeleton crew of six men. Over the next nine months a further one hundred and fifty-four names were entered in the muster. First among them was Captain Thomas Johnson. "A diligent man . . . [of good] carriage," Johnson had previous experience of command on the Jamaican station. The second in command, the Honourable Lieutenant Edward Neville, was the polar opposite of his captain. A highborn idler who owed his appointment to nepotism, Neville would not serve the frigate well. The majority of the sailors were pressed men. Spirited away from merchant vessels or kidnapped ashore, they were bundled aboard the *Swan* by press gangs armed with cudgels. Among a dozen men pressed at the Nore on December 12, 1689, were two brothers. On examination by one of the *Swan*'s lieutenants, Jonathan and Andrew Hodge were rated able seamen, testament to the experience they had garnered from service on merchantmen plying the English coast or the European or intercontinental trade routes. Once processed, the Hodges joined their new shipmates on the foul-smelling berth deck and slung their hammocks between the guns. Over the next two years, the brothers would barely leave the ship. Their lives would become a routine of hard work, poor diet, and limited sleep, for which they earned a pittance of ten shillings per month. The days were punctuated by corporal punishments dictated by the Articles of War. These included such indignities as keel hauling, flogging, hanging in the bilboes, ducking at the yard arm, paying the cobty, and running the gauntlet. Unlike the majority of their peers, over the next two-and-a-half years while the *Swan* was based at Jamaica, the Hodges would neither run nor be discharged nor killed in battle nor succumb to disease. Both would survive until the day the ship met its end at Port Royal in June 1692.[7]

ON FEBRUARY 15, 1690, taking advantage of a brisk westerly breeze, the West Indies fleet upped anchor and sailed east. Skirting the wrecks which littered the Kentish Flats, they tacked off the North Foreland, turned south, passed the castles at Deal, the Goodwin Sands, and Dover, and then headed west along the south coast, arriving at Plymouth Sound on March 6, where the rest of the ships bound for the West Indies awaited them.[8] Before leaving Plymouth, several passengers were taken aboard. A short-tempered, one-eyed Irishman, William O'Brien, the second Earl of Inchiquin and the newly appointed governor of Jamaica, was better suited to the battlefield to which he had taken in his youth than the Council meeting room that awaited him. Inchiquin's predecessors had ruled the kingdoms of Munster and Thomond since the late tenth century. Having switched their allegiance to the English crown in 1542, the family had been rewarded with the hereditary title of Baron Inchiquin on condition that they covert to the Anglican faith. The Inchiquins proved equally elastic in their loyalties during the Civil War. In 1641 Murrough O'Brien, the father of the new governor of Jamaica, had fought for the English during the Irish Rebellion. Murrough was later forced to submit to Parliament only to declare for Charles I in 1648, a move which saw the family forced into exile when Cromwell landed the following year. With his teenage son in tow, Murrough joined Charles II's court in France where he was created Earl of Inchiquin in 1654 as a reward for his loyalty.[9]

Like many exiled royalists, the O'Briens lived a peripatetic existence. Father and son served with the French against the Spanish in Catalonia before traveling to Paris in 1655 where they were implicated in Edward Sexby's plot to assassinate Oliver Cromwell. The Inchiquins spent the next four years between Catalonia and Paris, then turned up in London in December 1660 following the Restoration, where Inchiquin senior met the diarist Samuel Pepys at the Sun Tavern on Fish Street Hill, before sailing for Lisbon to fight for the Portuguese in their war of independence against Spain. En route the Inchiquins' ship was captured by Barbary pirates. In the melee, William lost an eye. Father and son were imprisoned in Algiers only to be released after the English Parliament had paid a ransom of 70,000 dollars. Subsequently, Inchiquin senior retired to his native Ireland where he died in 1663.

William O'Brien, the second Earl of Inchiquin. Appointed Governor of Jamaica by King William and Queen Mary as a reward for his loyalty, Inchiquin would exploit the post to restore his family's fortunes despite his ignorance of the difficulties that awaited him. (*National Army Museum, unknown, portrait, c.1680*)

As the second Earl of Inchiquin, William O'Brien took up a post in the Privy Council in 1671 and was made captain general of the colony of Tangiers three years later. Acquired by the English crown as part of Catherine of Braganza's dowry to Charles II, Tangiers was of strategic importance, but it was a problematic posting due to the interminable state of siege it was placed under by a hostile population. Nine governors would administer the colony in the two decades it remained an English possession. Inchiquin governed it for six years before returning to England in 1680 having lost the outlying fortifications to the Moors. It was a shameful reverse. Over one hundred of the garrison were captured and beheaded. Inchiquin's placatory gift to the king of a pair of ostriches did little to restore his reputation on his return home.[10] Following the death of his first wife, Margaret Boyle, with whom he had had three children, in 1683 Inchiquin married the Honorable Elizabeth Herbert, the coheiress of Lord Chandos. The couples spent the next five years in Ireland until the upheavals of 1688 presented an opportunity for Inchiquin to reinvigorate his stuttering career by siding with the Prince of Orange. Initially, the plan backfired. Inchiquin had his estate, O'Brien's Bridge in Clare County, sequestered and the family were forced to flee to England by superior Catholic forces under Major-General Macarthy. In London on September 19, 1689, William and Mary rewarded Inchiquin by commissioning him governor of Jamaica. The posting, which commanded a salary of £2,000 and would ensure a steady stream of additional income, could not have come at a better time. Inchiquin was in major financial difficulties: his estate had been attainted, he had been obliged to pawn his wife's jewels for £1,000, and he would spend the better part of his last two months in England squabbling with the Lords of Trade and Plantations, a subcommittee of the Privy Council responsible for administering the colonies, over the travel allowance he would be granted to accommodate his retinue on the voyage to the New World. As well as his wife Elizabeth, to whom the earl was particularly devoted, James O'Bryan, his third son from his first marriage, went aboard the flagship of the West Indies fleet along with the seventy-five servants deemed necessary to tend to the Inchiquins' every need.[11]

ON MARCH 9, 1690, two more passengers boarded the fleet. James Harlow and Alan Mullen were Irish scientists dispatched to Jamaica by Sir James Rawdon, a keen amateur botanist known as "the father of Irish gardening," their mission to collect plant samples and transport them home. Little is known about Harlow aside from the fact that he had traveled to Virginia on another plant collecting expedition in 1688. Mullen comes down to us as a more fully rounded character. After studying medicine at Trinity College, he had become a member of the short-lived Dublin Philosophical Society, but was best known for his work on the human eye and a bizarre account of the anatomy of the elephant, which he had published after dissecting an unfortunate specimen that had been burned to death in Dublin in 1681. Five years later, as the result of "an indelicate love affair," Mullen had been forced to leave Ireland for London where he met the Earl of Inchiquin. A few months later both men had boarded the West Indian fleet along with James Harlow. The latter sailed on HMS *Swan*. Mullen and Inchiquin traveled on the flagship, HMS *Mary*.[12]

Another passenger aboard the *Mary* was a Spaniard named Santiago Castillo. Born in Barcelona, Castillo had risen to prominence in Caribbean affairs as an agent of the *asiento*, a trade agreement aimed at keeping Spain's American colonies supplied with slaves. Lacking the resources to compete in the West African trade, the Spanish relied on foreigners to supply their overseas plantations. In the 1560s, the Portuguese, operating out of Angola, had been granted a monopoly. Thus had the situation remained until two Genoese merchants, Grillo and Lomelin, were awarded the contract in 1662. Unable to fulfil the terms themselves, the Genoese subcontracted the Dutch India Company and the English Royal Adventurers, the short-lived predecessor of the Royal African Company, to complete the contract. Both purchased their slaves at bases along the Guinea Coast in West Africa, before transporting them to the regional entrepôts of Curaçao and Jamaica for trans-shipment to Havana, Portobelo, and Cartagena. The Genoese struggled to fulfill their responsibilities, while the outbreak of the Second Anglo-Dutch War in 1665 crippled the English Royal Adventurers and in 1671 Grillo's contract was terminated. Various Spanish traders took over for the next ten years, but by 1680 Spanish agents were back in Jamaica, purchasing slaves from the newly established Royal African Company. Four years later Santiago Castillo, who had worked for fourteen years out of the Dutch colony of Curaçao, became the first asiento agent to be permanently based in Port Royal.

During the governorship of Hender Molesworth (1684–1687), Castillo's business had prospered. As Jamaica's principal agent of the Royal African Company, Molesworth engineered an agreement by which Castillo got the pick of the company's slaves in exchange for an annual "commission" of somewhat over 10,000 pieces of eight paid to the governor. When the Duke of Albemarle took over in 1687, Castillo's activities were curtailed. With no direct interest in the RAC, Albemarle favored the interests of the Jamaican plantocracy, who were in competition with Castillo for the company's slaves. After detaining several of the sloops the Spaniard used for trans-shipment, Albemarle had a warrant for Castillo's arrest issued on the pretext of a religious squabble between the Spaniard and Thomas Churchill, chief minister of the Catholic faith in Jamaica who had been appointed by James II. Castillo fled for Cuba, where he was detained for some time by the

Spanish authorities for having failed in his mission, before traveling on to England in 1689 with the hope that the Glorious Revolution would enable him to secure favorable terms. Granted an audience with King William's Privy Council, Castillo struck a deal to reestablish the Jamaican asiento and was awarded a knighthood by a government keen to promote friendly relations with Spain as a counterbalance to an increasingly hostile France. On September 17, 1689, it was agreed that the Royal African Company should furnish two thousand "negroes" for the asiento at Jamaica over the next twenty months with the price per head fixed at eighty pieces of eight, a little under £20. Thus Castillo boarded the fleet at Portsmouth with full sanction to purchase slaves for Spanish America and the new governor's unfettered support.[13]

BY EARLY MARCH the West Indian fleet was sixty-six sails strong. The largest of the fourteen men of war was the flagship, HMS *Mary*, a 54-gun third rate ship-of-the-line commanded by Captain Matthew Aylmer which had fought at the Battle of Bantry Bay the previous May. The *Mary* also carried the commander in chief of the West Indies fleet, acting admiral Matthew Wright, as well as Inchiquin and his retinue, James Kendall, the newly appointed governor of Barbados, and the scientist, Alan Mullen. Eight fourth rates of between 40 and 48 guns—the *Bristol*, the *Antelope*, the *Assistance*, the *Tiger*, the *Success*, the *Princess Ann*, the *Hampshire*, and the *Jersey*—were also present, along with two fifth rates: the *Swan* and the *Guernsey*, both of 28 guns. There was a small armed ketch, the *Quaker*, which would eventually join the *Swan* at Jamaica, and a fireship named the *Saint Paul*. The remaining fifty-one vessels were merchantmen. Most were bound for Barbados, but eleven would go on to Jamaica. In total the fleet carried over three thousand sailors, both Royal Navy ratings and merchantmen. Divided among the men of war there were also thirteen companies of the Duke of Bolton's regiment. Destined to fight the French in the Caribbean, the regiment had been embarked since mid-December 1689 to prevent desertion. Cramped conditions, poor provisions, and a lack of clothing and beds had led to the outbreak of disease. Despite the close attention of their senior officers, Lieutenant

Colonel Holt and Major Nott, the troops suffered terribly. On February 19, 1690, Nott complained that the men were "the wretchedest fellows that ever were seen." By March 1, with the fleet still at anchor in Plymouth Sound, sixty of the nine hundred and thirty strong regiment were sick of "a malignent fever" and "one or two bodies [were being thrown] overboard every day."[14]

On March 9, the fleet departed. The *Mary*'s gunner fired a signal cannon at 4 A.M. and a lantern was hung out on her maintop mast shrouds to advise the captains to raise anchor and prepare for sea. The *Mary* set sail at 7 A.M. with the entire fleet of sixty-six ships in company. Coming out of the sound with a fresh gale billowing out of the east, they made good progress and at 2 A.M. the next morning the Lizard was sighted due north three leagues distant. Over the next five days the fleet covered an average of fifty-five miles every twenty-four hours, but on March 15, as they traversed the Bay of Biscay, "a violent storm" sprung up out of the southwest. The following day the winds increased and by the afternoon of March 17 the waves were towering over the decks. "We were near foundering," Governor Kendall wrote. "The upper deck was full of water up to the gunwales, and the tarpauling not being good the water in the hold was above the ballast." As the men worked the pumps, the *Mary*'s foremast was sprung "about ye upper portions." Captain Aylmer ordered the foreyard hauled down to ease the strain, but at 4 P.M. a giant wave "stoved [in] all ye windows" in the state rooms. "[It] broak much carved work in ye ships stern," the log recorded, "and filled up ye great cabin half full of water." "A great sea pooped us," Governor Kendall recorded, and "filled the cabin so full that it set me and the other gentlemen swimming. . . . We had meanwhile lost sight of the fleet."[15]

The next morning the wind died and the waves abated. At 6 A.M. the *Mary* set its main topsails and stood off to the northeast, intending to return to England to make repairs, but the following day the wind began "blowing very hard" from the southeast, forcing Admiral Wright to turn once more toward his original destination: the Portuguese colony of Madeira. On March 23, the *Mary* came up with "8 Sails of Hollanders & an Englishman bound to ye Southward" and at daylight on March 28, an unidentified sail was spotted. Captain Aylmer gave chase and by 8 A.M. had caught the stranger, a hundred-ton French merchantman bound for Martinique. A prize crew was sent aboard and letters were found which spoke of "great preparations" to send a "considerable" French fleet to the Caribbean. Elsewhere, out of sight on the open ocean, HMS *Swan* suffered its first casualties of the voyage. After the briefest of ceremonies, the bodies of Henry Tewk, an able seaman pressed into service on August 1, 1689, and Garfield Welch, a young midshipman, were committed to the deep. Their clothes and the meager possessions they had crammed into their sea chests were auctioned off at the mast. Over the next few days the *Bristol, Hampshire,* and *Success* and eleven merchantmen rejoined the flagship, and on April 3, they sailed into Funchal Bay, Madeira, a deep cove dominated by two strong, stone castles perched on high cliffs to the north and east. Admiral Wright was delighted to find all but a handful of the rest of the men of war and merchantmen riding at anchor in fifty-five fathoms in the roads.[16]

The fleet stayed at Madeira for five days. While the sailors filled the ships' water casks and cut wood under the watchful eyes of armed sentries, the masters of the merchantmen loaded their holds with Madeira's most famous export. Both the rarer white and the longer-lasting red varietal fetched a good price in Jamaica: profits of 50 percent were commonplace. Its hold already packed with dry goods, the *Antelope* only had room for thirty pipes, each containing roughly one hundred and twelve gallons; Master Robinson of the *George* purchased sixty; while the smallest of the merchantmen bound for Jamaica, the eighty-ton pinks *Adventure* and *Bertue,* found space to load two hundred pipes apiece. Meanwhile, the officers and passengers went ashore to stretch their legs. Madeira had a pleasant climate and its hills were richly cultivated. There were abundant vineyards; apple, pear, fig, orange, walnut, apricot, peach, pomegranate, and lemon trees; and rambling plantations of banana, sugarcane, and plantain. The town of Funchal boasted five hundred whitewashed houses, a nunnery of the Order of Saint Clara, and two churches, as well as the governor's house at which Kendall and Inchiquin were received with "extreme civility." Confined to their ships, the soldiers of the Duke of Bolton's Regiment continued to suffer. "We are still . . . sickly," Governor Kendall wrote on April 4, "and have buried twelve [more] men since we left Plymouth." Six days later HMS *Mary* completed its watering and set sail for Barbados. In company were most of the merchantmen and all of the men of war that had left Plymouth with the exception of the fifth-rate HMS *Guernsey*. With his ship badly damaged in the storm, Captain Edward Oakely had called in at Cadiz for repairs before sailing on to Madeira. By the time Oakley arrived at Funchal, Admiral Wright had already sailed.[17]

The remainder of the voyage to Barbados was uneventful. As the ships cut their way westward, the temperature and humidity climbed and the sun straightened in the sky. The sailors caught the dolphins that played about the ships' wakes with ten-foot-long harpoons tipped with barbed arrowheads; flying fish and small whales were spotted. On April 11, the Coronation Day of William and Mary was celebrated, and the fleet reached the doldrums six days later. The wind fell away and the temperature soared. Occasional showers did little to ease the men's torment. Their sails limp, the ships averaged less than twenty miles a day. Several sharks were spotted. Hoisting heavy hooks overboard baited with salt beef, the sailors waited for them to bite, allowed them to run until exhausted, then hauled them aboard to add variety to the mundane fare doled out by the cooks. By April 24 the winds returned, on April 30 the *Mary* covered one hundred and twenty miles, and at 1 P.M. on May 10, the rocky east coast of Barbados was spotted. The following afternoon, passing between numerous "boats plying to and fro," the fleet dropped anchor in Carlisle Bay in twenty-two fathoms.[18]

SETTLED IN 1627 by a syndicate headed by Sir William Courteen, a wealthy Anglo-Dutch merchant, Barbados is a tiny island of a little over one hundred and sixty square miles. The colony had suffered from mismanagement in its early years. When Courteen's right to colonize the island was challenged by the Earl of Carlisle, a rival for Courteen's position as de facto governor, civil war erupted: agents on both sides were banished and one governor was executed before Carlisle's men gained the upper hand. The earl proved to be the first of a long line of disinterested absentee landlords. Real power rested in the hands of the governor, Henry Hawley, a petty despot who scraped together a living by levying a poll tax. The overwhelming majority of the initial settlers were single, young, and male. Many were indentured servants. Lured by the thrill and adventure of a new beginning, they were bound into servitude for five years in exchange for their passage out and the promise of a ten-acre plot on the expiration of their indenture. Most of the land was distributed in smallholdings of between thirty and fifty acres, although a few sizable estates of up to six hundred acres were acquired. Tobacco, planted in the rich tropical soils cleared of the cloying vegetation and "massive" trees which originally covered the island, was the principal crop. The work was labor intensive. Disease took a heavy toll and the tobacco was "earthy and worthless." Exports "could give them little or no return from England, or elsewhere."[19]

The island's fortunes improved in mid-century. After a failed experiment growing cotton and some success with the dye woods indigo and fustic, in 1640 a wave of Dutch settlers forced out of Brazil by the Portuguese arrived at Barbados and taught the English how to raise and process sugarcane. The new crop caught on, and although progress was retarded by the Civil War, by 1660 Barbados was dominated by "White Gold." Black slaves replaced white servants; smallholdings were amalgamated into large estates by a rising plantocracy of two hundred individuals. The climate and soil proved perfect and the new product flooded into the European market. What had previously been a luxury item farmed on a small scale in the Mediterranean became a staple used to sweeten tea, coffee, and alcoholic beverages and to make a dizzying array of cakes and pastries. From the trading hubs of London and Amsterdam the craze spread and the Barbadian economy boomed. Land prices soared from ten shillings per acre in 1640 to twenty pounds per acre after the Restoration. Soon the entire island was deforested. With sugar monoculture supreme, food had to be imported from the North American colonies while demand for labor fueled dealings in West African slaves. The era of triangular trade had begun.

By the time of Inchiquin and Kendall's arrival, Barbados had entered a third phase. With no more land available, the once-rich soil was becoming exhausted. Sugar prices had fallen in Europe due to competition from the Portuguese in Brazil; the newly founded English colonies of Antigua, St. Kitts, Nevis, Montserrat, and Jamaica; and the French sugar islands of Martinique, St. Lucia, and Guadeloupe. Although the profits of the 1660s had dwindled, the crop remained lucrative: the plantocracy was well established and its members among the wealthiest citizens in the empire. The island had a population of seventy thousand: twenty thousand whites, fifty thousand African slaves, and a handful of their mulatto progeny. No forest remained aside from a few clumps clinging to the cliffs of the east coast, exposed to occasional storms which howled in from the Atlantic. Row upon row of eight-foot-high sugarcane covered the hills broken only by the sugar mills, boiling houses, and ostentatious great houses of the elite. The capital, Bridgetown, stood in the sheltered southwest corner of the island, on the shore of Carlisle Bay. Over a league across, the bay was capable of harboring five hundred sail and was dominated by the cannon of the capital's twin forts and accompanying batteries. Bridgetown's streets ran parallel to the sea and were lined with fine houses, a string of shops, and "divers storehouses." The town played host to the offices of the Royal African Company, whose principal agent, Colonel Edwin Stede, also served as deputy governor. In the low ground beyond the town limits was a pestilent bog. Fed by annual spring tides, it was home to swarms of malarial mosquitoes. As Richard Ligon, a visitor to Barbados in 1673, remarked, "'[it] vent[ed] out so loathsome a savour, as cannot but breed ill blood, and is (no doubt) the occasion of much sickness to those that live there."[20]

Admiral Wright and Governors Kendall and Inchiquin went ashore at 10 A.M. on the morning of May 11, 1690. It was a beautiful day. The trades blew in from the east and the sun hung in an azure blue sky. As the boats departed, HMS *Mary* fired a 22-gun salute, answered by the guns of forts James and Willoughby. Kendall found Bridgetown "in a lamentable condition." With no men of war to protect it, the town had suffered the indignity of blockade by a single French ship. As well as taking all in-bound merchantmen at its leisure, the vessel, which had since departed on the approach of the English fleet, had ensured that no provisions had been landed for some time. While the rich had barely tightened their belts, the poor had struggled and the island's slaves were on the verge of starvation. To make matters worse, "a terrible earthquake" had struck on April 5. As well as destroying several buildings and killing a number of the inhabitants of

A Prospect of Bridgetown, Barbados, 1695. By the 1670s, sugar monoculture had made Barbados the most lucrative outpost of England's nascent Caribbean empire. (*Library of Congress, Samuel Copen, engraving, 1695*)

the nearby English colony of Antigua, the reverberations had caused panic throughout the region. "For a month afterwards," Sir Christopher Coddrington, the English commander in chief in the Caribbean, noted, there were "almost daily shakes, and even now there passes not a week without some tremblings."[21]

In contrast to their English opponents, who lacked uniforms, arms, ammunition, training, and discipline, the French had reacted swiftly to the outbreak of war in the Caribbean. After capturing the Dutch island of St. Eustatius in early April 1689, the governor general of French possessions in the Caribbean, the Comte de Blénac, had turned his attention to the English colony of St. Kitts. With the aid of the Irish residents, who turned against their English overlords, and bolstered by the presence of the much-feared privateer, Jean-Baptiste du Casse, the French took the island swiftly. The surrender was signed on August 15, 1689. In the first months of 1690 the situation stabilized. Sir Christopher Coddrington patched together an impromptu fleet of armed merchantmen and managed to quell the threat of further Irish rebellion on the islands of Montserrat and Nevis, as well as driving off a would-be invasion fleet hovering off the tiny colony of Barbuda. Coddrington then took the offensive. A force of eight hundred Barbadian volunteers under Sir Thomas Thorngill seized the undefended French possession of St. Bartholomew, but were then blockaded by du Casse when they attacked the nearby island of St. Martin. On the verge of surrender, Thorngill was rescued in February 1690 by a ragged gang of privateers led by Captain Thomas Hewetson, "a brutal scoundrel" who would make a considerable fortune in the Caribbean over the next two years by hiring out his services to the highest bidder. Since then, the French had failed to press their advantage. With the arrival of Admiral Wright's fleet and the five hundred or so soldiers of the Duke of Bolton's Regiment well enough to fight, Coddrington hoped to turn the tide against them.[22]

INCHIQUIN SPENT a little over a week at Bridgetown. Having recovered from the ravages of the Atlantic crossing and discussed the future cooperation of Barbados and Jamaica in the struggle against the French, on May 20 he transferred his retinue to the *Swan* and set out for Port Royal to take up his new post. Accompanying the frigate were eleven of the merchantmen which had sailed from Plymouth with Wright's fleet back in March. Each having lost at least one crew member to accident or disease on the outward voyage, all had recruited new hands at Barbados. The *Swan* had also lost several crewmen, including one Thomas Gee who had deserted on the very day of departure. Also absent was Alan Mullen, the colorful scientist whose tales of ill-fated love affairs and elephant autopsy had no doubt enlivened the voyage. Mullen had succumbed to the "effects of intoxication" soon after landing at Barbados, leaving James Harlow the sole representative of Sir James Rawdon's scientific expedition to Jamaica.[23]

Joining the Jamaica fleet was the *Lion*, a privateer of 50 guns captained by Thomas Hewetson, the "brutal scoundrel" who had rescued Sir Thomas Thorngill's men from the French at St. Martin. Having raised over £50,000 in England from several prominent backers, including the Earl of Clare and viscounts Longeirle and Falkland, in 1688 Hewetson had purchased four ships: the *Lion*, the *Albemarle*, the *Palermatan*, and the *Hunter*, which he had fitted out for a voyage of three years. Promising his investors a sound return, Hewetson left England in September 1688 for the Pacific, intending to make his fortune from trade and wreck salvage and with a vague idea of establishing a colony in southern Chile, home to the indigenous Mapuche and still unconquered by Spain. Willful and proud with a cruel streak in his nature, Hewetson proved an unsuitable commander and the expedition met with disaster. Unable to beat his way through the Straits of Magellan, in late 1688 Hewetson decided to cut his losses and turned back north for the Caribbean. The captains of the other three ships promptly lost faith in their commander and went their separate ways. The *Albemarle* broke convoy off the coast of Brazil and headed for the island of Montserrat in the Caribbean where it loaded with sugar and returned to London, the *Hunter* blew up in Bridgetown Roads, and the captain of the *Palermatan* hired his ship out to Governor Coddrington at Barbados. Left without a fleet to command, Hewetson also headed for Barbados after resupplying and refitting on the coast of Tobago. At Bridgetown he was awarded a privateer commission by Coddrington. After gathering a new fleet of three ships, two sloops, and more than four hundred men, among whom was the soon to be infamous William Kidd, Hewetson spent five days plundering the tiny French outpost of Marie Galante before sailing to Nevis and St. Martin. Hewetson then returned to Bridgetown and was at somewhat of a loose end until the arrival of Inchiquin's fleet provided exactly the opportunity he had been looking for. With the outbreak of war against France, Santiago Castillo, the asiento agent who had boarded the fleet at Plymouth, needed a vessel to transship the slaves he intended to purchase from the Royal African Company's agents at Port Royal. Heavily armed and with a capacious hold, the *Lion* was perfect. Castillo and Hewetson agreed to terms and the *Lion* joined the convoy for Jamaica.[24]

THE ROUTE FROM Barbados to Port Royal was a well-traveled one. In the days before longitude could be ascertained with any degree of accuracy, ships sailed within sight of land whenever possible. A day's voyage from Bridgetown were the French possessions of St. Lucia and Martinique. Originally settled by Cardinal Richelieu's short-lived

Compagnie des Îles de l'Amérique in 1635 and 1643, respectively, by 1690 both were dominated by sugar plantations worked with slave labor. A few days later, the ships skirted the shores of Dominica, the first of the Leewards, and one of just two islands in the Caribbean remaining under Carib control. Once spread over the majority of the region, the Caribs were a warlike people whose raiding parties had terrorized the other indigenous cultures, the Tainos and Arawaks, but had subsequently suffered at the hands of the Europeans. Disease and slave raiding had greatly reduced their numbers, and by the late seventeenth century the only other Carib stronghold remaining was St. Vincent, like Dominica a mountainous island whose inhospitable terrain had proved prohibitive to European settlement.

After skirting Dominica, the fleet passed Guadeloupe, another sugar-producing French colony, before sighting the diminutive island of Montserrat. A rocky atoll whose capital, Plymouth, was built at the foot of a volcano which rose abruptly out of the sea, Montserrat's mostly Irish, Roman Catholic inhabitants were smallholders who grew tobacco, a crop of superior quality to that attempted at Barbados due to the island's volcanic soils. As a consequence of their faith and history of persecution, the islanders were of doubtful loyalty to the English crown in the war against their French coreligionists. Soon after they left Montserrat, the island of Nevis was spotted. Another English possession, Nevis had 2,500 inhabitants, who were dedicated to sugar production. The island also served as the Royal African Company's headquarters for the Leeward Islands. Leaving Nevis behind, the fleet navigated round the war torn island of St. Kitts, discernible by "a ridge of Hills run[ning] . . . through the middle, lying East and West," before passing St. Eustatius, a colony governed by the Dutch West India Company whose chief business was the transshipment of African slaves and European goods to the neighboring French and English colonies. Next, St. Croix, another French sugar island, came into view, after which the *Swan*'s lookouts sighted Puerto Rico: a Spanish colony and the largest Caribbean island that Inchiquin and his fellow passengers had seen so far. Settled by Juan Ponce de León in 1508, Puerto Rico was one of the oldest colonial possessions of any nation in the region. The *repartimiento* and later the *encomienda* systems had seen the indigenous Tainos serve as chattels to their Spanish

THE WEST INDIES FLEET 21

overlords in the gold mines of the interior. Added to the casualties endured in the reprisals which followed several failed uprisings, widespread suicide, and endemic disease, these toils decimated the population to such an extent that Taino culture had all but disappeared from the island just fifty years after the Spaniards' arrival. From 1528 to 1655, the island had witnessed a series of French, English, and Dutch attempts at conquest. All had ended in failure and while Puerto Rico, in common with many of the Spanish possessions in the Caribbean, remained economically backward compared to the colonies of its European rivals, militarily the colony was relatively strong.

A day's sail beyond Puerto Rico, the fleet reached the tiny island of Mona, then skirted Hispaniola, an island divided between French and Spanish rule. Founded in 1496, the Spanish capital of Santo Domingo was the oldest European settlement in the Caribbean. French colonization had only begun in 1665. Although resisted by the Spanish, by 1690 the French had established themselves in the western third of the island. The day after passing Santo Domingo, Inchiquin's fleet passed the Ile de Vache. Known to the English as Cow Island, this tiny islet and the nearby settlement of Petit Guavos were notorious havens for pirates and privateers. Of various nationalities, these men paid token allegiance to the French, who would take advantage of the outbreak of the Nine Years' War to entice the privateers to raid the poorly defended plantations of Jamaica, which lay just over one hundred miles to the west.[25]

On May 30, Jamaica was spotted. At a little over 4,200 square miles, it was much larger than any other English colony in the Caribbean. The first sight to greet the visitors was the Blue Mountains. A lofty range, rising to a height of 7,400 feet, these rocky peaks dominated the eastern half of the island. Below, clinging to the middle and lower slopes, lay cloud forest, thick with vegetation. Lower down this gave way to woods, rainforests, and savannahs. As the *Swan* drew closer, Point Morant, the island's easternmost tip, hove into view. From the deck, the passengers could make out a string of houses and a battery built on a bluff covering several ships in the bay. The fleet then skirted the south coast, passing the salt pans of St. David's Parish and Cow Bay and, in the neighboring parish of St. Andrew's, the estuaries of the Hope and Cane Rivers which were interspersed with pestilent swamplands and flanked by sugar plantations built on the rich alluvial plains that dominated Jamaica's central southern coast. On the *Swan*'s approach, the seemingly endless rows of eight-foot-high canes were approaching maturity. Among this sea of green rose mills and boiling houses, the elegant homes of the planters and the squalid huts of their slaves. As the fleet was spotted, signal fires were lit on shore and the long-anticipated news of the new governor's arrival spread westward toward Port Royal.

The next landmark to appear to those watching from the deck of the *Swan* was Point Cagway, a low-lying sand spit which jutted out some ten miles into Kingston Bay. As the ships neared its western tip, firing a series of guns to alert the residents to their presence, Port Royal was spotted. The tower of St. Paul's Church, each corner of which was decorated with a large pendant to mark the occasion, rose above the headstones of a nearby cemetery lying on the goat-cropped scrubland just beyond the town limits. A mile to the west, the flags of the union fluttered with the land breeze above the low, gun-studded ramparts of Fort Rupert, named after Charles I's nephew, where two hundred militiamen dressed in bright scarlet coats lined with blue stood to arms. In the harbor to the north, guarded by Forts Walker, James, and Carlisle, a forest of masts rose above the warehouses lining the quayside; the star of David, mounted on the Jewish community's synagogue deep in the heart of the town, glinted in the sun. The multistoried residences of the town's chief administrators, merchants, and the factors of the Royal African Company abounded. Built in the English style, they appeared incongruous with the tropical clime. By the waterfront, fruit, vegetable, fish, and meat markets were alive with activity. Everywhere was industry, activity, and noise, while the smell of decay, a constant in a tropical town with little sanitation, wafted out to the ships on the land breeze. Mingling with the acrid tang of salt spray, the sweet, sickly stench permeated the air.[26]

CHAPTER 2

As Hot as Hell, and as Wicked as the Devil

JAMAICA AND PORT ROYAL

May–June 1690

The Dunghill of the Universe, the Refuse of the Whole Creation, the Clippings of the Elements, a shapeless pile of Rubbish confus'ly jumb'd into an Emblem of the Chaos, neglected by Omnipotence when he form'd the World into its admirable Order. The Nursery of Heavens Judgements, where the Malignent Seeds of all Pestilence were first gather'd and scatter'd thro' the Regions of the Earth, to Punish Mankind for their Offences. The Place where Pandora fill'd her Box, where Vulcan Forg'd Joves Thunderbolts, and that Phæton, by his rash misguidance of the Sun, scorch'd into a Cinder. The Receptacle of Vagabonds, the Sanctuary of Bankrupts, and a Close-stool for the Purges of our Prisons. As Sickly as a Hospital, as Dangerous as the Plague, as Hot as Hell, and as Wicked as the Devil.

—Edward Ward, *A Trip to Jamaica*, 1698

THE ENGLISH INVASION of Jamaica in 1655 was born out of failure. Admiral William Penn and General Robert Venables, the commanders in chief of the naval and army forces appointed by Oliver Cromwell to lead his great Western Design, had originally been ordered to capture the Spanish possessions of Puerto Rico and Hispaniola. Flushed with success following victories over the Scottish, Irish, and Dutch, in the mid-1650s England's warmongering Lord Protector set his sights further afield. What better target than the Papists'

American colonies? While Louis XIV's France was a fearful prospect, the Spanish possessions in the West Indies were believed to be both immensely wealthy and poorly defended. They promised great commercial opportunities and appeared ripe for the taking. Such Caribbean buccaneering also raised fond memories of the Elizabethan golden age. The stories of Hawkins, Raleigh, and Drake battling the Spanish in the tropics and returning home with their ships laden with booty for their virgin queen were regularly reprinted in the 1650s as safe patriotic fare after years of divisive civil war. The Black Legend of Spanish cruelty had been given further impetus by the first English-language release of Bartolomé de las Casas's classic *A Short Account of the Destruction of the Indies*. Under the title *The Tears of the Indians*, the publication was instigated by Cromwell himself. Not only would the Western Design bring territory and wealth to England, it would also free the inhabitants from the "Miserable Thraldome and bondage both Spiritual and Civill" of Spain.[1]

Despite such promising propaganda, the expedition was a disaster. Poorly prepared, armed, and equipped and with a dizzying ignorance of both their opponents and their destination, Penn and Venables set out from Portsmouth in December 1654 with an army of roughly three thousand men. A mixed bag, comprising a core of veterans of the New Model Army mingled with the flotsam and jetsam of the poorer neighborhoods of the cities of the British Isles, the army was "bolstered" on its arrival in the Caribbean by six thousand men recruited at Barbados and St. Kitts. According to Venables's wife, who accompanied her husband, these men were "the Devil's instruments." Many were indentured servants and of even worse quality than those recruited in England. By the time the fleet reached Hispaniola, the troops were already on half rations; issues of divided command and arguments over the distribution of plunder further lowered morale. Landing forty miles west of Santo Domingo on April 14, 1655, the troops found the conditions unbearable. A lack of fresh water and enervating heat and humidity decimated the ranks. The tatterdemalion band struggled eastward for three days only to find that their siege equipment was inadequate when they reached their destination of Santo Domingo. Skillfully timed sallies by the garrison's cavalry made up of lance-wielding slaves, volleys from the great guns mounted on the city walls, and a constant drain on manpower brought about by dysentery resulted in just two thousand men being fit enough to fight by the end of April. Faced with the imminent fragmentation of his army, Venables abandoned his mission and on May 4, 1655, the remaining troops reembarked. Neither he nor Penn relished the prospect of returning to England empty-handed: the Lord Protector was not known for taking failure lightly. Penn and Venables decided to make a descent on another of the Spaniards' Caribbean possessions instead.

WHEN FIRST EXPLORED by Christopher Columbus in 1494, Jamaica had been home to as many as fifty thousand Tainos. After a hostile reception and a brutal demonstration of strength typical of early European encounters with the indigenous people, Columbus had departed only to return in 1503 when shipwrecked on the south coast. Later colonists, under orders of Columbus's son, Diego, built a city on the north coast and forced the Tainos to dig for gold. Little was discovered, the workers died in droves from European diseases to which they had no immunity, and the town was abandoned for a more wholesome site in the south. Built on plains six miles from the sea, by the mid-seventeenth century San Jago de la Vega (Spanish Town) consisted of several churches, a monastery, and one hundred brick-and-timber houses, roofed with tiles and low-built to resist the earthquakes which frequently shook the island. The surrounding plains were cultivated with sugarcane, cacao, pimento, and cassava. The crops were principally for domestic consumption and, by 1655, were tended by African slaves, who had long since replaced the much diminished Tainos. Hides taken from the cattle which roamed free in the savannas were occasionally exported, but the island had little economic importance.

Jamaica was soon overwhelmed by Penn and Venables's troops. The island's defenders fled on first contact and the governor, Juan Ramirez, surrendered. The terms were harsh, however, and led to a prolonged resistance. Orchestrated by Spanish officers leading bands of slaves, the guerrillas were ably supported by the maroons, escaped Africans who had established themselves in the heavily forested and mountainous interior. Their rapid strikes, combined with disease and a lack of provisions, took a heavy toll. Within twelve days of landing, Venables's companies were at half strength and the guerrillas grew increasingly daring. English stragglers were picked off and found later with their throats cut and their bodies mutilated. At one stage the guerrillas even entered the capital, now known as Spanish Town, and burned several buildings before being driven off. First Penn and then Venables chose to sneak back to England with the majority of the fleet. Both were imprisoned in the Tower by Cromwell on their return.[2]

Determined to salvage some pride from the ruins of his Western Design, Cromwell's reaction was swift. By promising every man who chose to immigrate to Jamaica twenty acres of land and offering ten to each woman, the Lord Protector attracted an eclectic combination of colonists: Quakers from Barbados who had made themselves unwelcome in Bridgetown by refusing to take up arms in the militia; Portuguese Jews expelled from Brazil; two thousand boys and girls sent out from Ireland as indentured servants; several dozen Scottish "robbers and vagabonds" rounded up by county sheriffs and transported; one thousand men from the English colonies in the Leeward Islands together with their women and slaves; and numbers of half-savage buccaneers of a variety of nations whose rudimentary bases on the island of Tortuga and the wild north coast of Hispaniola were coming under increasing pressure from the Spanish military. In exchange for a pledge to act as an auxiliary defense force in case of foreign attack, the latter were offered sanctuary in Jamaica from where they could refit their ships and sell the booty they captured. This unlikely amalgamation of settlers survived the guerrilla warfare waged by the Spanish holdouts in the first five years of Jamaica's history as an English colony and, once Juan de Bolos, the leader of the Spanish maroons, had been encouraged to switch sides, the fear of reconquest by the Spanish waned. By 1660 the last of the holdouts had been expelled to Cuba and Jamaica was firmly in English hands.[3]

With the colony's survival assured, the next step was economic self-sufficiency. Several ex-soldiers turned their hands to farming. The soil was rich and land abundant, but the tobacco, indigo, and cotton produced by the scattered smallholdings brought little revenue. The island's location offered a far better alternative. Strategically positioned at the heart of the Caribbean, Jamaica made an ideal base for raiding

the Spanish Main, Hispaniola, and Cuba whilst also providing un-
paralleled access to the sea lanes used by the annual treasure fleets
bound for Cadiz. For the veterans of Penn and Venables's expedition
and the recent influx of buccaneers, the temptation was irresistible.
At first, these attacks had an official veneer. As well as the buccaneers'
vessels, the strike force consisted of a handful of English naval ships
left behind on Admiral Penn's departure commanded by Captain
Christopher Myngs, an aggressive young officer from Norfolk related
to the much-celebrated Sir Cloudesley Shovell. This motley crew
proved the scourge of the Spanish Caribbean. In 1658 they destroyed
the ports of Tolu and Santa Marta in present-day Colombia, and the
following year Cumana, Puerto Cabello, and Coro in what would become Venezuela were sacked. In 1662 Santiago de Cuba was targeted.
The following year Myngs gathered fourteen ships and 1,400 men
and raided Campeche in Central America. About 150,000 pieces of
eight were looted, but Myngs was severely wounded and returned to
England to recuperate. He would never see Jamaica again.[4]

THE RISE OF THE buccaneers fueled the growth of Port Royal, the island's principal naval base. Situated on the end of a sand spit known
to the English as Point Cagway which jutted out into Kingston Bay,
the port boasted a superb natural harbor where "a ship of 1000 tunn
may lay her sides to the shore . . . and load or unload with planks a-
float." The Spanish had used the area to careen their ships, but had
left it undeveloped—perhaps due to its susceptibility to earthquake.
Two months after Penn and Venables's arrival, the English, ignorant
of such concerns, began building a fort, which was named after the
Lord Protector, on the southern shore from locally quarried limestone.
Twenty guns were mounted on firing platforms of timber and sand,
and in 1656 a round central tower was added. Houses were built to
the north, and naval and merchant vessels began anchoring in the
sheltered roads beyond. Warehouses and a quayside were built, sutlers
(merchants or victualers who sold provisions to an army in the field)
were granted licenses, and a fortified house was constructed for the
commander in chief. By 1658 there were at least three rows of houses
and a church was under construction, and by the following year the

A Hispaniola buccaneer. Welcomed to Jamaica by the first English governors as a potent auxiliary force, by the 1690s, as the island sought its future wealth from sugar and slavery, the buccaneers had been forced to return to their haunts in and around French Hispaniola. (A. Exquemelin, *Buccaneers of America*, 1678)

entire northern shore had been occupied. By 1662 the residents had begun to refer to the burgeoning settlement as Port Royal. New buildings crept ever southward across the point and Fort Cromwell was rebuilt in stone.[5]

ENGLAND, MEANWHILE, was undergoing dramatic change. Cromwell had died, Charles II had been restored to the throne, and peace had been made with Spain. Unwilling to antagonize his new allies, the king forbade further Caribbean raids. The Jamaican buccaneers, unconcerned about official policy, continued regardless. So lucrative was the business that the king's officials got involved, and Lord Windsor, governor from 1661 to 1663, was recalled to answer for his complicity. His replacement, Sir Thomas Modyford, proved no more compliant. After twenty years' residence on Barbados, Modyford was one of several of the island's planters who had decided that their future lay in Jamaica. Barbados' lands had all been claimed and its soils were nigh-well exhausted. In his seven years in office, Modyford proved a capable and energetic administrator. He granted over 1,800 land patents totaling upward of 300,000 acres—triple that of the total available land in Barbados, and encouraged the immigration of a thousand poor, white Barbadians to oversee the new allotments. Each man was granted thirty acres and given an additional thirty for each member of his family. Sugar production took off as large-scale plantations emerged from the former pattern of smallholdings, especially along the fertile southern-coast parishes of St. Catherine, St. John's, and Clarendon. By 1670 forty-four planters held 1,000 or more acres, and sixteen held 2,000 or more—larger individual estates than any seen in the Lesser Antilles. The island's rising plantocracy began importing African slaves to raise the labor-heavy crop. They also moved into local government. The thirty-two-man island Assembly, Jamaica's equivalent of England's House of Commons, held the power to veto any new laws proposed by the island's Council. The latter bore some resemblance to the House of Lords. A body of thirteen "of the Gravest and Chiefest Gentlemen of the Island," the council was made up primarily of members of the plantocracy chosen by the king on the governor's advice. The same planters dominated the judiciary system and militia. Appreciating the wealth they brought to the island, Modyford also tacitly supported the buccaneers, thus enabling the twin developments of agriculture and government-sponsored piracy that would characterize the island's early history.[6]

In the 1660s the most notorious of all Jamaica's buccaneers rose to prominence. A Welsh farmer turned Caribbean immigrant, Henry Morgan is thought to have been among those who invaded Jamaica under Venables. Turning his hand to buccaneering, Morgan rose to the rank of captain and took a leading role in Myngs's raid on Campeche. Between 1665 and 1669 attacks on Providence Island, Portobelo, and Maracaibo followed. Morgan used surprise, speed, ruthlessness, and daring to deadly effect. The Spanish authorities, slaves to central command and incapable of acting on their own initiative, proved unable to stop him. By selling plundered trade goods to Port Royal's growing merchant class, Morgan and his men became rich while squandering the Spanish pieces of eight they stole in the town's ever increasing number of taverns and brothels. They thus not only boosted Jamaica's economy but also provided a much-needed source of coinage in a colony that was frequently bereft of currency. Modyford was only too happy to accommodate such high-living guests. As well as aiding the colony's growth and hindering that of its colonial rivals, the actions of the "brethren" personally benefited the governor to the tune of £1,000 per year.[7]

Morgan's greatest filibustering exploit, the sacking of Panama in 1670–1671, also proved his last. With England and Spain having ratified a new peace treaty in the same year, the conquering hero of Jamaica was arrested not long after his return with a reputed £70,000 in loot and conducted back to England. As Charles II was desperate to regain control of the situation in the Caribbean and anxious to mollify his Spanish friends, Modyford was also recalled. While Morgan's popularity saw him granted the freedom of the City of London, the ex-governor spent two years in the Tower only to return to Jamaica in 1675 as a change in the political climate once more saw England distancing itself from Spain. Although he never again held public office, Modyford remained an influential figure and his plantation became the wealthiest on the island. Morgan had returned one year before. As well as being knighted by the king, the former buccaneer was also the proud bearer of a new title: lieutenant governor of Jamaica. Besides protecting the island from foreign attack, Morgan was charged with controlling his former comrades in arms.

Modyford's successor, Sir Thomas Lynch, who was governor from 1671 to 1675 and again from 1681 to 1684, took up the cause of the rising plantocracy. As the sugar trade grew, the planters saw the buccaneers as a threat to their livelihoods: they destabilized the region, raised insurance costs on merchant shipping, and interrupted trade. The two parties were also in direct competition for white labor. While the planters required overseers to keep their slaves in check, they struggled to compete with the profits and adventure to be had from a life at sea. Lynch, himself one of the leading landowners with over 6,000 acres, turned Jamaica away from its privateering past and toward a sugar-fueled future. The former champions of Port Royal were pardoned on condition they abandoned their free-booting ways, forced to relocate to Hispaniola where they received tacit protection from the French, or hunted down to end their days swinging from the

hangman's noose erected at Gallows Point. During Lynch's governorship, the population of Jamaica increased by eighteen thousand, two
thirds of them African slaves. More land was parceled out until few
choice plots remained, although considerable tracts to the north and
west of the island were as yet uncultivated. Among the beneficiaries
were one hundred families led by Major Thomas Banister who had
been forced to leave their sugar plantations in Suriname in 1671 following its capture by the Dutch.

After Lynch's death in 1684, Sir Hender Molesworth assumed the
governorship. As well as being the owner of eight farms and two sugar
plantations spread over 7,500 acres, Molesworth was also Jamaica's
principal agent for the Royal African Company, a role which brought
him into conflict with his fellow planters. As sugar production grew,
the Royal African Company struggled to keep up with the demand
for slave labor. Unwilling to expand operations when it was already
losing money due to the costly forts and trading stations it was required to maintain on the West African coast in the face of stiff Dutch
opposition, the company was also reluctant to supply the Jamaican
planters, who habitually demanded credit in lieu of future harvests
when the Spanish agents of the asiento were willing to pay hard currency to purchase slaves for transshipment to Portobelo or Cartagena.
Furthermore, Barbados was still a larger and more reliable market than
Jamaica despite the deterioration of its soils, and as it was a week's sail
closer to the Guinea Coast, it made a far more attractive point of sale
than its Leeward counterpart. Consequently, the Jamaican planters
often bought slaves from Dutch and English interlopers. Plying the
Middle Passage in small, swift ships, these prototype free traders dared
to breach the terms of the company's monopoly as well as undercut-
ting its prices to a considerable degree.

Conflict between the island's factions continued on the appointment of Molesworth's successor. Christopher Monck, the second
Duke of Albemarle, was the son of Lord General Monck, a much-
lauded military officer who had fought on both sides during the Civil
War and had gone on to become England's leading commander during the Anglo-Dutch Wars. His son, by contrast, had little to recom-
mend him. A profligate and irresponsible man, Albemarle had been
appointed, it seems, for no better reason than England's newly

crowned king, James II, wanted to be rid of him. Albemarle divided
his time on the island between heavy drinking and carousing and fur-
thering his interest in Jamaica's profitable wreck-salvaging business,
a sideline which had previously netted him £50,000 following an investment of just £800 when a sunken Spanish galleon had been found
off the coast of Hispaniola. Albemarle's governorship also saw a brief
reversal of fortunes for the diminishing band of buccaneers remaining
in Port Royal. To counter the growing power of the plantocracy and
thereby facilitate the Assembly's adoption of his policies, the duke
championed the buccaneers' cause while also garnering support from
the smallholders who continued to scrape a living on the least attractive plots in the island's hinterlands, the formerly downtrodden
Catholic minority, and the white servants who toiled in the fields.
Bribery, intimidation, and other heavy-handed tactics were used by
the duke's supporters. Among Albemarle's adherents was Henry Morgan. Pot-bellied, prematurely aging, and alcoholic, the Welshman was
in rapidly declining health. He died in August 1688. Albemarle followed Morgan to the grave one month later after a debauched celebration to mark the birth of James II's son and would-be heir.

Shortly after Albemarle's death, news of William of Orange's invasion of England threw Jamaica into turmoil. The Glorious Revolution proved less disruptive than feared, but the outbreak of war with
France was more serious. Having pushed the buccaneers into the arms
of their rivals on Hispaniola, the colonists feared that the brethren
would turn against them. Equally frightening was the rise of a fifth
column from among Jamaica's indentured servants, many of whom
were Irish Catholics, or, most terrifying of all, the possibility of the
French somehow instigating an island-wide slave revolt. Out of this
chaos Sir Francis Watson, the island's longest-serving Council member, emerged as the prominent political player. A hard-drinking ex-
soldier, Watson had fought under Albemarle's father toward the end
of the Civil War and had gone on to win laurels for his role in a death-
or-glory charge at the siege of Maastricht in the Third Anglo-Dutch
War in 1673. Declaring martial law, Watson executed a virtual coup
d'état. Having awarded himself the title of lieutenant governor, he
garnered support, as had his predecessor, from among the middling
and lower classes, cementing his position through a combination of

bribery and intimidation. Unable to challenge Watson directly, his opponents in the plantocracy sent a series of missives to England begging for the restoration of the status quo. William and Mary duly obliged. As well as appointing Inchiquin as the island's new governor, the monarchs issued an edict canceling Albemarle's appointments along with any made subsequently, thus allowing Watson's opponents to return to their former posts. With the balance of power restored, an uneasy stalemate ensued.[8]

SUCH WAS THE STATE of affairs as HMS *Swan* and its convoy of eleven merchantmen dropped anchor off Port Royal on Saturday, May 31, 1690. Boarding the frigate's barge, which was decked out with gaily colored bunting, Inchiquin and his family were rowed ashore through a sea of small boats crammed with those keen to get a glimpse of their new leader. A series of salutes fired from forts Charles, Walker, James, and Carlisle as well as by the island sloops and armed English, North American, and Spanish merchantmen in the roads, coughed clouds of lingering, acrid smoke across the water. Port Royal was in the mood for celebration. As well as welcoming a new governor whose arrival promised to put an end to the chaos which had reigned since Albermarle's death, the inhabitants were relieved by the arrival of new supplies. With the threat of French attack, no fleet had reached Jamaica from England for some time: provisions were scarce and the wine, spirits, dry goods, and salt meat brought out in the ships' holds were very welcome indeed.[9]

On the sun-baked quayside a cosmopolitan crowd awaited. Among African slaves wearing loincloths and threadbare shirts were sunburned white servants dressed in coarse canvas breeches and smocks. Others had lined the length of Thames Street and gathered in and around the busy fish market, where hawkers tried to keep the flies off the barracuda, manatee, snapper, shark, tuna, stingray, and swordfish slowly putrefying in the heat. Crammed onto the balconies above and behind the glass windows of the two-, three-, and four-story houses overlooking the sand-surfaced thoroughfare, were the town's chief merchants and their families, well-to-do shopkeepers and artisans, planters who had left their country residences to be in town, and sev-

eral employees of the Royal African Company. Waving hats and hand-
kerchiefs, with the ladies resplendent in their best flowered silks
adorned with gold and silver lace, the crowd gave three cheers as
Inchiquin's barge approached. A militia band added to the jubilation,
rattling their drums and sounding their trumpets as the governor
stepped ashore at the Wherry Bridge in the heart of Port Royal's commercial district.[10]

The first to meet the new governor were the island's ruling elite.
At their head stood Sir Francis Watson, a heavy man, prone to asthma,
no doubt sweating heavily in the heat.[11] Also present were several
councilors. Dressed in their finest wigs, silk coats, patterned cottons
and vests trimmed with silver, and mohair shirts, they carried silver-
tipped canes and wore broad-brimmed hats, stockings, and gloves to
keep off the sun. Among them were Thomas Ballard, a veteran of the
1655 invasion, a colonel in the militia, and the owner of a 2,391-acre
sugar plantation in St. Catherine's Parish; Peter Beckford, a Council
member and colonel in the militia who had risen from humble begin-
nings to become the owner of a 1,000-acre estate in Clarendon Parish
and a house and several warehouses in Port Royal; Simon Musgrave,
the island's attorney general since 1686 and a major in the militia;
John White, a respected administrator, former chief justice, and Council member since 1671; Thomas Freeman, an ensign during the invasion, now the aging owner of plantations in St. David's and St.
Thomas's Parishes as well as of several properties in Port Royal including the Three Tunns, one of many taverns located in town; James
Walker, a forty-seven-year-old who suffered from chronic gout and
had been suspended from the Council for a year for daring to challenge Watson's right to govern; Samuel Bernard, a resident since the
mid-1660s who owned a large property on the quayside at Port Royal
and had held the post of chief justice since 1685; John Bourden, an
Irish Protestant and retired soldier who owned a considerable tract of
land near Spanish Town; and Peter Heywood, a former Royal Navy
captain who had risen to prominence as a planter despite having lost
his frigate, HMS *Norwich*, within sight of Port Royal after striking
the rocks on the East Middle Ground in 1682.[12] In the words of John
Pike, one of several Quaker residents, these were "great men," but full
of faults. "[They] were so swallowed up with pride," Pike had written

to his brother, "that a man could not be admitted to speak with them." The councilors' women, "whose top-knots seemed to reach the clouds," were equally guilty of ostentation and arrogance, a mix all too prevalent in the fundamentally flawed societies of the English West Indies.[13]

After greeting the councilors Inchiquin was ushered across Thames Street. Proceeded by Major Smith Kelly, the provost marshal carrying his ceremonial sword, and Charles Boucher, the recently appointed secretary of the Council, who bore a mace and the governor's seal, Inchiquin stepped onto a field of green cloth laid on the street's sandy surface, flanked by twin files of scarlet-coated militiamen standing to attention with their muskets presented.[14] The governor's train moved east down Thames Street away from the fish market, past the brick-built Feathers Tavern, with its second-floor billiard table, and skirted the entrance to Honey Lane.[15] Another company of militia fired a musket volley into the air as Inchiquin entered the grounds of King's House. A large, "timberwork" building surrounded by a high brick wall, it had last been occupied by Governor Molesworth and, until recently, had been used, with Watson's consent, by the Reverend Thomas Churchill for Catholic mass, much to the Protestant majority's displeasure.[16] Despite recent work carried out by slaves hired by the Council and a certain Margaret Boone, who had been paid £20 to whitewash the place, the building remained in a state of disrepair.[17] The refreshments arrayed on a long table in the yard were lavish. Two "tunns" of French claret had been decanted into bottles for the reception along with two whole pipes of Madeira wine.[18]

Jamaican feasts were noted for their extravagance. Eyewitnesses to similar scenes as that which confronted Inchiquin mention a wide selection of dishes: turtles cooked in their shells, imported salt beef and pork, wild jerked hog, roasted goat, tongue, fricasseed rabbit, brawn, capons, hashed pullet, fried and baked fish, roasted turkey, duck, turtledove, and pigeon. Other contemporary Jamaican dishes included potato pudding, pickled oysters, anchovies and olives, Irish butter, apples from New England, and English cheese. The Jamaican elite also enjoyed the great variety of fruit available on the island, many of which Inchiquin and his entourage had probably never seen. Watermelons, plantains, bananas, avocados, prickly pear, custard apples, and pineapples, the latter considered by many visitors to be the finest island fruit of all, would have been served along with pies, tarts, and pastries. Numerous toasts would have been drunk: to the longevity of the new king and queen, to the health of Inchiquin, and to the imminent defeat of the French.[19]

The next stop for the governor was St. Paul's Church. Heading south down Sweeting's Lane, a passage lined with shops, storehouses, and two-and three-story residences, the crowd passed beneath a covered stone walkway whose roof was supported by "large cedar pillars of ye dorrik order" where the town's merchants met in the cool of the morning to discuss fluctuations in prices and the state of international trade. The adjacent church was a small, sturdy structure, built in the shape of the cross and boasting a tall crenelated tower. Entering via the northern cloister, Inchiquin crossed the marble floor and was ushered into a chair of state, "cover'd with azur velvet, richly bost, fringed and embroider'd with . . . golden lions like Solomon's throne." Once Inchiquin was seated, the secretary of the Council, Charles Boucher, read his commission from King William and Queen Mary. The new governor was sworn in and an order read, proclaiming that all those holding public office were to continue in their posts until further notice.[20] A final tradition in the English colonies of the Caribbean was the presentation of a "Jew Pie" to the newly inaugurated governor. The "gift," consisting of a piecrust covering a purse of gold doubloons presented by the island's Jewish community as a means of currying favor, was no doubt warmly received.[21]

COVERING AN AREA of sixty acres, the Port Royal that welcomed Inchiquin that day contained over two thousand buildings crammed along a series of crooked streets and meandering thoroughfares and wedged into the intersections of narrow alleyways. Principal among them were the forts: Rupert, Charles, James, and Carlisle. Stone-built with strong ramparts and bastions, they housed magazines stocked with powder, muskets, pistols, hand grenades, fuses, and round shot and were manned by two companies of regular soldiers as well as two specialist gunners, Nathaniell Frigg and Richard Arnold, respected professionals who earned a salary of £27. The southern shore was guarded by a long breastwork known as Morgan's Line, studded with fourteen cannon. In all, the fortifications mounted over ninety guns, including heavy mortar which could lob shells high over the water to fall upon enemy shipping. Designed to prevent a naval descent, the guns covered the sea approaches which meandered between the numerous shoals and keys that dotted the bay, as well as dominating the shipping in the roads. On the eastern boundary of town, near the port's parade ground, was a wooden stockade known as the Pallisadoes which guarded the land approaches to the east. This common land, thickly planted with prickly pear to hinder infantry attack, was used for grazing goats and cattle, and a cleared area housed the town's principal burying place. Along with the resident battalion of one thousand militia armed with muskets and swords and divided into ten companies, at least one of which was on duty at all hours of the day and night, these fortifications made Port Royal one of the best defended towns in the Americas.[22]

Other buildings of note included the Jewish synagogue, the Audiencia where the courts of judicature were held, and the Marshalsea Prison, a brick building on Thames Street a few hundred yards east of the Wherry Bridge where the wharfs gave way to a strip of sand lined with canoes. Along with the town's second holding house, the Bridewell Prison, the Marshalsea housed Port Royal's "lazie strumpet[s]," pirates awaiting the gallows, mariners, and any others whose crimes were deemed too serious to be dealt with by the stocks, cage, or "ducking stoole."[23] Among those who had had the misfortune to be incarcerated in the period before Inchiquin's arrival was Lucretia Hall, "imprisoned . . . on pretence of witchcraft,"[24] and Roger Elleston, the former chief judge of the colony. Once a friend of Henry Morgan's and one of Francis Watson's principal supporters, Elleston was described by one contemporary as "one of the most pernicious &Vexatious sheriffs that was ever known." Charged with corruption and the illegal seizure of a Dutch merchantman and its cargo which had been divvied up by Watson and his supporters, Elleston had been arrested in October 1689.[25]

Port Royal had three markets: the fish market on Thames Street, where "for a royall you may have enough . . . to satisfie fouer reasonable men's appitites"; a "herb and fruit market held in the hart of the high street," where "fruitts and fowles" were available "fresh every morning, unless on the Sabbath"; and the "fleash and turtle" market at the west end of the High Street. "Plentifully stored with beef, mutton, hog, veal, lamb, kid and tortoise," the latter did its principal business "in the cold of ye morning and eavenings." The turtles in particular attracted the interest of first-time visitors, who often afforded these strange animals human traits. "This creature is . . . exceeding[ly] sencible,"one recorded, "for when he is layn on 's back, and he perceiveth the butcher coming to cut his throat, he will sigh, groan and weep like a child that is beaten, or a woman when she wants mony from hir husband." Turtle meat provided the principle source of protein for Port Royal's poor, identifiable by the fact that they "develop[ed] a strange yellowish tint to their skin and clothes" as a result. "[The meat] infect[s] the blood of those feeding on them," one of Port Royal's doctors explained, "whence their shirts are yellow, their skin and faces the same colour, and their shirts under the armpits stained prodigiously."[26]

Of Port Royal's private buildings, roughly six hundred were built of stone. According to John Taylor, a visitor in the late 1680s, many were "fouer story high, cellar'd, covered with tiles and glazed with sash windows." They had "large shops and comodious store-houses belonging to 'em." Due to the climate, the only fires used were those kept burning in the kitchens, typically built apart from the main buildings to reduce the heat. "These houses," Taylor continued, "yield as good rents as those in Chepeside in London, seldom less than £80 or £60 yearly rent, and lodgings are here very cleane, soe that you must give six dollars a month for one chamber reasonably furnished." Many were private residences; others were used as bakeries, butchers' shops, or artisans' workshops, their dim interiors partially illuminated by candle light. There were also several whorehouses, principally catering to the town's transient seafaring population, as well as numerous taverns and inns where customers could enjoy "a good glass of wine, a sangaree, or a joly bowl of good punch." Other attractions in Port Royal included "a bull and bear [kept] . . . for sport at ye bear garden and billiards, cockfitting, shotting at the target, etc." Others spent their leisure time playing shuffleboard or walking or riding in the common land beyond the Pallisadoes, where a tavern known as Barre's served excellent "silabubus, creamtarts, and other quelquechoses."[27]

On Inchiquin's arrival, Port Royal had a population of 6,500. A little over half were white: 1,500 men, 1,400 women and 1,000 children.[28] Although the majority of the remainder were enslaved Africans, there was also a smattering of free mulattoes and blacks. The former were largely the manumitted offspring of white fathers, the latter were all that remained of the community of Spanish-speaking maroons who had allied themselves to the English in the aftermath of the invasion of 1655.[29] Port Royal's slaves were mainly domestics. As such they were relatively better off than their peers on the plantations. Most were from Africa, but a growing minority were Jamaican-born creoles. There were also a small number of mulattoes and several Indians from the Mosquito Coast, the wilds of Florida, or the North American colonies, who had been enslaved after being captured in war. Although notorious for their propensity to commit suicide when faced with the monotonous hard work of the plantations, male Indian slaves were sought after for their expertise at hunting and fishing, while the women were valued for their ability to turn the ubiquitous yet highly poisonous cassava root into a nourishing flour with which to make bread.[30] Among the Indians resident in Port Royal on Inchiquin's arrival was a boy named Jack Straw, who was valued at £12 and owned by William Turner; Cupid, a boy worth £20 belonging to Thomas Gunn, a Quaker cooper who had been fined five shillings for his refusal to bear arms with the militia in 1687; and Andrew, an Indian man valued at £20 who was owned by John Griffin, a former pirate turned wreck salvager and legally sanctioned privateer.[31]

Port Royal's female slaves were cooks, cleaners, and concubines. Many of the men were liveried personal servants. Decked up in garish regalia, their chief task was to boost their master's prestige. Other Port Royal slaves worked as artisans in cottage industries, served in shops or taverns, or worked as merchants' assistants.[32] It seems likely that some of the fifty-four slaves belonging to John Willmaott, a Quaker shoemaker, helped their master with his trade. John Pike, another of the town's resident Quakers and a joiner by profession, owned fourteen. The most skilled slaves were of considerable value and may even have commanded some respect from their masters. While £20 to £26 was typically paid for a healthy male slave straight off the ships from Africa, Mino, "a negroe cooper" belonging to John Phillips, a Port

Royal merchant, was valued at £50 "with his tooles," and Pompey, another slave belonging to Phillips, was worth £60.[33]

Port Royal's white population was diverse. At the bottom of the social standings were the indentured servants. In exchange for their passage to Jamaica and board, clothing, and lodging, they were bonded to their masters for a period of between four and ten years. Though unpaid and frequently punished, they were often awarded, on the expiration of their contracts, a small plot of land, a cash bonus, or a parcel of colonial trade goods. It has been estimated that in the 1670s indentured servants were arriving in Jamaica at the rate of three hundred per year. Most merely hoped to improve their economic prospects, the more adventurous sought to escape a lack of opportunity at home; others were running from tiresome or abusive apprenticeships or the law. The majority were young single males from ten to twenty-four years of age. About a third came from agricultural backgrounds. Others were artisans, tradesmen, or unskilled laborers. There was also a smattering of professionals and young gentlemen fallen on hard times. Many, especially the children, had been tricked into signing on by unscrupulous "spiriters" who worked the poorer districts of London and the other large cities of England, Ireland, and Scotland, preying on "all the idle, lazie, simple people they . . . [could] entice." Once lured into holding houses near the docks with sweets or alcohol, they were detained for up to a month, before being bundled aboard ships bound for the Americas.[34]

Details of the lives of Jamaica's indentured servants are sparse. Most were employed in the plantations of the interior where they worked as overseers and served as a white counterbalance to the preponderance of potentially rebellious black slaves. Those who resided in Port Royal worked as domestic servants, housekeepers, and cooks.[35] Some female indentured servants were employed in "low class drinking establishments." Others worked as prostitutes.[36] A census conducted in Port Royal in 1680 revealed that a certain John Starr lived with twenty-one white women and two blacks, making it likely that he owned the largest whorehouse in town.[37] Some of Port Royal's prostitutes even earned considerable notoriety, none more so than Mary Carleton, known as "the German Princess." Born in Canterbury around 1634, Carleton was charged yet acquitted of bigamy in 1663, then briefly took to the stage before being arrested for theft and sentenced to transportation for life to Jamaica in 1671. There she wrote *News from Jamaica in a letter from Port Royal, to her fellow collegiates and friends in Newgate.* "A Stout frigate she was," recorded one contemporary, "or else she would never have endured so many batteries and assaults . . . but as common as a barber's chair: no sooner was one out, but another was in. [She was] cunning, crafty, subtle, and hot in pursuit of her intended designs." Carleton's tale ended in tragedy. Arrested for theft on her return to London, she swung from the hangman's noose at Tyburn in 1673.[38]

Port Royal's male indentured servants were sometimes apprenticed to craftsmen and manufacturers. Andrew Orgill, a planter turned Council member who owned properties in St. Mary's Parish on the north coast as well as in Port Royal, had six white servants in 1685. Most were men whose terms would expire before 1690, but one, a "Boy" named Christopher Gibbons, whose indenture had cost Orgill £8, still had nine years and two months left to serve when the record was taken. If he had not succumbed to disease, signed up on board a passing merchantman, or been pressed onto one of their Majesties' ships, it is possible that Gibbons was among the crowd on the quayside who witnessed Inchiquin's arrival on May 31.[39]

Some of Jamaica's indentured servants were convicted criminals, political prisoners, and religious dissidents. With no means to hold them in England, transportation to the colonies was an attractive alternative: as well as ridding England of undesirables, it also provided a source of cheap labor for the plantations while acting as a counterbalance to the ever-increasing number of African slaves. In the 1660s and 1670s about one hundred Quakers were forcibly transported to the Americas and eight hundred Scottish Covenanters were sent between 1660 and 1688, the majority in the aftermaths of the Battle of Bothwell Bridge in 1679 and the ill-fated Argyll Rising of 1685. Many were shipped to Jamaica by John Ewing, an Edinburgh merchant.[40] Among them was William Marshall, an Edinburgh smith, who wrote a letter explaining that the voyage from Leith to Port Royal had taken twelve weeks and that he and his fellow transportees were sold on arrival for £15 each. Several ended up working as overseers in the plantations. Others remained in town.[41]

Another group transported to Jamaica en masse were the Monmouth rebels. Seeking to place Charles II's illegitimate son on the throne in 1685 in lieu of the Catholic James II, they had been defeated at the Battle of Sedgemoor. The Duke of Monmouth was executed along with one hundred and fifty of his followers. Eight hundred and fifty others were sentenced to ten years' indenture in the Americas, of which two hundred and thirty arrived at Port Royal.[42] Among them was a Somerset carpenter and dissenting preacher named John Coad, who later published an account of his experiences. Taken to London in October 1685, Coad was bundled aboard the *Jamaica Merchant* along with one hundred others. Conditions aboard were comparable to those on the slave ships running the Middle Passage. Locked "under deck in a very small room where . . . [they] could not lay . . . down without lying upon one upon another," twenty-two died in transit. At Port Royal, the rest were auctioned and distributed around the island. Those who survived the initial seasoning period found good work in the plantations. Coad was sold to Colonel Samuel Bach, a leading planter. Freed after four years' service, Coad eventually made his way back to England along with half of the men he had been sent into exile with.[43] The rest were still in Jamaica when Inchiquin arrived carrying a missive from James II's successor, King William, ordering their immediate pardon.[44]

Above the indentured servants of Port Royal was a "middle class" of professionals, artisans, shopkeepers, and tradesmen. The lower rank, semi-skilled workers such as porters, watermen, blacksmiths, bricklayers, carpenters, tailors, and glove makers, typically acquired estates worth £50 to £150 by the time they died. More specialized and skilled craftsmen such as cabinetmakers, pewterers, goldsmiths, silversmiths, and glaziers and those who produced goods in bulk, such as the tanners and coopers, stood to amass goods worth between £250 and £500. The wealthiest of the middle rank were those who sold food and drink. Port Royal's bakers, butchers, tavern keepers, victuallers, and vintners were often worth in excess of £700. Among the individuals plying such trades on Inchiquin's arrival were a tanner named Thomas Buckley who owned two slaves; Robert Howard, a butcher with a nine-room property and twelve white servants; and Moses Watkins, a carpenter turned innkeeper who presided over the Catt

Sir Hans Sloane. An Anglo-Irish doctor, author and naturalist, Sloane's *A Voyage to Jamaica*, compiled in the late 1680s when he was resident on the island as Governor Albemarle's personal physician, is an invaluable historical source for the period. (*Engraving from a portrait by T. Murray, c. 1700*)

and Fiddle. There were also several gold and silversmiths, masons, sailmakers, pipe makers, and a handful of craftsmen who used the turtle shells they purchased from the fish market to make intricately decorated combs, snuff boxes, and mirror backs.[45]

Several doctors, chemists, and surgeons resided in Port Royal. John Taylor, the visitor quoted above, considered many no better than "a parcell of pittyfull quacks, empericks, and illiterat pretendors," while conceding that others, including the druggist William Matthews, and doctor Christopher Love Morley, a forty-four-year-old graduate of Leiden University—the oldest such institution in the Netherlands— were "honest . . . learn'd, skillful and men of known integrity."[46] Undoubtedly the best-known doctor to visit Jamaica in the period was Hans Sloane. An Irish Protestant born into a family of influence in County Down in 1660, young Sloane had studied medicine, chemistry, and botany in Paris and Montpellier before returning to London, where he was admitted into the Royal College of Physicians on April 13, 1687. In the same year he became the personal physician to Christopher Monck, the second Duke of Albemarle, who had recently been appointed governor of Jamaica. Sloane would spend over two years on the island. As well as treating both white and black residents for a variety of ailments, principally those related to excessive alcohol consumption, the doctor collected over eight hundred plant samples and compiled detailed notes on the island's flora, fauna, and natural phenomena before his return to England in March 1689.[47]

Another of Jamaica's doctors was Thomas Trapham. Arriving in 1673, Trapham lived with his wife, Susannah Coxe, and several children in a house near the quayside, whilst also co-owning the Hermitage, a 1,500-acre plantation in St. Mary's Parish where the doctor's slaves were branded "with TsT on ye right shoulder." Trapham had served as personal physician to Lord Vaughn, governor of Jamaica from 1675 to 1678, and as a member of the island Assembly in 1677. Two years later Trapham's *Discourse of the State of Health in the island of Jamaica* was published. According to the accepted theory of the day, the book maintained that good health was a matter of keeping the body's four humors: black bile, yellow bile, phlegm, and blood, in a state of balance—a juggling act only possible through the judicious use of bleeding, purging, and scarification and the administration of various medicines which included infusions made with rare and costly herbs, roots, and spices. In 1688, Trapham was called upon to treat the ailing Lord Albemarle in consultation with the governor's personal physician, the aforementioned Hans Sloane. Despite their best efforts, the duke, a hopeless alcoholic, died on October 6, 1688. When a rumor spread that Albemarle had been badly treated, "Dr. Trapham and the rest of his Grace's physicians . . . desired that . . . [the Council] appoint someone to view his Grace's corps[e], which they are now going to Embalme" in an attempt to clear their names. Two days later, "Coll Freeman and Coll Ballard," the dignitaries appointed by the Council for the purpose, "made their Report, that they went to view his Grace's Body, which being opened by the doctors and Chirurgeons present: they saw that his Vitals were very defective except his Heart and it was the opinion of all those present that he could not longer subsist." Trapham and Sloane had been exonerated. While the latter returned to England shortly afterward, Trapham remained resident in Port Royal on Inchiquin's arrival.[48]

A significant minority of Port Royal's middling set were Quakers. A few were former servants forced into indenture as a punishment for their nonconformity, but the majority had chosen to immigrate to Jamaica, an unusually tolerant society for the age, to escape persecution at home.[49] One such was Thomas Hillyard, a Friend who owned a shop at the junction of New Street and Common Street. Another was John Pike, the enterprising joiner mentioned above who shared his home with his wife, Ann, his son, an apprentice, a white maid, and six of his fourteen slaves. It seems Pike's business was a roaring success. He owned two empty lots of land, a rare commodity in chronically overcrowded Port Royal, on which he intended to build ten houses. Another Quaker tradesman resident in Port Royal was Thomas Gunn, the cooper who owned the Indian boy named Cupid. Gunn also kept £100 worth of wooden hoops and iron bindings in his shop, which he and his slaves made into barrels to sell to the masters of the merchantmen anchored in the roads.[50]

Another notable minority were Port Royal's Huguenots. French Protestants who were persecuted for their beliefs by the Catholic majority in their homeland, the Huguenots had fled France in the thousands over the course of the sixteenth century, a trend which increased dramatically following Louis XIV's 1685 Revocation of the Edict of Nantes, a bill previously granting them a measure of religious toleration. With the full apparatus of the Sun King's draconian regime operating against them, forty to fifty thousand emigrated to England in the late 1680s. They were welcomed by King William's new regime: as well as being famed for their enterprise, industry, and aptitude for trade, the Huguenots were known for their military prowess, while England's hatred of Papists, perhaps the strongest emotional force in the country in the post–Glorious Revolution period, ensured that the native population was largely sympathetic to their plight. Many emigrant Huguenots worked in the textile industry, a craft at which they were among the most skilled in Europe. Their move to London proved a boon for the trade. Others immigrated to England's colonies in North America, or the West Indies.[51]

Among the Huguenots resident at Port Royal on Inchiquin's arrival were two figures of note. Born in Montpellier in 1659, Lewis Galdy had immigrated to Jamaica in the late 1680s to set himself up as a merchant. Initially of modest means, Galdy was a wealthy man by 1690. As well as dealing in the sugar and slave trades, he dabbled in local politics and had become a figure of "Great Reputation" in Port Royal "beloved by all who knew him."[52] Peter Bratelier had fled France in 1685. Granted English citizenship two years later as part of James II's amnesty to French refugees, Bratelier relocated to Jamaica where he worked as a sloop captain. Although not of Galdy's stature, Bratelier was successful in his own way. Alternating between captaining the *Newcastle* sloop and the *Mayflower* brigantine, he traded for codfish with the Dutch at Curaçao as well as occasionally trying his hand as a wreck salvager when the opportunity arose.[53]

Of paramount importance to the economy of Port Royal were the town's merchants. Between 1674 and 1701 at least twenty-three were resident. Their average estate was well over £1,000. Most had premises and storehouses along Thames Street bordering the wharfs to the north of town. From their garret windows they could keep an eye on the comings and goings of the two hundred or so merchant vessels that arrived annually from ports all across the Caribbean and the wider Atlantic world. As well as the large convoys, typically of between six and a dozen vessels, which arrived from England three or four times per year with dry goods, beer, cider, spirits, and Madeira wine, there were weekly arrivals from England's North American colonies. These ships carried much-needed provisions. As the Jamaican plantations specialized in sugar monoculture, they were unable to supply their own needs. Barrels of salt pork and beef, beer, flour, frying oil, mackerels, herrings, onions, apples, and bacon; bags of bread; bushels of pease; rundlets of hog's lard; firkins of butter, and whole cheeses were shipped from Boston, Salem, and Marblehead in New England, as well as from New York, Rhode Island, Pennsylvania, Virginia, and Carolina. Another cargo commonly shipped from North America were the hoops and staves of red and white oak the Jamaican plantation owners used to make barrels in which to export their sugar and rum. Barrels of cod and salt fish caught off the Grand Banks were imported directly from Newfoundland; hundreds of chests of candles (both the inferior variety made of beeswax and the costlier variety made of spermaceti wax) were shipped to Jamaica from locations across the North American seaboard. Other goods arrived in Port

Royal from a variety of Caribbean locales. Rosewater was shipped from Bermuda; mules and stock fish came from Rio de la Hachain in modern-day Colombia; logwood, a timber much sought after for the red dye which could be extracted, was shipped from the bays of Campeche or Honduras in Central America; and salt was imported from Curaçao.[54]

All these ships also required homebound cargoes. While sugar, either packed in barrels or measured by the hundredweight, was the principal Jamaican export, ships bound for England also took barrels of rum; bundles of logwood reexported from Campeche; indigo, a purple dye-wood grown in Jamaica; cacao; ginger; and small quantities of sarsparilla, the latter much prized for its medicinal properties. Other minor exports included bags of cotton and barrels packed with pimento, a fiery Jamaican spice. Fustic, a plant from which a yellow dye could be extracted, was also shipped to Europe to serve the clothing industries of northern England and Flanders.[55]

Another important export was transhipped Spanish bullion and gold and silver coin. Jamaica was the hub of the Caribbean reexport trade. Many of the English manufactured goods landed at Port Royal never got any further into the island than the merchants' warehouses on the quayside. Instead, they were either sold to one of the Spanish merchantmen that regularly called in at Port Royal in defiance of Madrid's strict trading regulations, which entirely prohibited trade with foreigners, or smuggled into the Spanish colonies by one of Jamaica's fleet of small, swift-sailing sloops. These vessels sailed for Havana in Cuba, Portobelo (in modern-day Panama), or Cartagena, on the Spanish Main. Anchoring at spots distant from the prying eyes of the few uncorrupted customs officials, they waited for local traders to arrive with whom they exchanged their goods for treasure and hard currency, the one remaining commodity that the Spanish colonies had in relative abundance. According to Francis Hanson, a resident writing in 1682, Port Royal was awash with "bars and cakes of Gold, wedges and pigs of Silver, Pistoles, Pieces of Eight and several other Coyns of both Mettles . . . wrought Plate, Jewels, rich Pearl Necklaces, and of Pearl unsorted or undrilled." Added to this was the high-quality gold dust which the Guinea men brought from West Africa which was occasionally used in Port Royal to pay for supplies and repairs.

Much of this wealth eventually found its way back to England where it was used to fuel the war effort against France.[56]

The Port Royal merchants who profited from such transactions were an eclectic mix. William and Francis Hall were brothers who had relocated to Port Royal in 1687 from London to act as Jamaican factors for a variety of individuals and firms based in the English capital.[57] Peter Qoudan and Dirck Wessels originally hailed from the provinces of the United Netherlands. The former had moved to Jamaica from Curaçao in the 1660s after finding himself in financial difficulties, while the latter had relocated from New York following its capture by England in the Second Anglo-Dutch War.[58] Other factors resident in Port Royal were Thomas, Isaac, and Joseph Norris, part of Jamaica's growing congregation of Quakers. Originally from London, the Norrises had relocated to Port Royal in 1678 due to the wave of religious persecution sweeping England in the wake of the Civil War. While the father, Thomas, and his eldest son, Joseph, were permanently based in Port Royal, the younger sibling, Isaac, regularly traveled between Jamaica and Philadelphia to manage the family's business connections in the North American colonies. Despite objecting to the debauchery and ostentation prevalent among Port Royal's elite, occasional harassment from the town militia for their refusal to bear arms, and the fact that Joseph and his wife, Martha, had lost both their children to disease, the Norrises prospered in Jamaica. As well as working as a factor, Joseph co-owned Thomas Hillyard's shop on New Street and had a share in at least one London-built broad stern which visited Port Royal roads. By 1690 his estate was worth some £4,000.[59]

Another powerful mercantile contingent in Port Royal were the Portuguese Jews. Many of them, or their ancestors, had formerly been residents of the Dutch colony established in 1630 in Recife in Brazil, where they had been respected for their mercantile skills and enjoyed the religious freedom afforded them by the laws of the United Netherlands. Driven by sugar production and trade, the colony initially prospered, but in 1645 came under guerrilla attack from the former owners of Recife, the Portuguese. After a decade of struggle, the Dutch were forced to surrender. Under threat of persecution by the Inquisition if they remained, the Jewish community emigrated. Many went to Holland, twenty-three sailed to New Amsterdam (later to be renamed New York), while others chose to settle in the Caribbean. Several of the latter made their way to Spanish Jamaica, where a handful aided the English in their invasion of 1655. Others reached the island later via Suriname or Barbados, and a Jewish cemetery was established at Hunt's Bay, across the water from Port Royal, in the late 1660s. Immigration became especially notable in the following decade under Governor Molesworth, who valued the new arrivals for their international connections and understanding of global trade, and in 1677 land was purchased on Port Royal's New Street, or Jew Street as it came to be known, to build a synagogue. In 1683 Rabbi Haham Josiau Pardo, a Jew from Amsterdam who had also lived in Curaçao, arrived to administer to the spiritual needs of his coreligionists, and by 1690, despite the ever-present threat of anti-Semitism, the community is estimated to have numbered between one hundred and three hundred individuals. Many of Port Royal's Jews were wealthy and the community was of considerable economic importance. The Jews had interests in the sugar and slave trades and the manufacture of items in gold and silver, as well as being the island's principal moneylenders. Among the most prominent at the time of Inchiquin's arrival were Isaac Rodriguez de Sousa, a moneylender whose estate was valued at over £9,000; Moises de Lucena, a leading merchant whose trade interests stretched from Jamaica to New York and London and beyond; and Moses Cordoso, a merchant who specialized in buying sick slaves from the Royal African Company at low prices to sell on to the planters at a profit after they had recovered their health to some extent.[60]

Equally powerful economically (and considerably more so in the political realm) were Port Royal's resident factors for the Royal African Company. Charles Penhallow was a captain in the Port Royal militia with his own company to command, a churchwarden, and the owner of The Three Mariners, a tavern on Honey Lane. As well as holding 204 acres of land in the prime planting parish of St. Thomas, Penhallow owned a valuable plot in Old Harbour, the largest settlement in Clarendon.[61] His fellow agent, Walter Ruding, lived with his wife and family on Thames Street, directly opposite the wharfs and warehouses lining the bay on the north side of town. Even better connected than his partner, Ruding was immensely rich and would soon be nominated for a seat on the island's Council. As well as the salary he earned from the company, Ruding held various trade interests and received regular commissions from the slave auctions held on board the company's ships upon their arrival from Africa. It is also apparent that he accepted payments from favored customers, principal among whom was the representative of the asiento, Sir James Castillo, in exchange for allowing them first selection when purchasing slaves. Although this angered the planters, who were left to squabble with the Jews over the "refuse negroes" surplus to Castillo's requirements, it also brought Ruding great riches. Unlike the planters, who lacked currency, demanded credit, and were often only able to pay for purchases in sugar during harvest time, the Spanish had access to silver and gold coin. According to one associate, James Wale, who lived in the house next door on Thames Street and was married to Ruding's sister-in-law, by the 1690s Ruding's estate was worth in excess of £10,000.[62]

The final significant element of Port Royal's population were several hundred itinerant mariners.[63] Although of no fixed abode, this peripatetic band spent the majority of their earnings in Port Royal. Most found work with the island's fleet of one hundred sloops. Small, well-built, fast, well-armed, and well-manned, these vessels were based out of Chocolata Hole, a bay on the western edge of Cagway Spit near a line of turtle pens under the guns of Fort Charles. The sloops were engaged in a variety of trades. With the outbreak of war, a few would find work privateering; others were engaged in the coasting trade, shipping goods between the island's secondary ports and Port Royal. Wreck salvage was a potentially profitable yet intermittent alternative. Preying on the half-sunken hulks of the Spanish galleons which occasionally met their ends on the rocks and banks surrounding the island, the wreckers were allowed to keep 90 percent of their findings providing they gave the remainder to the crown. Other options included making the run to the Cayman Islands to fetch breeding turtles to sell at Port Royal's fish market; shipping logwood harvested at Campeche or Honduras; inter-island trade with the other English colonies in the Caribbean; running the triangular routes between London, Jamaica, and North America; interloping for slaves in West Africa; and the lucrative yet risky option of dealing in contraband with the Spanish Main. Despite the threat of the crew's arrest and the seizure of the ship (as many as four hundred of Jamaica's residents could be found languishing in Spanish jails at any one time), the potential profits and wages of up to forty-five shillings per month ensured the business was well served.[64]

Among the sloops operating out of Chocolata Hole on Inchiquin's arrival were the *Rebecca*, a fifteen-ton, ten-gun vessel which traded with London and whose master and sometime privateer, William Peartree, would go on to become the twenty-eighth mayor of New York;[65] the *Speedwell*, a sloop occasionally registered to Cornelius Essex, a former pirate who had raided Portobelo in 1680 and had since turned his hand to wreck salvage;[66] the *Samuel Barque*, whose master, Giles Shelley, traded between New York, Jamaica, and Curaçao;[67] the *Ann*, a thirty-tonner commanded by a wrecker and trader named Daniel Plowman who regularly sailed between Gambia and Jamaica breaking the RAC's monopoly;[68] the *Diligence*, whose master, a slave-owning privateer and wrecker named Robert Scroope, also had a quarter share in the vessel's ownership worth £75;[69] and *George's Adventure*, an eight-tonner registered to Thomas Craddock, the unlikely owner of one of Port Royal's better stocked libraries which featured over one hundred tomes including "4 new gilt Bibles," "6 common prayer books," and "thirty plays," as well as Craddock's *Apostolocall History*, Edmund Spenser's *Faerie Queen*, *The Golden Fleece*, and a history of the reign of Richard II by Buck Gusman.[70]

In charge of marshaling this disparate group, as well as the masters and sailors who arrived from North America, West Africa, England, Ireland, and elsewhere, was another of Port Royal's leading players: the naval officer Reginald Wilson. One of eight sons born in Bradfield, England, in 1645, Wilson had served as an apprentice tailor before arriving in Jamaica prior to 1675 when he was appointed to his current post, yet another example of the opportunities available for those willing to relocate. As well as recording all ships' arrivals and departures in a leather-bound ledger kept in the property he owned on the quayside where he lived with his son and several slaves, Wilson was charged with ensuring the Navigation Acts were enforced; collecting port fees; apprehending pirates; providing pilots for masters unfamiliar with the rocky shoals which had bested Peter Heywood in 1682; keeping a quayside storehouse stocked with wood and provisions; and taking care that no masters or sailors violated rules concerning the proper disposal of ballast. Typically for the age, Wilson also had several other roles. As well as serving as one of the island's assemblymen, he was a churchwarden for Port Royal and a judge at the court of common pleas. He also found time to dabble in trade and corresponded regularly with William Blathwayt, the Westminster-based secretary of trade and foreign plantations.[71]

As INCHIQUIN WOULD LEARN, seventeenth-century Jamaica had given rise to a peculiarly debauched society. With a population consisting largely of recent immigrants, both black and white, who had had little or no exposure to the virulent diseases of the tropics, mortality rates were high: one in three new arrivals would die in their first three years on the island. Due to the physical demands of plantation work, male immigrants were much more valued than females, leading to a considerable sexual imbalance and a corresponding prevalence of self-destructiveness and lack of restraint.[72] The majority of the population had been coerced into migrating, and many of the whites, even those who had somehow risen to the ranks of the island's elite, came from the lowest reaches of society, and a significant minority had already been criminalized. Immense wealth could be garnered rapidly for little work from investment in trade or sugar production, there was a notable lack of culture and religion, and a climate of gross brutality governed the everyday lives of both blacks and the majority of whites—capital and corporal punishment were frequent, and public, events.

All these factors enabled the residents to develop a self-indulgent attitude toward sin: if one was to die tomorrow, why not enjoy today? As early as 1671 the North American merchant John Blackleach was shocked by the "high presumptuous sinning" in Jamaica; another North American, Samuel Sewall, worried that a young relative would lose his religion if he spent long on the island; and the Quaker Isaac Norris advised his friend to steer clear of Jamaica—"though we do not live so flash and fast [in the North American colonies]," he warned, "yet we live well and enjoy life with a better gust."[73] Alcoholism was rife in Jamaica and gluttony was widespread. Both resulted in a number of common health complaints, not least of which was gout, an illness that the doctor Hans Sloane had had to treat frequently during his fifteen-month hiatus at Jamaica in the late 1680s. Visitors frequently commented on the indolence of the population; sexual morals were loose; and corruption at all levels of society, even by the standards of the age, was endemic.[74]

GOVERNOR AND LADY INCHIQUIN were allowed precious little time to recover from the ordeal of their transatlantic crossing. After a whirlwind of ceremonies and introductions in Port Royal, the new governor and his family made their way to the administrative capital of Spanish Town to set up home.[75] The journey was typically undertaken by wherry, a clinker-built rowing boat with overhanging bows which allowed passengers to step ashore dry-shod. From the quayside of Port Royal these craft regularly ferried passengers six miles across the bay to Passage Fort, a small settlement built in a low marshy valley between two hills where the Rio Cobre entered the bay. Founded by the Spanish to defend the route to the capital, the site's eponymous fort had long since been demolished and by 1690, the village, a place Taylor noted was "both day and night miserably torment[ed] with stinging insects," consisted of "thirty houses, ten taverns, and as many storehouses" where the planters from Sixteen Miles' Walk and the other plantations of St. Catherine's Parish stockpiled their sugar for dispatch to Port Royal.[76] From Passage Fort, the Inchiquins traveled six miles by hackney carriage along "a smooth, sandy road," flanked by sugar plantations, past a limestone rise known as Craigellachie Hill, before emerging onto "a spacious, grassy plain, sprinkled with wild flowers." In the shadow of the Blue Mountains, the meadow was fed by the Rio Cobre, "an excelent cleare river of sweet water" on the banks of which the capital of Jamaica lay.[77]

Santiago de la Vega, or Spanish Town as its English residents referred to it, had been a large city under Spanish occupation. Built on a regular grid system, its broad streets had covered an area of six square miles. The city had since entered a period of decline with the advent of English control. Three quarters of the buildings had been burned during the invasion, and, on Inchiquin's arrival, just three hundred remained. In contrast to the towering, four-story brick homes crammed into Port Royal's twisting alleyways, most of the houses in Santiago de la Vega were built in the Spanish style. Low, sturdy, and spacious with deep wooden foundations, large doors, latticed windows, and palm-thatched roofs, they were designed to provide a cool, breezy retreat as well as being able to withstand the seismic activity which regularly shook the island. Of the original four churches, only St. Paul's survived into the English era, while the old Spanish monastery, a large, brick building encompassed by a curtain wall, had been converted into the governor's residence. In the town center stood a vast parade ground, capable of holding five thousand troops, and the Audiencia, a large building used to host the Grand Court of Judicature four times a year.[78]

Having taken up residence in the old monastery which his wife, Elizabeth, would furnish with such exotic paraphernalia as a Japanese bedstead, table stands and looking glass, a Russian leather couch and twenty chairs, and a patriotic portrait of William and Mary valued at £20, on Wednesday, June 4, Inchiquin presided over the first Council meeting to be held at Spanish Town since his arrival.[79] Seated on five of the Council Chamber's twelve "leather chaires" which were positioned around a central table, Sir Francis Watson, Thomas Ballard, Thomas Freeman, John White, and John Bourden attended. Once oaths of allegiance had been sworn, the governor was presented with a long list of grievances authored by Jamaica's principal landowners. They complained about Watson's illegal and partisan government; his use of "arbitrary and despotical power"; his use of violence and intimidation to achieve his aims; his promotion of "ye meanest tradesmen" to positions of power; and the fact that he had "govern[ed] . . . absolutely by ye sword" during his brief tenure.[80] For Inchiquin the process was both confusing and exhausting. "I find the animosities here far greater than I imagined," he later confessed in a letter to the Lords of Trade, "not due to the late transactions but to fifteen or sixteen years standing of turbulent and pernicious advisers. . . . Since the disease has been of so long duration you will not expect a sudden cure. . . . The Courts of Judicature have fallen [silent] nearly two years. People have lived without law or justice, to the great encouragement of malefactors and to the strengthening of pretensions to martial law. Such exorbitances have been committed as I believe were never heard of, but now that the Courts are open again the offenders will be brought to condign punishment, though all that they are worth will never make amends for the mischief they have done."[81]

A second, related order of business for the Council that Wednesday morning was the fate of a long-detained Dutch merchantman, the *St. Jago de la Victoria*. Under service of the asiento and flying Spanish colors, the ship had left Cadiz for Portobelo sometime in 1689. On its return voyage, laden with eight chests of Spanish silver, its captain, Mr. Daniels, had called in at Port Royal for provisions. Learning that such a wealthy vessel had been dropped into his lap, Watson moved fast, detaining it on the premise that it was a Dutchman trading in Jamaica and therefore in contravention of the Navigation Act. With the aid of Roger Elleston and several other officials, each of whom received a cut of the spoils, Watson stripped the *St. Jago* of its silver as well as eight of its cannon, which were promptly remounted on the *Calapatch*, a sloop occasionally used for coastal defense. As Inchiquin soon realized, the charges of unwarranted detention and illegal profiteering leveled against Watson as a result of the incident were clear cut: although the accused had assumed the title of governor, he was not legally so at the time and therefore not permitted to convene a court of seizure; furthermore, specific instructions had been received from England that no new courts were to be held; and the items that Captain Daniels had purchased in Port Royal were merely provisions for use onboard ship and therefore not covered by the terms of the Navigation Act. Nevertheless, due process had to be followed. Once a date had been set for hearing an appeal from Captain Daniels's lawyers, the Council was dismissed until further notice.[82]

Friday, June 6, brought news of the death of one of the longest-serving members of the Council. Having first set foot in Jamaica in 1655 as a "soldier of fortune" linked to Penn and Venables's invasion force, Thomas Fuller had become a Jamaican institution. The owner of a 1,309-acre plantation in St. Catherine's Parish, he had been a member of the Council since 1678, had served as a colonel in the island militia, and had donated the land on which the sparsely attended Tamarind Tree Church in Old Harbour, St. Dorothy's Parish, had been built in 1681. "Much troubled with gout" aggravated by an excessive consumption of red meat and managed with regular doses of opiates, Fuller had been in deteriorating health since at least 1687 when he had been treated by Hans Sloane. Buried in the church which he had patronized, Fuller left a son, Charles, who inherited his estate, and his fifty-year-old wife, Catherine, whom Sloane had once treated for "a swimming in her head" and "a great many incoherent and troublesome Fancies and Chimeras in her thoughts."[83]

On June 12, the Council met at Port Royal. Peter Heywood, the former Royal Navy captain who had had the misfortune to wreck his ship within sight of Port Royal, was present, along with Inchiquin, Watson, White, Freeman, Bourden, and Ballard. The ongoing dismantling of Watson's regime was the order of the day. A petition written by Roger Elleston requesting release from the Marshalsea Prison was read. The former chief justice was duly granted bail, but Samuel Mayo, another of Watson's adherents, was ordered to pay securities of £400 to ensure he did not flee the island while awaiting prosecution at the next Grand Court "for words tending to sedition and rebellion." Inchiquin was then called upon to read William and Mary's order of January 9, declaring that the Monmouth rebels sentenced to transportation were to be released forthwith. The order proved somewhat belated. Half of the rebels, having served four years' indenture, had already left the colony. The remainder had settled, having found well-paid work as boilers, distillers, refiners, and overseers on the sugar plantations inland.[84]

Mid-June saw a momentous arrival. One of many effects of the outbreak of war with France was that Jamaica had been starved of slave deliveries. Only a single Royal African Company vessel, the *Blossom*, which arrived from Angola with 280 "negroes" on October 14, 1689, had reached the island from West Africa in the previous twenty-two months.[85] Although some undocumented interlopers had no doubt arrived in the interim, the large ships of the Royal African Company, which could deliver up to six hundred slaves at a time, had been sorely missed. Due to high mortality rates and frequent desertions, slave owners had to constantly top up their labor forces or risk them diminishing despite the occasional boon of new births. In 1688, for example, it was estimated that Jamaica would need to import ten thousand slaves annually to maintain its population of thirty thousand—meaning that one in three was expected to die every year.[86]

Slave prices had risen as a result of the recent dearth and many planters were left with no other recourse but to buy low-quality or sick "refuse negroes" from "Jews and beggarly sub-brokers."[87] On Monday, June 16, 1690, all this was about to change. That morning, news spread around town that the *Hannah*, a Royal African Company vessel of 170 tons and 22 guns, was in the offing. On board were 359 slaves to be auctioned at Port Royal to the highest bidder.[88] Although hugely profitable, the *Hannah*'s voyage had been far from straightforward. One third of the slaves it had picked up in West Africa and nearly half of the crew with which it had left London over eighteen months before had died.[89]

CHAPTER 3

Black Ivory

The *Hannah* and the West African Slave Trade
July 1689–June 1690

The stench became absolutely pestilential. The closeness of the place, and the heat of the climate, added to the number in the ship, which was so crowded that each had scarcely room to turn himself, almost suffocated us. This produced copious perspirations, so the air soon became unfit . . . from a variety of loathsome smells, and brought on many a sickness . . . of which many died. . . . The wretched situation . . . aggravated by the galling of the chains . . . became insupportable; and the filth of the necessary tubs, into which the children often fell, and were almost suffocated. The shrieks of the women and the groans of the dying, rendered the whole a scene of horror almost inconceivable.

—Olaudah Equiano, *The Interesting Narrative*, 1789

ON DECEMBER 8, 1689, Charles Danvers, the master of the Royal African Company's slave vessel the *Hannah*, opened his account book for trade. In response to a series of smoke signals emitted on shore, the 22-gun sloop had dropped anchor at its first port of call: the estuary of the Sanguin River. Located in the Malaguetta, "Tooth," "Grain," or Quaqua Coast, the Sanguin emptied its muddy waters into the Atlantic at a point roughly equidistant between the capes of Sierra Leone and Palmas, six degrees south of the equator on the Windward Coast of West Africa. As Danvers scanned the shoreline through the heat haze, with flies and malarial mosquitoes buzzing around his head and his clothes steaming from the frequent tropical downpours, he

spotted movement off the palm-fringed beach. Several three-man canoes were paddling out through the muddy waters from an area dominated by a stand of high trees. Dressed in wide-sleeved shifts which
hung to their knees, the Quaquas, as the Europeans called them, had
a terrifying appearance. "Well-limb'd," strong, and athletic, they
daubed their skin "with a sort of dark reddish paint." Their hair, which
hung down to their shoulders, was plaited with flax and their teeth
were filed to razor sharp points. As well as being rumored to practice
cannibalism, the locals of Sanguin were notorious for theft. As they
boarded the *Hannah*, Danvers warned his thirty-strong crew to be on
their guard.[1]

Danvers's voyage had begun in London six months earlier. After a
seemingly interminable delay, enforced by port authorities who tightly
regulated all merchant ships' departures during wartime to ensure that
enough sailors remained in the country to man the ships of the Royal
Navy, the *Hannah* had set out from Custom House Quay with a special license on July 20, 1689.[2] Like all outbound vessels of the Royal
African Company, the sloop was deeply loaded: forty bales of perpetuanas, a hard-wearing, cheap textile manufactured in England's West
Country; twenty-two cases of pewter, containing basins of one, two,
and three pounds in weight; two bales of boysadoes, a heavy, expensive
cloth imported from Holland; one bale of Welsh plains; eight bales
of bays, another British textile; twenty-three casks of knives; 450 iron
and lead bars; 156 gallons of French brandy; twenty barrels of gunpowder; and 150 half firkins of tallow along with numerous scales and
measures with which Danvers would weigh out his goods were packed
in the hold. The cargo, when customs and other charges were included, was worth a total of £2,617, 14 shillings and sixpence. Also
on board were £910, 17s. 10 d. worth of stores, goods, and provisions
which Danvers had been entrusted to deliver to the company's principal African outpost at Cape Coast Castle on the Gold Coast.[3]

The trade goods were intended for the first of the *Hannah*'s desti-
nations, the Windward and Gold Coasts. The former, reached after a
brief stop at the company's outpost on the Gambia River, stretched
some five hundred miles between Cape Mount and Cape Palmas and
had become increasingly important for the Royal African Company
since 1680. More goods were consigned to the region than to any of

the other seven regions into which the Europeans divided West Africa. With the outbreak of the Nine Years' War, however, trade had slowed considerably. Unlike the Gold Coast, where Danish, French, German, Dutch, and English forts provided safe haven, the Windward Coast was almost entirely devoid of European settlement. As such it was frequented by pirates and French privateers: the latter had already taken five of the company's ships in African waters that year. The Windward Coast's remoteness also resulted in uneven trade. Business, as Danvers was discovering, was uncertain and slow. Specific ports of call were left entirely to the discretion of the ship's captains and although trade could be plentiful, it was invariably carried out in small amounts. To make matters worse, the Royal African Company's rivals, not to mention the countless illegal interlopers, also did business there, resulting in oft-flooded markets.[4]

The crew of the *Hannah* had less trouble at Sanguin than expected. In exchange for twelve iron bars, Danvers received 630 ozier, or wickerwork, baskets filled with malaguetta which were promptly stowed in the ship's hold. Known as paradise-grains or Guinea pepper, malaguetta was a fiery condiment that grew on shrubs inland. As well as giving the coast one of the names by which it was known to its European visitors, the pepper was an essential purchase for all slavers. "[We] give [it to] our negroes in their messes to keep them from the flux and dry belly'ach, which they are very incident to," Captain Thomas Phillips, another of the Royal African Company's captains, explained in his journal written two years after the *Hannah's* voyage had been concluded. Although Danvers was yet to begin picking up a human cargo, he would need the malaguetta soon enough.[5]

On the afternoon of December 8, Danvers left Sanguin for the Bay of Boffoe, one mile to the east. Watching for the half-submerged rocks, shoals, and sandbanks for which the region was notorious, Danvers took the *Hannah* toward shore where a series of smoke signals were rising into the sky. Once more several round-bottomed native canoes, their crews standing and dipping their paddles into the water in unison to the beat of a drum, rowed out to the sloop. Two bales of perpetuanas were bartered for nineteen "elephant's teeth." Captain Phillips left a description of the peculiarities of such a trade.

[The natives came alongside the ship in their canoes and] invited us to come to anchor; but ere the[y] . . . would come aboard, they requir'd the captain come down the out side of the ship, and drop three drops of the sea water into his eye, as a pledge of friendship, and of safety for them to come aboard . . . I . . . readily consented," Phillips recalled, "[but] seeing so many on deck, [they] were mistrustful, and went into their canoes again . . . with much perswasion [I] prevail'd on them to return . . . and having given each . . . a good coge of brandy, I shew'd then some of my commodities, and they brought in some teeth."[6]

The *Hannah* was a typical Royal African Company sloop. Built in London prior to 1687 in the broad-stern style common in England (as opposed to the lighter, flat-bottomed, round-stern ships favored by the Dutch), its current voyage was at least its second to the Guinea Coast.[7] About eighty feet long from stern to bowsprit, the sloop had a displacement of 170 tons, it carried thirty crew, and its hull was pierced by twenty-two cannon. Triple heavy masts rose from its main deck, carrying a vast array of sails and miles of standing and running rigging. Although not the fastest of sailors, the *Hannah* was a sturdy, reliable, seaworthy craft. In the stern, under the quarterdeck, was Danvers's cabin and those of the first, second, and third mates. The men's quarters in the steerage, later used to hold the slaves, was a cramped, fetid space. Swinging with hammocks and littered with seamen's trunks, it was accessed via the hatches in the spar deck beside the ship's main mast. Below lay the hold. Tightly stowed with trade goods, ballast, gunpowder, round shot, small arms, and ship's stores, it was infested with rats and awash with foul-smelling bilgewater.[8]

Charles Danvers, the *Hannah's* master, was a sailor of considerable experience. He had probably been to Africa before, was paid in the region of £5 per month, and would receive a considerable commission on all sales. In his will, written on the day of the *Hannah's* departure from London, Danvers had named his father, John, as his sole heir and executor.[9] The *Hannah's* first mate, John Zebbett, was married. He had two children and owned a property in the village of Ratcliffe in Stepney in London's East End. Bordering the Thames, "Sailors Village," as it was commonly known, was a shipbuilding center, had a notable community of Presbyterians and Quakers, and was infamous for its transient population and numerous lodging houses, bars, and brothels.[10] The ship's second mate was Thomas Cooper, and the third was David Cheyn.[11]

Among the remaining twenty-six crew members were a surgeon, a carpenter, a boatswain, and a gunner. The rest were rated able or ordinary seamen. The average age of merchant seamen on English vessels of the period was twenty-seven, although the youngest, the ship's boys, would have been barely into their teens. It is likely that they hailed from a variety of countries. Germans, Swedes, Dutch, French, Spaniards, Portuguese, Irish, Scots, North Americans, Africans, Indians from the subcontinent, and men from the Caribbean colonies were frequently found manning English ships, especially in times of war, when many English seamen were impressed by the Royal Navy. Typically, the crew of a slave ship were drawn from the dregs of society. The trade, which traversed the disease-ridden tropics, was notorious for high mortality rates, and although a reasonable wage could be secured, especially in wartime when sums of over £2 per month for able seamen were not unheard of, and the men habitually boosted their earnings through "clandestine trade," the route was not for the faint-hearted. Dalby Thomas, a veteran of the "Guinea Trade," recalled that those who signed up "must neither have dainty fingers nor dainty noses [and] few men "[were] fit for . . . it. It is a filthy voyage," he opined, "as well as a laborious [one]."[12]

On December 9, Danvers stopped at Sestre Crou.[13] A wide estuary marked by two "Great rocks on the Shoar," the area was dominated by a "large" and "beautiful" village and set against a backdrop of giant trees. Willem Bosman, a factor of the Royal African Company's main rivals, the Dutch West India Company, recalled that "the Negroes [t]here seemed to be a good sort of People, honest in their Dealings, and much more regular than those who live [in Sanguin]," although their language—a series of clicking, or quaqua noises—was "utterly unintelligible."[14] Relying on signs and gestures, Danvers bartered eight iron bars and a single bale of perpetuanas for 415 units of malaguetta and seventeen "elephants teeth." The *Hannah* then continued east, doubling the prominent point of Cape Palmas, before arriving at Cape Lahoue on December 12.[15] The site of a "very large" village stretching a mile along shore which was dotted with "multitudes of Coco Trees,"

Dutch and Africans trading ivory. While the Portuguese had been the first to exploit West African trade, by the late seventeenth century the English and the Dutch were the principal European players. (*Rutger van Langervelt, pen and ink drawing, c. 1690*)

Lahoe was renowned for the quality of its ivory. "The negroes" were "affable and civil," according to Bosman, "and very easy to be dealt with." Over the next two days, Danvers oversaw his briskest trade to date. In fifteen separate transactions, he exchanged 152 iron bars and fifteen dozen knives for 124 tusks. December 16 saw the *Hannah* anchored off Cape Apolonia, an area "in all parts furnished with great and small villages." The cape itself was unremarkable. "[It] appears to be low ground," Bosman wrote, "behind . . . are three high hills, which are its distinguishing marks . . . [and] without [which it] . . . would be sailed by without ever being seen."[16] From Apolonia eastward, Danvers traded for gold. On the first day business started slowly: the *Hannah* received a little over two ounces in exchange for four iron bars and 517 knives, but when Danvers moved on the next day, trade picked up and off Axim the *Hannah* took six and a half ounces.[17]

Both the Dutch and the Brandenburgers, subjects of an independent German principality, were drawn to Axim by its gold. Mined in the dry season from shallow shafts dug in the forested interior, from the sixteenth century the mineral had been transported to the coast and exchanged for goods bartered with Europeans.[18] In late 1689 it was the *Hannah*'s turn to profit from the trade. The site of a Dutch and a Brandenburger fort, Axim was the first European settlement the crew of the *Hannah* had seen since leaving the Gambia River. Fort St. Anthony, originally a Portuguese settlement, had been captured by the Dutch West India Company in 1642, and, by the time of the *Hannah*'s voyage, was the company's principal outpost to the west of the Gold Coast. The fort was "neat and beautifully Built," according to Bosman, "as well as [being] strong and conveniently situated." It boasted "three good Batteries besides Breast-works, Out-Works, and high Walls on the Land side, as well as a sufficient quantity of Guns" so as it "might hold out against a strong Army of the Natives." Gros Frederic'sburg, the fort of the Brandenburgers, was situated three miles to the east. Named after the principality's Elector, Frederick I, the fort, which had been founded in 1685, was "situate[d] on the Hill Mamfro' . . . . near the village Pocquesoe." It "is handsome and reasonably large," Bosman related, and "strengthened with four large Batteries furnished with forty six Pieces of Ordinance. . . . The Gate . . . is the most Beautiful of all the Coast, [but] . . . the Breast-works are built no higher than a Man's knee, and the . . . [defenders] thereby are continually exposed . . . no small Incovenience in Wars with the Blacks, for . . . the Negroes [can] easily reach . . . [them] with a Musquet-shot."[19]

On December 20, Danvers reached Cape Three Points, a headland ten miles southeast of Gros Frederic'sburg which marked the start of the Gold Coast proper. From this point onward the number of transactions recorded in the *Hannah*'s account book increased considerably. In just four days, in exchange for numerous iron bars and knives and bales of boysadoes and perpetuanas, Danvers took over ten marks of gold, a local measurement equivalent to £322.[20] "The way of receiving the gold upon this whole coast," Captain Phillips explained, "is by weight, of which the several kinds us'd, and in which we keep out accounts, are marks, ounces, achies, and taccooes. A taccoo is a small berry as big as a pea, 12 of which make an achy . . . 16 Achies are 1 ounce . . . [and] 8 ounces are 1 mark gold; value about 32l. Stirling. . . . The gold is most in dust," Phillips went on, "with some pieces of rock among it; and sometimes in wire, and wedges . . . We first sift and blow the dust . . . until it be well clear of dirt . . . then it is carefully pick'd, and all the bad or suspicious taken from it by a negroe that understands gold well, and we entertain aboard for that purpose, giving him a gratuity when we have done trading. . . . Indeed we had need of all the caution imaginable to avoid being cheated by the negroes, [who] . . . mix . . . filings of brass with the gold dust, and fill . . . the middle of their cast ingots with lead, so that we never take any of them without cutting them with a chizel into small pieces . . . We are always very kind to good traders," Phillips concluded, "giving them store of good punch and brandy, but such as bring very bad gold, we sometimes chastize . . . [by] turn[ing them] away with severe threats . . . [or] put[ting] them in irons." Another means of punishment, which was reserved for Africans who defaulted on their debts, was to pinion them below decks until a ransom was paid by friends and relatives. If the money was not forthcoming, the captives were taken to the Americas and sold as slaves.[21]

THE PEOPLE OF THE GOLD COAST, as distinct to the Quaqua from the Windward, were Akan. A loose conglomeration of multiple ethnicities bound by composite cultural, religious, and linguistic traits and a high degree of ideological conformity, the Akan were recognizable to Europeans by an intricate system of facial scarification practiced at puberty. Originating among the inland forests of West Africa, over time Akan culture spread and by the early seventeenth century the Akan language, Twi, had become the lingua franca of the entire Gold Coast (modern-day Ghana). Its usage stretched from the Komóe River in the west to the Volta in the east, from the Atlantic coast to the edge of the forest belt to the north. As well as practicing goat and sheep herding, the Akan exploited the region's rich gold deposits. It was this resource that had given impetus to the formation of Akan states, which sold the gold to Wangara traders, who took it north of the Sahara to Islamic merchants some four hundred years before the arrival of the Europeans. The Akan were also notable for their expertise in medicinal plant use, their complex spiritual practices, warlike nature, and their skill in political and military organization.[22]

By the late seventeenth century, the inland gold-producing areas of modern day Ghana were dominated by two Akan states, the Denkyria in the west and the Akwamu in the east. Both had risen to prominence by means of aggressive expansionist policies fueled by the European arms for which they exchanged their gold. The trade with the Europeans itself, however, was carried out by a third group of Akan people, the Akani, a multiethnic, seminomadic mercantile community who linked the inland areas with the coast. Relying on diplomacy rather than warfare, the Akani caravans carried gold from the interior to the Atlantic. There they entered the territory of several Akan coastal polities, principal among them the Fante and Asebu to the east of the central Gold Coast area and the Fetu to the west. Having traded their gold with the Europeans, the Akani then returned to the interior with their newly acquired trade goods. To the Portuguese, who had some understanding of the political complexities involved, the Akan were known as Mina, a name derived from the village-turned-trading-post on the central Gold Coast which the Portuguese had occupied from the 1480s to 1637. The name was also used by the French, Spanish, and Danish. The English and the Dutch, the latter of whom took over Elmina, as the outpost became known, in the mid-seventeenth century along with many of Portugal's other settlements in the region, preferred the term Cormonatee, a corruption of the name Kormantin, another Akan settlement-turned-trading-post ten miles to the east of Elmina.[23]

ON CHRISTMAS DAY, the *Hannah* reached the ruined Dutch fort of Takoradi.[24] Founded in 1653 by the short-lived Swedish Africa Company, the fort had been held by both the Brandenburgers and the Danes before falling into the hands of the Dutch only to be besieged and captured ("by Clandestine means," according to Bosman) by an English fleet led by Admiral Robert Holmes in 1664 on the eve of the Second Anglo-Dutch War. The next year the fort was retaken by the renowned Dutch admiral DeRuyter. Considering it a place of "little Importance" and difficult to maintain, De Ruyter promptly "raz'd it to the Ground," while nine hundred "negroes" raised by the local Dutch governor plundered the nearby Akan village, "destroying it with Fire and Sword, and cutting off the Heads of all that they took Prisoners. . . . Since that time it hath yet once [more] changed Masters," Bosman related, "but fell at last into . . . [Dutch] Hands" near the end of the seventeenth century.[25]

By the time of the *Hannah*'s visit, all that remained of Takoradi was a single "Negroe's House" where trade was conducted. Nevertheless, Danvers did good business. Anchored off the coast for two weeks, the *Hannah* took over eighty-two marks in gold, worth £2,634 sterling, in exchange for 19,097 knives; 2,310 pewter basins; 760 pieces of perpetuanas; 117 half firkins of tallow; 33 says (a cloth from Leiden in the United Provinces); 65 iron bars; 16 chests of sheets; 3 pieces of boysadoes; and 14 barrels of gunpowder, thus turning a profit of £1,119 on the £2,634 purchase price of the goods in London.[26] The sale of gunpowder was a particularly risky business, as Phillips explained: "The negroes are so little apprehensive of danger, that when we have sold them two or three barrels of powder, and they have got it in their canoe, they have . . . fallen to drinking [spirits] and smoking tobacco till they were drunk," he explained, "all the while sitting a top of the barrels . . . and letting the sparks from their pipes fall upon them without any concern, which created a terror in us to see, and by which means they are frequently blown up; so that it is our custom, as soon as we have sold them any powder, to make them take it into their canoe, and put off, and lie about 200 yards from the ship till the rest of their business be completed, lest we might be injur'd by their stupid carelessness."[27]

On January 6, 1690, sitting significantly lighter in the water, the *Hannah* sailed thirty miles east-northeast.[28] En route the sloop was buffeted by the freshwater outflow of the Pra River estuary, a sacred spot for the Akan, before passing the "moderately large" town of Chama, site of yet another Portuguese-built fort, since captured by the Dutch.[29] The seventh of January saw the *Hannah* reach Komenda. A Royal African Company factory had once stood outside the native village, but in 1687 the English had been "forced from there by the blacks." The Dutch, whom the English were in little doubt had instigated the move, had proceeded to build a fort on the site the following year. Since then, due to events in Europe, there was some hope that the intermittent warfare and double-dealing that plagued Anglo-Dutch operations on the Gold Coast might be coming to an end.[30] "As affaires now are," one London-based Royal African Company employee wrote in June 1689, "wee need not much feare the Dutch; their Prince of Orange being now our King, our alliances are very close & such as that wee now beleive none of their servants abroad dare violate." Nevertheless, Europeans paid little heed to treaties negotiated in their homelands once beyond the line. "You must not trust them," the scribe had added in a postscript. It was to prove wise advice indeed.[31]

On January 8 and 9, Danvers was trading once more. In a series of transactions "to Windward of Comenda," he bartered his remaining knives, iron bars, tallow, perpetuanas, says, gunpowder, brandy, and pewter basins for thirty-four guineas of gold (£1,088 sterling). Danvers even managed to rid himself of eight pieces of boysadoes which had been "Damidged" in transit.[32] The company's leading agents, based at Cape Coast Castle on the Gold Coast, often complained about the Windward trade. Many ships, failing to sell all their goods, were forced to dump them at Cape Coast Castle so as to be able to fill their holds with slaves farther east. These abandoned goods, for which the Cape Coast factors were obliged to pay in gold, proceeded to spoil in the humid conditions and had a negative effect on the Castle's account books, thus causing considerable discontent.[33] The *Hannah*'s voyage, however, had been inordinately successful. As well as entirely clearing his hold, aside from the two hundred lead bars he had ill-advisedly shipped in London, Danvers had turned a considerable profit. The ivory picked up at Sanguin and Cape Lahoe was worth roughly £3,000 on the London market, while the 132 marks of gold acquired to the east of Cape Apolonia would fetch £4,224. After deducting the cost of the trade goods purchased in London, the *Hannah* had made a profit of £4,728, a total which compared favorably with the accounts of ninety-five other Royal African Company voyages to the region made between 1680 and 1687. Three had shown a net loss, while the average profit was 38 percent. Even the most successful, which recorded net gains of 141 percent, pales by comparison with Danvers's gains of over 170 percent, a result perhaps explained by the voyage's timing. Due to the threat of French privateers, the *Hannah* had been the first Royal African Company vessel to visit the Windward Coast for five months.[34]

On January 10, Danvers arrived at Cape Coast Castle. Built by the Swedes in 1652 on the territory of the Fetu, a small coastal Akan kingdom, Cape Coast Castle had since been acquired by the English and was now their principal base on the entire Gold Coast. Thomas Crispe, the factor involved in the original deal, had paid £64 worth of trade goods to the Fetu for the privilege of living on their territory, and by the time of the *Hannah*'s arrival the English were paying a ground rent of nine marks of gold, or £288, per year. According to Captain Phillips, Cape Coast Castle made for a "handsome prospect from the sea. . . . [It] was . . . very regular and well-contriv'd, and as strong as . . . can be. . . . It has four flank[ing batteries] . . . which have a cover'd communication with each other and are mounted with good guns; and . . . [there] is a noble battery of fifteen whole culverin and demy cannon, lying low, and pointing upon the road, where they would do good execution upon any ships that should pretend to attack the castle." Bosman, for his part, noted an array of small lizards and salamanders which sunbathed on the castle walls, occasionally breaking into movement to snatch a passing spider, fly, or worm. The whole fort was built on a massive rock upon which the Atlantic rollers broke with such force "that the noise thereof is hear'd all over." Below the fort, a water tank had been cut out of the rock which was capable of holding four hundred tons. Above was "a most pleasant walk" from which Samuel Humphreys, the company's chief merchant since 1687, could observe the ships in the roads. Through his telescope, Humphreys could also spy on the Dutch headquarters of Elmina, the largest European fortification in the whole of West Africa, which lay just seven miles to the west.[35]

Having fired a salute from the *Hannah*'s cannon, which was promptly returned from the fort, Danvers boarded his longboat and was rowed to within a cable's length of the beach, where he was met by a flat-bottomed native canoe which took him ashore through the breakers. Once on dry land, Danvers was escorted inside Cape Coast Castle. A "well-secur'd and large gate" that faced a Fetu town to the north led to a courtyard, which was surrounded by a barracks built for the hundred-strong garrison, a wretched and unhealthy bunch of malarial alcoholics and whoremongers, according to Bosman, who were fortunate indeed if they survived their first year. Also present were several "gromettos" or castle slaves, brought from other areas of Africa to perform the duties the Europeans considered beneath them, as well as numerous Akan employees who served as porters and canoeists. "Genteel convenient lodgings" housed Humphreys, Richard Wright, and John Boylston, the first, second, and third merchants, respectively, while less commodious rooms were occupied by at least five minor factors, as well as the commander of the garrison, a chaplain who, according to Captain Thomas Phillips, "read the church prayers" to the men "every morning at nine o'clock . . . and preach'd every Sunday," and a surgeon who had "a mate and a barber under him." Elsewhere was a "spacious warehouse" and several smaller ones, some granaries, rum vaults and workshops, a pigeon roost, a chapel, and two gardens full of "lime and orange trees." Below ground, cut out of the rock alongside the water tank, were dark, gloomy dungeons which could house up to one thousand slaves. A single iron grill afforded the "poor wretches" some light and air.[36]

By the late 1680s, the nature of the trade conducted between the Akan peoples and the Europeans on the Gold Coast was changing. Previously, the area had been known for its gold. By the time of Danvers's arrival, it was becoming apparent that the slave trade was more lucrative for all parties. Some two thousand slaves were being exported from the Gold Coast to the Americas every year. This development caused increasing instability in the interior where the Denkyria and Akwamu were conducting systematic and widespread warfare to enable them to acquire captives to sell to the Europeans. This also had implications for the coastal region. Among several others, the polities of the Fetu and Fante, the former of whom dominated the area around Cape Coast Castle, while the latter were based around the village of Anomabu some fifteen miles to the northeast, were locked in a struggle for control of the gold and slave trades on the coast. Previously characterized by low-level skirmishes and assassinations of political leaders, by the late 1680s the fighting had become endemic, as evidenced by a joint Fante-Asebu attack on the Fetu in 1688 which involved a column of some 5,400 warriors. The fighting, which would last until the turn of the eighteenth century, came to be known as the Komenda Wars. Although the Europeans played little role in actual combat, they exploited the situation to further their own ends, aiding one side or another with arms and ammunition or financing campaigns to secure better trading conditions with the victors. The Dutch and English also encouraged native attacks on each other's outposts: 1688 had seen a failed siege of Cape Coast Castle by the Fetu.[37]

Among those to lose influence in this period were the Akani traders who had acted as middlemen between the coastal polities and those of the interior. By the 1690s they were gradually being replaced by Fante and Fetu *caboceers* (middlemen or merchants).[38] Perhaps the most successful were the mulatto sons of African mothers and European fathers. Since the mid-fifteenth century, when the Portuguese had first arrived and taken local mistresses, the mixed ancestry, bicultural understanding, and linguistic skills of such people had made them ideally suited to the role. By the end of the seventeenth century, each European fort and settlement had its share of such entrepreneurs who grew rich from taking a cut, or *dashy*, "of a knife or two" on every transaction. Around the time of the *Hannah*'s visit to the Guinea Coast two of the most prominent *caboceers* were Johnny Kabes, "a Kommenda negroe" who had originally been a "friend" of the Dutch but was equally willing to do business with the English and only too happy to play each side off against the other, and Edward Barter, a mulatto who had grown all-powerful at Cape Coast, despite the reservations of the Royal African Company.[39]

THE *Hannah* remained at Cape Coast Castle for three weeks.[40] As well as loading the ship with Indian corn with which to feed the slaves they were to pick up at Ouidah, two hundred miles farther east, the crew unloaded the stores brought from London, which proved to have been spoiled in transit, and the gold acquired on the Windward Coast while Danvers and his officers were entertained onshore. This may have involved a banquet with their Dutch "allies" at Elmina or even an expedition into the interior to hunt for "tyger" or elephant. The latter, Bosman noted, were particularly difficult to kill, "unless the Ball happens to light betwixt the Eyes and Ears" as "their Skin is as good proof against the common Musquet Lead-Balls, as a Wall."[41] Further tasks at Cape Coast Castle were to fill the *Hannah's* water butts and hire several Akan canoeists. As the landing at Ouidah was even more perilous than the others along the West Africa coast, and as the locals had not developed their seafaring abilities, picking up Gold Coast canoeists before doing business on the Slave Coast was essential for all captains proceeding there.[42]

On January 31, Danvers fired a parting salute, upped anchor, and sailed on.[43] En route to Ouidah, the *Hannah* passed several Akan villages and European outposts. There were English factories at Anashan, Anomabu, Tantamkweri, Lagoo, Winnebah, and Shido, a "neat" Dutch fort "of about twenty guns" stood on a hill at Koromantin, there was a Danish fort at Christianborg, and at Accra English and Dutch forts had been built a mere musket shot apart. Beyond, the coastline was less densely populated. The English factory at Alampo was all that was seen for several miles. Afterward, the ship reached the estuary of the mighty Volta River, marking the boundary of the Gold and Slave Coasts. Sounding with the ship's lead as he inched forward, Danvers negotiated the double river bar with care before sailing on into deeper water, and the *Hannah* arrived off Ouidah on February 14.[44] As the town was situated three miles inland, Danvers dropped anchor in eight fathoms in the roads two miles off shore, a location visited by as many as fifty European slave ships per year. With a hoist rigged to the ship's capstan, the Akan canoes were lowered into the ocean and Danvers, accompanied by the ship's surgeon and several sailors, armed with muskets from the ship's stores, was paddled ashore to where a line of tents on the beach pitched among a "great thick tuft of trees" marked the start of the route inland.[45] The journey ashore was a treacherous one. As well as the possibility of being capsized and drowned in the breakers, there was the risk of sharks to contend with, as John Atkins, a surgeon employed by the Royal African Company, related on a visit in 1721: "A canoe was going on shore from a merchant-ship, and in attempting to land, overset: a shark nigh hand seized upon one of the men in the water, and by the swell of the sea, they were both cast on shore; notwithstanding which the shark never quitted his hold, but with the next ascent of the sea, carried him clear off."[46]

The route to Ouidah traversed a marsh and several rivers and lagoons where fishermen carried on a brisk trade. Salt production was another major factor in the local economy.[47] The swampland was home to pheasant and partridge and the dazzling crown bird, easily identified, according to Bosman, by the "yellowish Tuft . . . intermixed with speckled Feathers, strutting like Hogs Bristles; with which their heads are adorned."[48] Europeans typically undertook the journey in hammocks borne by native porters. "The traveller . . . either lies . . . or sits as he is dispos'd," Captain Phillips explained, "then . . . is mounted on the heads of two negroes . . . and away they will . . . run as fast as most horses can trot, cheerfully singing in parts to each other till they are quite tyr'd, when . . . they are reliev'd by two fresh, and they in course by two more." Phillips recalled, "The motion of the negroes attracts a fine cooling air, [and] I have often taken pleasant naps in them."[49]

Ouidah was a town of roughly one thousand inhabitants, each family living in a separate hut or *caze*. Standing low near the marshes it was considered a most unhealthy place by the Europeans who visited. Nevertheless, due to its primary importance in the slave trade, the French and English maintained factories in town, and there was also a significant Dutch and Portuguese presence. The English, who dominated the trade by the late seventeenth century, had built a settlement a small distance from town.[50] Two hundred yards in circumference, their complex was enclosed "with a mud wall, about six-foot high" which was regularly washed away in the rainy season from May to August. "On the south side is the gate," Phillips recalled, "within is a large yard, a mud thatch'd house, where the factor lives, with the white men . . . a store-house, a trunk [or holding cell] for slaves [where six hundred to eight hundred could be held at a time] . . . a good forge and some other small houses; To the east are two small flankers of mud, with a few pop-guns and harquebusses, which serve more to terrify the poor ignorant negroes than to do any execution." In the courtyard was a collection of graves. Among them was one belonging to Captain Wyborne, the officer who had built the complex some years earlier. Wyborne had succumbed to disease and been buried days before the *Hannah*'s arrival.[51]

Unlike the Gold Coast, where European infighting and Akan attacks were a regular occurrence, Ouidah was a relatively peaceful town. The entire region and all dealings with Europeans were governed by King Agbangla and his numerous subordinates.[52] Agbangla's dominion, the Kingdom of Hueda, was a region which encompassed ten miles of coastline and stretched some twenty-five miles inland. Ouidah itself was merely a trading town, which Agbangla's predecessors had designated fit for European habitation. No stone forts were permitted, hence the mud-walled enclosures, and fighting was punishable by either a fine of eight slaves or exile. All Europeans were obliged to employ local porters, and all purchases of slaves were conducted exclusively through the king, who resided in a "palace" at the capital of Savi, a settlement of over thirty thousand located five miles to the north of Ouidah. The slaves themselves, ten thousand of whom were sold annually by the 1690s, came via yet another polity twenty miles farther inland, the kingdom of Allada, which was said to have a population over twenty times that of Hueda.[53]

The traders of Allada came by their slaves through a variety of means. Many would have traveled hundreds of miles, passing through the hands of several different owners before reaching the coast. Those acquired by wide-ranging pillaging, banditry, kidnapping, and systematic warfare with neighboring states were supplemented by unfortunates who had been sold by their families to pay debts. Others were orphans or had been sold to allay fines imposed due to extramarital transgressions, while some fell victim to kidnappers or opportunistic bands of robbers. Social rank, wealth, or status were often not enough to save a person from such a fate: prosperous merchants, aristocrats, and even kings were sold into slavery in the period.[54]

While no accounts of slaves embarked from Ouidah are extant from either the seventeenth or eighteenth century, some roughly contemporary tales of Gold Coast captives survive. Abu Bakr, born in Timbuktu, was a prisoner of war who was sold to the English at Cape Coast Castle and spent thirty years in Jamaica. Belinda Royall was from the Volta River in northern Ghana. Aged twelve, she was kidnapped while her parents were praying at a local shrine, carried to the coast, and shipped to Antigua. William Unsah Sessarakoo, a young prince of Anomabu, was duped, shipped, and sold to a planter in Barbados around 1744.[55] Another Akan, a wealthy man who was the cousin of a subking and commanded three thousand warriors in battle, was enslaved to pay off his gambling debts, while Quacco, a slave who eventually became the property of John G. Stedman, a British officer who fought maroons in Dutch Guiana in the mid-eighteenth century, was stolen from his parents as a young child along with two brothers. Carried off in a bag and sold to a "king on the coast of Guinea," Quacco was given to one of the king's officers as a gift, before being purchased by the captain of a Dutch ship for some "[gun]powder and a musket."[56]

Two accounts of slaves known to have been sold out of Ouidah in the mid-nineteenth century survive. Mahommah Gardo Baquaqua was kidnapped at Djougou in northern Benin. He changed hands "7 or 8 times from market to market before arriving" at Ouidah. In his account, published in 1854 by an American abolitionist, Baquaqua wrote of his hope that he might escape en route or that his mother might purchase his freedom, but once he had reached Allada little hope remained: "When we arrived," Baquaqua wrote, "I began to give up . . . [on] getting back to my home again . . . the last ray seemed fading away, and my heart felt sad and weary within me, as I thought of my mother, whom I loved most tenderly, and the thought of never more beholding her, added very much to my perplexities. I felt sad and lonely . . . and my heart sank within me, when I thought of the 'old folks' at home."[57]

On February 18, 1690, Captain Danvers, the *Hannah*'s surgeon, and an armed escort of sailors travelled to Savi to do business with King Agbangla.[58] The journey, according to Phillips, took the English "thro' very pleasant fields, full of India and Guiney corn, potatoes, [and] yams, in great plenty." At Savi, they were carried to the palace, "the meanest" Phillips "ever saw . . . being low mud walls, the roof thatch'd, the floor the bare ground, with some water and dirt in it," where they "were met . . . by several [*caboceers*]," who shook their hands "with great demonstration of affection: when we enter'd the palace-yard," Phillips continued, they all fell on their knees near the door of the room where the king was, clapping their hands, knocking the ground with their foreheads, and kissing it, which they repeated three times . . . they [then] led us [in]to the room . . . upon their knees . . . and crawl'd to their several stations. . . . When we enter'd, the king peep'd upon us from behind a curtain, and beckon'd us to him, whereupon we approach'd close to his throne, which was of clay, rais'd about two foot from the ground. . . . He had two or three little black children with him, and was smoking tobacco in a long wooden pipe . . . with a bottle of brandy and a little dirty silver cup by his side; his head was tied about with a roll of coarse callicoe, and he had a loose gown of red damask to cover him. . . . We saluted him with our hats, and he . . . told us we were very welcome . . . that he lov'd Englishmen dearly, that we were all his brothers, and that he would do us all the good offices he could.[59]

After drinking a series of toasts to the Royal African Company and King William and Queen Mary among others, Danvers and his men were shown to their rooms. They stayed in Savi for the next thirty nights.[60] Sickness and fevers soon set in among the visitors. Malaria was the most common ailment to afflict the men of the Royal African Company. It began, one contemporary recorded, "with a violent pain and dizziness of the head. . . . Nausea, vomiting and restlessness" followed, after which "the patient . . . falls into excessive sweats, inextinguishable thirst and involuntary urinating." Finally, "delirium, convulsions or speechlessness" set in and could lead to the victim's death within four or five days. The bloody flux, or dysentery, was another killer, and river blindness took its share of victims. During the *Hannah*'s voyage, four of her crew of thirty succumbed to various ailments.[61]

Each morning at Savi, after a breakfast "of stew'd fowls and potatoes," Danvers got down to business.[62] According to Bosman, all transactions were conducted "on a large Plain. First the king's slaves were exhibited for sale, then each of the . . . [*caboceers*], taking turns according to their rank, displayed theirs."[63] "Our surgeon examin'd them well in all kinds," Phillips explained, "to see that they were sound wind and limb, making them jump, stretch out their arms swiftly, [and] looking in their mouths to judge of their age; for the [*caboceers*] are so cunning, that they shave them all close before we see them, so that . . . we can see no grey hairs in their heads or beards; and then having liqour'd them well and sleek with palm oil, 'tis no easy matter to know an old one from a middle-age one, but by the teeths decay." Phillips continued, "Our greatest care of all is to buy none that are pox'd, lest they should infect the rest aboard, therefore our surgeon is forc'd to examine the privacies of both men and women, with the nicest scrutiny."[64] The surgeons were well-rewarded for conducting such thorough checks: each received a commission of five shillings for each slave delivered alive to their destination, while the Portuguese, who were particularly keen on purchasing only adolescent males for sale to the plantation owners in Brazil, were even known to lick the faces of the slaves they were considering purchasing to check their cheeks for stubble.[65]

Those rejected, Bosman informs us, were "thrown out." These included "the lame or faulty . . . such as are above five and thirty Years old, or [those who] are maimed in the Arms, Legs, Hands or Feet, have lost a Tooth, are grey-haired, or have Films over their Eyes; as well as all those which are affected with any Veneral Distemper, or with several other Diseases."[66] What became of such individuals is uncertain, but it seems likely they were killed. Certainly, those prisoners of war considered unfit for the slave trade were typically slaughtered on the field where they were taken, while infants, thought to be more trouble than they were worth, were commonly left on the outskirts of town for the hyenas.[67]

'When we had selected . . . such as we liked," Phillips continued in his account of a slave transaction he conducted two years after the *Hannah*'s visit, "we agreed in what goods to pay for them, the prices being already stated before the king, how much of each sort of merchandize we were to give for a man, woman, and child, which gave us much ease, and saved abundance of disputes and wranglings[. We then] gave the owner a note, signifying our agreement of the sorts of goods; upon delivery of which the next day he receiv'd them; then we mark'd the slaves we had bought in the breast, or shoulder, with a hot iron, having the letter of the ship's name on it, the place being before anointed with a little palm oil . . . [it] caus'd but little pain."[68] Bosman, when writing of branding, felt the need to explain himself to his readers. "I doubt not," he began, "but this . . . seems very barbarous to you, but since it is followed by meer necessity it must go on; but we yet take all possible care that they are not burned too hard, especially the Women, who are more tender than the Men."[69]

On the first day of sales at Ouidah, conducted on February 19, 1690, Danvers bought three lots of male slaves. The first consisted of nineteen individuals, the second of thirty-one, and the third of six. The first two lots were paid for in cowries, sea-mollusk shells long used as currency in West Africa, which were obtained by the East India Company at Bengal. The third lot was exchanged for seventy pounds of tobacco. Over the next nineteen days, as he and his men grew gradually sicker, Danvers continued to purchase slaves in lots of between two and forty-four individuals. Prices varied wildly. The king's slaves, bought in the first transactions, were the most expensive. Subsequently, males brought in the first week cost up to one hundred cowries per head, but by March, the price had fallen to just one cowrie per individual. "Negresses" were generally cheaper than males, three selling for just forty-five cowries on the second day of transactions.[70] Once purchased, the slaves were sent to a holding bay known as "the trunk." From there they were dispatched to the coast in lots of fifty or sixty at a time. This operation was overseen by a *caboceer* known as the captain of the slaves, "whose care it was to secure them to the waterside."[71] By the time he had exhausted his trading goods, Danvers had purchased 399 Africans, 126 of them females, in exchange for 11,417 cowries, 900 bales of tobacco, and 589 brass pans. The fee included a 10 percent commission paid to King Agbangla, who also received an additional *dashee* of forty-five smoking pipes.[72]

Virtually nothing is known of the backgrounds of the men, women, and children Danvers purchased. We can only speculate as to who they were. A number of them were probably Akan, or Coromantee to the English. These may have traveled from west of the Volta River or perhaps were from the numerous Akan migrants then inhabiting territories inland of the Slave Coast. Others may have been Papas (also known as Popos or Papaws). Lighter skinned than the Akan, the Papas were natives of Dahomey, a rising polity to the north of Allada, and spoke Gbe languages.[73] It is just possible that one of the Akan may have been a warrior, aristocrat, or even a king named Cudjoe. A typical Akan "day name" meaning a male born on Monday, countless Cudjoes were shipped to the Americas as a result of the slave trade.[74]

"Tradeing on Ye Coast of Africa." By the late 1690s the English were beginning to dominate the trans-Atlantic slave trade. In exchange for base metals, gunpowder, knives, pewter bowls, and textiles, the Royal African Company acquired human cargoes for shipment to the West Indies. (*Nicholas Pocock, watercolor, c.1746*)

The Cudjoe that may have traveled on the *Hannah*, however, would leave a legacy which remains well-known to this day.

Once at the beach, Danvers's slaves were carried by the canoes he had hired at Cape Coast Castle to the *Hannah*'s longboat.[75] For many, this short passage across the breakers was the most terrifying part of their ordeal so far. John Duncan, a nineteenth-century English explorer, related the experience of one seven-year-old Mahi slave girl. "[She] had never seen the sea [before]," he explained, "and consequently felt much alarm. She could scarcely be urged to get into the canoe, though I told her she was going back to her . . . mother, of whom she was very fond. Unfortunately the sea was very high and the surf heavy, and though the canoe men displayed great skill in managing their boat, . . . a sea passed completely over us from bow to stern. . . . The little girl, who was upon her knees in the bottom of the canoe . . . [was distraught and] as soon as the little creature was able, for she was almost suffocated by the surf, she called out for her . . . mother."[76]

Once aboard ship the men were all put in irons. "Two and two [were typically] shackled together," Captain Phillips explained, "to prevent their mutiny, or swimming ashore."[77]

While none of the slaves bought by Danvers left a written record of their feelings as they boarded the *Hannah*, the words of one eighteenth-century survivor, Olaudah Equiano, may be used to illuminate the scene. "The first object which saluted my eyes when I arrived on the coast," Equiano related in his 1789 book, *The Interesting Narrative*,

was the sea, and a slave-ship, which was then riding at anchor, and waiting for its cargo. These filled me with astonishment, which was soon converted into terror, which I am yet at a loss to describe, nor the then feelings of my mind. When I was carried on board I was immediately handled, and tossed up, to see if I were sound, by some of the crew; and I was now persuaded that I had gotten into a world of bad spirits, and that they were going to kill me. Their complexions too differing so much from ours, their long hair, and the language they spoke . . . united to confirm me in this belief. . . . When I looked round the ship . . . and saw . . . a multitude of black people of every description chained together, every one of their countenances expressing dejection and sorrow, I no longer doubted of my fate, and, quite overpowered with horror and anguish, I fell motionless on the deck and fainted.[78]

Equiano's fears about the "white devils" were not unusual. John Barbot, a French Huguenot who made two voyages to Guinea in the employ of the Compagnie du Sénégal between 1678 and 1682, recorded that "all the slaves from [Allada and Ouidah] . . . especially those whom we transport to the islands of America . . . firmly believe when they are embarked that we have bought them to have them fattened in our own country, so that we will be better able to sell them when they are more suitable to be eaten."[79] Another theory is that the transported slaves believed the Europeans to be witches who were taking them to the land of the dead, a common African association with the European and American continents, which they often seem to have conflated.[80]

THE *Hannah* set sail on the third leg of its journey on March 10, 1690. By this stage, as Danvers was too sick to make entries in his account

A former slave, Olaudah Equiano lived an extraordinary life. Following a series of adventures in West Africa, Barbados, the United States, and Britain, he wrote *The Interesting Narrative*, a book endorsed by London's increasingly powerful abolitionist movement. (*Engraving by Daniel Orme from a portrait by William Denton, c.1794*)

book, David Zebbett, the *Hannah*'s first mate, took over. Before reaching Jamaica, Zebbett was to make two stops: the first at the island of St. Thomas (Sao Tome), a tiny volcanic atoll lying 155 miles off the shore of West Africa in the Gulf of Guinea which had been colonized by the Portuguese since the 1470s; the second at Barbados in the Caribbean. As the sloop was now carrying over four hundred passengers and crew, both detours were required for the purchase of provisions and water as well as wood to fire the galley stove.[81]

The first day after leaving Ouidah was the most dangerous for the crew. Slave revolts typically occurred while still in sight of the coast, the Africans believing that some hope remained of their returning to their homes.[82] As a result, the traders ensured security was tight. "We shackle the men two and two while we lie in port, and in sight of their own country," Phillips recorded, meaning that each slave was shackled to the ankle of those immediately to his left and right. "We always keep sentinels on upon the hatchways, and have a chest of small arms, ready loaden and prim'd, constantly lying at hand upon the quarterdeck, together with some granada shells; and two of our quarter-deck guns, pointing on the deck thence, and two more out of the steerage, the door of which is always kept shut and well barr'd. They are fed twice daily," Phillips continued, "at 10 in the morning and at 4 in the evening, which is the time they are aptest to mutiny, being all upon deck; therefore all that time, what of our men are not employ'd in distributing their victuals to them, and settling them, stand to their arms; and some with lighted matches at the great guns that yaun upon them, loaden with partridge, till they have done and gone down to their kennels between decks."[83]

Despite such precautions, slave revolts were relatively commonplace. "I have twice met with this Misfortune," Bosman related.

> The first . . . proved very unlucky to me, I not in the least suspecting it; but the Up roar was timely smashed by the Master of the Ship and my self, by causing the Abettor to be shot through the Head. . . . The second time it fell heavier on another ship, and that chiefly by the carelessness of the Master, who having fished up the Anchor of a departing English Ship, had laid it in the Hold where the Male slaves were lodged; who, unknown to any of the . . . Crew, possessed themselves of a Hammer; with which, in a short time, they broke all their Fetters in pieces upon the Anchor . . . came above Deck and fell upon our Men; some of whom they grievously wounded, and would certainly have mastered the Ship, if a French and English Ship . . . who perceiving by our firing a Distressed-Gun, that something was in disorder on Board, [had not] immediately came to our assistance . . . and drove the Slaves under Deck: Notwithstanding which before all was appeased about twenty of the . . . [slaves] were killed.[84]

The ships of the Royal African Company had also experienced several uprisings. In 1686 Captain Latton, commander of the *Charlton* sloop, was killed along with his entire crew.[85] The following year on the *Lomax*, several slaves were killed in a botched uprising and the crew regained control.[86] The *Hannah* was not to share these ships' fate. As the coast slipped out of sight, Zebbett and his crew no doubt breathed a sigh of relief. Not only was the chance of rebellion diminished, but also, as the ship left the malarial mosquitoes behind, the risk of falling prey to disease also fell significantly.[87]

For the Africans, losing sight of the shore had the opposite effect. Many gave up hope. Preferring death to confinement, some would refuse to eat. In such situations slavers typically force-fed their charges, either whipping them or breaking their teeth to push their rations down. "On my refusing to eat," Olaudah Equiano recorded, "one of [the crew] . . . held me fast by the hands, and laid me across . . . .the windlass, and tied my feet, while . . . [an]other flogged me severely."[88] Other slaves "escaped" by throwing themselves into the sea. "This afternoon," Captain Blake of the *James* recorded in his log on April 17, 1676, "I had a stout man slave leaped overboard . . . I hoysted out my pinnace and sent her after him, and just as they came upp with him hee sunke down. . . . My cockswaine runn downe his oare betweene his armes, but he would not take hould of it and soe drowned."[89] Those who did manage to kill themselves had their bodies burned or mutilated: one account speaks of heads being cut off and limbs scattered "about ye deck." This was done as a warning to the rest: it was commonly believed that West Africans thought that their souls would only return to their homelands after death if their bodies remained intact.[90]

Conditions on slave ships were appalling. Stripped naked and separated by gender to prevent the spread of sexually transmitted diseases, the adults were chained below decks. Wanting to maximize their profits, the crew packed them as tightly as possible. "The stench," Equiano recalled, "became absolutely pestilential. The closeness of the place, and the heat of the climate, added to the number in the ship, which was so crowded that each had scarcely room to turn himself, almost suffocated us. This produced copious perspirations, so the air soon became unfit for respiration, from a variety of loathsome smells, and brought on many a sickness among the slaves of which many died. . . . The wretched situation . . . aggravated by the galling of the chains . . . became insupportable; and the filth of the necessary tubs, into which the children often fell, and were almost suffocated. The shrieks of the women and the groans of the dying, rendered the whole a scene of horror almost inconceivable."[91] Another survivor, a young boy called Louis Asa-Asa from the country of "Bycla" who was shipped on board a French slaver named the *Pearl*, left the following description of his confinement. "The slaves . . . were chained together by the legs below deck, so close they could not move. They were flogged very cruelly: I saw one of them flogged till he died; we could not tell what for. . . . The place they were confined in . . . was so hot and nasty I could not bear to be in it. A great many of the slaves were ill, but they were not attended to. They used to flog me very bad."[92]

Mahommah Baquaqua's voyage to the Americas was equally horrendous: "The only food we had . . . was corn soaked and boiled . . . [and] we suffered very much for want of water," he recalled. "A pint a day was all that was allowed . . . and a great many slaves died upon the passage. There was one poor fellow became so very desperate . . . that he attempted to snatch a knife from the white man who brought in the water. . . . He was taken up on deck and I never knew what became of him. I supposed he was thrown overboard. When any one of us became refractory," Baquaqua continued, "his flesh was cut with a knife, and pepper or vinegar was rubbed in to make him peaceable. I suffered, and so did the rest of us, very much from sea sickness at first, but that did not cause our brutal owners trouble. Our sufferings were our own, we had no one to share our troubles, none to care for us, or even to speak a word of comfort to. . . . Some were thrown overboard before breath was out of their bodies; when it was thought any would not live, they were got rid of in that way."[93]

The deaths on board the *Hannah* were recorded by Zebbett on the final page of the vessel's account book. One male died on March 9, before the *Hannah* had even left Ouidah. No more perished for the next three weeks, but from March 24, they began to die with alarming regularity. On March 25, another expired and on March 26, two more died. One perished the following day and another died on the last of the month.[94] Smallpox, dry belly ache, measles, scurvy, yaws (a sexually transmitted disease similar to syphilis), gonorrhea, and the bloody flux, overcrowding, suffocation, heat exhaustion, lack of water, and starvation all proved fatal during the so-called Middle Passage. One crew member recorded seeing "steam coming through the gratings, like a furnace" from those confined below. All fatalities were flung overboard without ceremony. Sharks, which commonly trailed slave ships across the Atlantic, made the most of the free meals.[95]

The majority of Europeans involved in the slave trade seemed to have little or no sympathy for their charges. Most regarded the

Africans as "barbarians," "heathens," or "savages." The slavers justified their cruelty by labeling the Africans practitioners of cannibalism, infanticide, and witchcraft, incapable of human emotion and therefore not to be pitied. Phillips's rantings, written toward the latter part of his voyage to Barbados during which 334 of the 700 slaves he had shipped on board died, show such a dizzying lack of empathy that they have to be read to be believed. "After all our pains and care to give [the slaves] . . . their messes in due order and season," he wrote, "keeping their lodges as clean and sweet as possible, and enduring so much misery and stench so long among a parcel of creatures nastier than swine; and after all our expectations to be defeated by their mortality. . . . No gold-finders can endure so much noisome slavery as they do who carry negroes; for those have some respite and satisfaction, but we endure twice the misery; and yet by their mortality our voyages are ruin'd, and we pine and fret ourselves to death, to think that we should undergo such misery, and to take so much pains to so little purpose."[96]

Occasionally, some contemporary Europeans were able to empathize. Aphra Behn, the author of what is regarded as the first English novel, *Oroonoko, or the Royal Slave, a True History*, was one example. Written shortly before her death in 1689, the book is a romance which recounts the tale of the eponymous hero's capture on the Gold Coast along with his beloved, their subsequent shipment to Suriname, and their attempts to gain their freedom which end with Oroonoko's execution after he leads a failed rebellion against the planters. Notably, Behn is full of praise and admiration for her lead character and, one hundred years after its publication, the book was used by abolitionists to promote their cause. On a closer reading of the novel, however, it is apparent that Behn's feelings about slavery were somewhat ambiguous. Her sympathy for Oroonoko was not born out of an abhorrence of the institution of slavery, nor from a belief in racial equality, but rather grew from the fact that Oroonoko was a prince in his native West Africa and therefore not fit to be enslaved. Nevertheless, the fact that she chose to make her lead character an African was certainly significant and a radical decision for the time. Oroonoko is portrayed as an intelligent human being and his fate and that of Imoinda, his beloved, perhaps spurred feelings of sympathy among Behn's readers and even outrage against such a barbaric institution.[97]

Among slavers such feelings are harder to identify. The journal of William Chancellor, a surgeon from Philadelphia who sailed on the *Wolf* to West Africa in 1749, reveals him as a man capable of some empathy. "These sort of vessels are terrible things to have Slaves in," he wrote, "especially so great a number. Sick, & none but myself to look after them." On August 8, while the *Wolf* lay off Cape Coast Castle, Chancellor continued: "To my mortification died this morning a Boy Slave, of the Dropsy. . . . These misfortunes are I think sufficient to make me repent my coming to Africa."[98] One of Olaudah Equiano's jailers also briefly showed a human side: "During our passage . . . I first saw the use of the quadrant," Equiano explained, "and I could not think what it meant. The [sailors] . . . at last took notice of my surprise; and one of them, willing to increase it, as well as to gratify my curiosity, made me one day look through it. The clouds appeared to me to be land, which disappeared as they passed along. This heightened my wonder: and I was now more persuaded than ever that I was in another world, and that every thing about me was magic."[99]

Other slavers allowed their charges to come up to the deck in shifts and encouraged them to grind their own corn upon "cancy stones" they provided for the purpose. Although this principally reflected a concern for lost profits rather than for the wellbeing of their cargo, it perhaps briefly served to alleviate the slaves' suffering. Women and children, believed to be the least likely to attempt to escape, were commonly the recipients of such benefits, although the men were also brought up occasionally for exercise and fresh air. On the *Hannibal*, Captain Phillips allowed the men to eat on the main deck and forecastle. The women ate on the quarter deck with the crew, while the children used the poop. The slaves were sometimes given a little salt, palm oil, and malagueta pepper to season the ubiquitous ground corn mash known as *dabbadabb* which provided the bulk of their meager rations. Others were occasionally provided with horse beans (a smaller, harder variety of the broad bean) or fish.[100] One general order issued by the Royal African Company stated that "to prevent the mortality of the negroes you must observe frequently to wash the decks [with] vinegar and divert them as much as you can with some sorts of musick

& play."[101] Phillips's journal provides more detail. "We often at sea in the evenings would let the slaves come up into the sun to air themselves," he wrote, "and make them jump and dance for an hour or two to our bag-pipes, harp, and fiddle, by which exercise to preserve them in health."[102]

THE *Hannah* reached the Portuguese island colony of St. Thomas on April 5.[103] Having secured all the "negroes" in irons below, Zebbett anchored in the roads of the capital, São Tomé, which was dominated by twenty old guns mounted in a castle. The boats were sent ashore to purchase provisions and wood and to fill the *Hannah*'s water butts. According to Phillips, St. Thomas was a majestic-looking place. "Full of high mountains" whose peaks were obscured by an ever-present cap of cloud, the island was covered by dense tropical rainforest and alive with the squawks of abundant parakeets. Farms planted with lime and orange trees, yams, plantains, and fields of Indian corn and expansive sugar plantations surrounded the town, which boasted some two hundred "large and well-built" houses with "galleries and great open windows about them, for conveniency of air."[104] Besides the usual purchases of provisions, water, and wood, another possible reason for Zebbett's calling in at St. Thomas may have been Captain Danvers's increasingly serious condition. If this was the case, any medical treatment the captain may have received failed to revive him. The next time the slaves were mustered on April 7, Zebbett recorded in the account book that he was "Captain John Zebbett, Commander of the Hannah." Danvers had died. By this stage at least three other crew members had also succumbed, their bodies thrown overboard surreptitiously at night so the slaves would not realize that the strength of their tormentors was diminishing. Having restocked, Zebbett left St. Thomas at the end of April on the final leg of the voyage.[105]

As the *Hannah* cut its way across the Atlantic, the slaves continued to perish. Three men and three women died in April. The muster of May 5 recorded that just 257 of the former and 128 of the latter remained alive, revealing a total loss of sixteen men and two women. By May 27, when the *Hannah* reached Bridgetown, Barbados, another eleven had died. The crew were also in "a very sickly condition." Many had perished and, as Edwin Stede, the Royal African Company's resident factor, noted, only eight remained fit enough "to stand on ye deck." Zebbett remained in port "for 17 or 18 days." Stede provided fresh provisions "for ye negroes to ye value of 12 l. 12s 6d" at the company's expense, while Zebbett managed to recruit several new seamen to replace the hands that had died. By mid-May, with the ship's muster complete once more, Zebbett gave the signal to depart.[106]

Zebbett reached Jamaica on June 14, 1690. Of the 399 slaves who had boarded at Ouidah, 246 males and 115 females remained alive. Compared to the Royal African Company's average mortality rate in the period of 23.5 percent, the *Hannah*'s rate of just under 10 percent was remarkably low, especially considering the number of deaths among the crew. As he guided the ship into Port Royal harbor, Zebbett was no doubt rather pleased with himself. Not only had he earned somewhere in the region of £36 for the voyage so far, but he would also be paid a large commission when the slaves were auctioned as well as rising to the rank of commander. Furthermore, Zebbett had timed his arrival to perfection. The sugar harvest, which began in January, was reaching its conclusion. Finding a return cargo would be relatively easy and, as the planters had an excess in their warehouses, sugar prices would be comparatively low, making it likely that the *Hannah* would make a handsome profit on the return leg of its journey.[107] For those below decks, the arrival was just another ordeal in a voyage of confusing and frightening events. "[When] we came in sight of [our destination]," Equiano related, "the whites . . . gave a great shout, and made many signs of joy. . . . We did not know what to think of this; but as the vessel drew nearer we plainly saw the harbour, and other ships of different kinds and sizes; and we soon anchored amongst them."[108] Equiano and his companions were right to be afraid. Conditions at the English sugar plantations of the Caribbean were among the worst in the entire history of slavery. The planters ruled with unprecedented savagery. Only the very strongest or most fortunate would survive.[109]

CHAPTER 4

Plantation Slavery in the New World

We are bought and sold like apes or monkeys, to be the sport of women, fools, and cowards, and the support of rogues.

—Aphra Behn, *Oroonoko, or the Royal Slave*, 1689

NEWS OF THE *Hannah*'s arrival soon spread around Jamaica. Riders, dispatched by Walter Ruding and Charles Penhallow, Port Royal's resident Royal African Company factors, departed on the track leading down the Pallisadoes to alert the planters of St. Andrew's, St. David's, and St. Thomas' to the east. Others took wherry boats across the bay to Passage Fort then rode to the western parishes of St. Catherine's, St. Dorothy's, Clarendon, and Vere. Back at Port Royal, Ruding and Penhallow had gone aboard the *Hannah*. Their first duty was to ensure Master Zebbett had not smuggled any slaves ashore. Seeking to do a little business on the side, many captains bought slaves off the books in Africa for private sale on arrival in the West Indies. Such were the profits to be had, that it was even known for rank-and-file sailors to engage in such contraband, regardless of the risk of being fined or imprisoned for daring to break the Royal African Company's monopoly.[1] Also on board the *Hannah* that morning was Reginald Wilson, the port captain of Port Royal. Charged with ensuring all ship arrivals were recorded, Wilson noted that the *Hannah* was carrying twenty-six crew, 359 slaves, and 4,000 elephant's teeth from Ouidah on the Slave Coast of West Africa.[2]

Ruding and Penhallow's next task was to revise Zebbett's account books. They checked that the sales and purchase figures added up, tallied the mortality rates, and had the slaves mustered on deck.[3] At least two were unable to comply. One of the females died a few hours after the ship's arrival, while a male was so sick that he would succumb the following day.[4] The rest were inspected to ascertain their quality and divided into lots or "parcels" of equal numbers, each of which was to be sold as a single item to ensure that buyers could not select the best individuals and discard the remainder.[5] "They . . . examined us attentively," recalled Olaudah Equiano of the moment he arrived at Barbados. "They . . . made us jump and pointed to the land, signifying we were to go there."[6] Thomas Thistlewood, an eighteenth-century Jamaican overseer and diarist, noted that the best slaves should have "a good Calf to their Leg and a small or moderate Sized Foot."[7] Agents also assessed the slaves' ages, inspected their teeth, felt the plumpness of their muscles, and checked their genitalia for signs of sexually transmitted disease—a major cause of mortality during the Middle Passage. Another sought-after sign was callused hands—an indicator that a slave was used to physical work and could therefore stand up to the grueling routine of plantation life. Such examinations were terrifying for the slaves. "We thought by this we should be eaten by these ugly men," Equiano recalled. "Soon after, we were all put down under the deck again, there was much dread and trembling among us, and nothing but bitter cries to be heard all the night."[8]

Ruding and Penhallow divided the *Hannah*'s slaves into three categories. The first, comprising forty-four men, twenty-two women, six boys, and three girls, was handed over to John Zebbett. Along with £1, 8s. 11d. in cash, the slaves were the captain's payment for freighting his cargo from Africa.[9] In wartime such a service was deemed to be worth £11 for each slave delivered still capable of "going over the side."[10] The remainder would face auction. The 170 deemed of high quality, or "lusty" as the parlance of the trade would have it, were priced at £26 per head and divided into thirty-four lots, each containing three males and two females. The remaining one hundred (sixty-six men, seven women, eighteen boys, and ten girls) were to be sold only once all those of the first category had been purchased. The adults in this group, being considered of inferior quality, would go for £25 per head, while the children would be sold at either £17 or £13, depending on age, health, attractiveness, muscle development, and fitness.[11]

Another factor which may have influenced Ruding and Penhallow's categorization was the region from which the slaves were thought to have hailed. The English most valued the Akan, or Coromantees. "They are . . . the best and most faithful," opined Christopher Coddrington, the Barbados-based commander in chief of all English possessions in the Caribbean. "[They are] grateful and obedient to a kind master, but implacably revengeful when ill-treated."[12] Captain John Phillips of the *Hannibal* and the author Aprha Behn both shared Coddrington's opinion. "[The] gold coast negroes . . . are very bold, brave and sensible," wrote the former, noting they "yield 3 or 4 l. a head more than" other slaves, while the latter recorded that they were deemed both "warlike and brave."[13] By comparison, the Papa, or Popos, from the Slave Coast, were thought docile and agreeable, although not as hard working as the Coromantee, while Hans Sloane wrote that the few who were transported to the West Indies from Madagascar were "reckoned good enough" in terms of workload, "but too choice in their Diet. . . . Being accustomed in their own Countries to Flesh . . . [they] do not well here, but very often die."[14] Ibos from the Niger delta were held to be timorous and despondent; there was no market in Jamaica for slaves from the Gambia River; while the worst of all, according to the English planters, were the Bantu-speaking Angolans, who were considered both rebellious and lazy.[15] Curiously, Spanish slavers held different opinions. They were happy to purchase Papas, Angolans, and Gambians and preferred darker-skinned slaves with tightly curled hair. The Spaniards also believed that the bellicose Coromantees, whose reputation for rebellion was universal, were more effort than they were worth, while scarification, also practiced by the Akan, and the habit of filing teeth, common among the natives of the Tooth Coast, were also disapproved of.[16]

Once Ruding and Penhallow had left the *Hannah*, Zebbett and his crew prepared the slaves for auction. Over the course of the next two days, the Africans were exercised and well fed—£3, 15s. 7½d. being spent on extra rations on June 18;[17] fresh water was provided for washing, and tobacco and pipes were handed out, to render the slaves cheerful and calm prior to sale. Their heads and beards were shaved "and their Bodies . . . anointed all over with Palm-Oil," the latter being thought to "add . . . a great beauty to them."[18] A doctor, who charged £4, 17s. for his services, was brought aboard to treat the sick, while armed guards were hired to ensure that none escaped while the *Hannah* was moored so tantalizingly close to shore.[19] It was common practice to send seasoned plantation slaves on to newly arrived ships "to pacify" the arrivals. This happened when Olaudah Equiano reached Barbados. "They told us we were not to be eaten, but to work," he explained, "and were soon to go on land, where we would see many of our country people. This report eased us much," Equiano recalled.[20]

On June 19, the sale began. Zebbett hoisted an ensign at the *Hannah*'s masthead and ordered a single cannon fired, "according to custom," to announce that the auction was about to commence. Ruding and Penhallow came aboard and had the slaves stripped and mustered on deck by the previously arranged lots, while two dozen potential purchasers, chiefly planters and farmers, were rowed out from the quayside and helped aboard. Typically, such sales were conducted as auctions, with each lot timed "by inch of candle," a system which meant that buyers were free to bid while the candle burned, with the greatest price offered by the time the prescribed amount had expired being accepted. With human judgment a deciding factor, such a procedure was open to abuse. As such it is little wonder that a high number of contemporary complaints about the method were registered in the Royal African Company's files. Due to the fact that the prices had been preordained, it would appear that such a system was not used during the sale conducted on board the *Hannah*. What is recorded is that Santiago Castillo, the agent of the asiento who had traveled to Jamaica with Inchiquin, purchased the majority of the slaves sold that day. The twenty-one lots bought by the Spaniard included sixty-three males and forty-two females, valued at £26 per head, as well as a further fifty-eight males and five females for which he was charged £25 per head, and thirteen boys and seven girls valued at between £13 and £17 each.[21]

As well as infuriating the Jamaican planters, who believed subjects of the English crown should be favored customers, the sales also left Castillo unsatisfied. In London the previous year, William and Mary had decreed that the Spaniard was to be supplied with two thousand slaves by the Royal African Company over a period of twenty months at eighty pieces of eight (roughly £20) per head. With prices increasing due to the outbreak of war with France, it appears that Ruding and Penhallow were reluctant to stick to the terms of the agreement. Not only was Castillo forced to pay more than he had bargained for, but he was also restricted in the total number of individuals that he was allowed to buy. In due course the Spaniard would address an official complaint to Westminster. For the time being, however, he chose to pay the price demanded, while ordering Captain Hewetson of the *Lion*, the English privateer he had contracted in Barbados, to sail to Curaçao and purchase six hundred more slaves from the Dutch as a means of making up for the shortfall.[22]

The remainder of the slaves auctioned at Port Royal that day were sold in smaller quantities.[23] As the second purchaser paid in cash, his or her name went unrecorded. The third, who took credit in lieu of future commodity sales to the company, as was normal in such circumstances, was Jeremiah Tilley, a Quaker from Bristol who had lived in Port Royal since at least 1685 and owned a house in town along with seventy-four cattle and several horses.[24] The next four buyers were Samuel Lewis and George Ivy, John Hillyard of St. Thomas, and James Banister, the son of a former governor of Suriname who had been ousted by the Dutch in 1671 and murdered in Jamaica three years later. The island's surveyor general had subsequently been hanged for the crime.[25] Anthony Swimmer, a Bristolian by origin who rented an estate in Clarendon for £300 per year, took a single lot, as did Peter Shuler and Smith Kelly, the provost marshal of Port Royal who was also one of Jamaica's principal planters, while Reginald Wilson, the port captain, purchased two lots. Other buyers included Fulke Rose, a noted physician, long-term resident, and planter of St. Thomas and the father of three illegitimate mulatto children, and Governor Inchiquin, who bought two men, one woman, and two boys for £100.[26]

Most of the purchasers, with the possible exception of the newly arrived governor, would have been perfectly accustomed to "the noise and clamour" typically attendant at such scenes. One witness commented on purchasers' "eagerness" to buy, while Richard Ligon noted how they made their selections "as they do Horses in a Market; the strongest, youthfullest, and most beautiful, yield the greatest prices."[27] For the slaves themselves, the moment of sale was often the most traumatic of their entire ordeal, particularly when it involved being separated from family members or fellow countrymen with whom they had shared the miseries of the Middle Passage. On the ship which carried Equiano to Barbados, for example, were "several brothers, who . . . were sold in different lots. . . . It was very moving . . . to see and hear their cries at parting," he recalled.[28] Other sources state that the most experienced slave owners were careful to keep families together. As separating relatives could result in suicide, avoiding this possibility was a sound financial expedient.

Following the tribulations of the auction, the slaves bought by Santiago Castillo faced the further ordeal of transshipment. Their immediate destination was Cartagena, the principal port of the Spanish Main, located on the coast of the Viceroyalty of New Granada in modern-day Colombia. Due to the ravages of the voyage from Ouidah, Castillo decided to delay the next leg of the journey to allow the 188 men, women, and children he had purchased time to recuperate.[29] After the auction, they were landed and taken to a holding pen, probably located in Port Royal, where they would remain for two weeks. Guards were hired to prevent their escape while a physician would probably have been on call. Sick slaves were routinely bathed in "sweet herbs" to speed their recovery, others had their mouths washed out with lime juice to prevent scurvy. Slaves due for transshipment were normally well fed, receiving meals of beef, rice, flour, yams, biscuits, fish, or bananas twice a day. There may even have been rum and tobacco, and they were likely to have been exercised on occasion.[30] Castillo, meanwhile, hired a vessel to transport his cargo to Cartagena. By the first week of July he had chartered "a small ship" and the slaves were taken back to the quayside and hustled on board.[31]

Loath to have such a valuable cargo intercepted en route to the Main, Castillo arranged to have HMS *Swan* assigned as an escort. No doubt Inchiquin helped to broker the deal and was compensated by Castillo as a result. To give the mission a veneer of respectability, Inchiquin ordered Captain Johnson to deliver "some letters to the Spanish Ambassador for the release of certain English prisoners" held in Cartagena, most likely the crews of Jamaican sloops who had been detained for engaging in illegal trade.[32] The *Swan* was also loaded with trade goods. Starved of supply from home due to the inefficiency of the flota system, the colonists of the Spanish Main were a ready market for English manufactures.[33] The trade also provided a cash-strapped Jamaica with a supply of hard currency: the silver Spanish pieces of eight which had long since become the unofficial coinage of Port Royal. The crew of the *Swan*, for their part, had spent their first month in Jamaica acclimating to the tropical heat, wooding and watering their vessel and making minor repairs. As well as the six men who had been lost to illness and accident during the transatlantic voyage, several more had died in Jamaica, among them the gunner, Robert How, who had been discharged dead on June 23. On July 1, in preparation for his imminent departure, Captain Johnson had Jonathon Stephens entered into the *Swan's* muster. Listed as a pilot, Stephens would have had valuable local knowledge of the shoals and keys surrounding Jamaica and may even have had experience of the waters off Cartagena.[34]

On July 6, 1690, the *Swan* and the small ship Castillo had hired departed from Port Royal.[35] Sailing due south, they reached Cartagena within ten days without incident. With a population of several thousand Spaniards, creoles, and Indian and negro slaves, the walled city boasted numerous whitewashed churches, forts, convents, and cathedrals built on a spit of land projecting into the sparkling Caribbean. To the south lay a magnificent double bay, the inner of which was projected by a series of booms and fortifications bristling with over one thousand cannon. The whole was dominated by the San Felipe de Barajas Castle rising above the city to the south. While the *Swan* beat back and forth off shore, Castillo's hired ship sailed into the harbor, where it was boarded by local officials charged with ensuring that the slaves were not infected with disease. Having passed the inspection, Castillo's slaves were unloaded and taken into town, housed in temporary holding bays known as "casas del cabildo," branded once more in preparation for resale, and divided into lots which typically numbered between fifteen and thirty individuals. Some may have been sold to residents, while others were purchased by agents who would keep them in Cartagena until a sufficient number had been gathered to dispatch inland for resale. Some of these went north to Panama, others headed south for the sugar plantations of southern and central New Granada, while a significant number traveled as far as northern Peru.[36] The *Swan* picked up six prisoners at Cartagena before returning to Port Royal laden with Spanish pieces of eight. The voyage proved difficult: the frigate was a remarkably poor sailor. Beating up against the prevailing winds, it would not arrive back at Jamaica until September 12, some six weeks after its departure.[37]

MOST OF THE *Hannah*'s slaves who had remained in Jamaica were destined for a short, brutal life on one of the island's sugar plantations. By the 1690s Jamaica's economy was coming to be dominated by such concerns. By examining inventory records dating from between 1674 and 1701, it is possible to identify some two hundred planters. Perhaps half were smallholders. With an average of two slaves or indentured servants each, most owned provision farms aimed at supplying regional markets and the central hub of Port Royal with pork, poultry, fruits, and vegetables for local consumption. Others owned cotton plantations or cacao walks. These were businesses which required relatively little investment but were diminishing in importance. Jamaican cotton, being considered an inferior crop, struggled to compete with that grown in the North American colonies, while the island's cacao crop was regularly ruined by blight and the hurricanes which swept the Caribbean annually in August and September. Many of the other small to mid-sized estates were cattle pens which supplied fresh beef for internal markets. Hog farming was also popular, but by 1690, all the largest and wealthiest planters were dedicated to sugar production. In the sample of two hundred mentioned above, some fifty-four can be assigned to this category due to the mill rollers, boiling coppers, sugar pots, and stills listed among their inventories. Of these, six were small scale. Owning less than twenty slaves each, they would have struggled to make their labor-intensive businesses profitable. The majority of the remainder owned at least forty slaves, while the biggest seven planters had more than one hundred slaves each and owned estates valued in excess of £3,000.[38]

At the time of the auction held on board the *Hannah*, the largest and most profitable sugar plantation in Jamaica belonged to Thomas Sutton, an assemblyman and colonel in the island militia. Sutton's estate, valued by contemporaries at over £10,000, covered 1,100 acres on either side of the upper Minho River near the hamlet of St. Jago in Clarendon Parish.[39] The single most valuable asset, representing 70 percent of the estate's total value, were the four to five hundred slaves who lived on the plantation. Three hundred were "working" slaves. At least sixty were women and children. The estate also contained a great house: a grand, fortified building which combined luxury with the need for defense.[40] Built on rising ground some distance from the sugar works, thus allowing Sutton to keep an eye on his charges, the great house would have been surrounded by formal gardens, while the interior would perhaps have featured finely cut stone, seasoned timber, and highly polished floors.[41] Sutton lived with his wife, Judith, his infant son, John, and his daughters, Anna and Sarah.[42] Nearby was a dwelling house, home to six or seven indentured servants and the plantation's caretaker, who looked after the estate when Sutton was away on business in Spanish Town or Port Royal. Inside was an arsenal. As well as four small cannon, perhaps 2 or 4 pounders, it also housed at least six barrels of gunpowder and fifty firearms, including blunderbusses and muskets.[43] Elsewhere on the grounds, on the far side of the extensive cane fields, was a watermill powered by the Minho River, a boiling house with furnace and coppers, a still, a curing house, and a village for the slaves.[44] The plantation produced roughly four hundred hogsheads of sugar per year, roughly a thirtieth of that produced by Jamaica as a whole.[45] Each hogshead sold for about £10 at Port Royal. Judging by the inventories of contemporary estates, Sutton's would have also contained various livestock pens and provisions grounds. Cattle, goats, and sheep were commonly raised for their meat and manure, while horses served as mounts or beasts of burden.[46]

Nothing is known of Thomas Sutton prior to his arrival in Jamaica in 1670. On November 26 of that year, he emigrated from Barbados, along with several other planters who made the move during Mody-

ford's governorship, and purchased his Clarendon estate from Henry
Tennant for twenty-two slaves and £80.[47] Sutton was acting as an
agent for his brother John, a ship's captain, merchant, and planter of
Barbados.[48] This seems to have been a common pattern at the time:
Richard Guy and William Drax, both of whom became prominent
planters in the 1680s, also arrived on the island in the same period as
agents for wealthier elder siblings.[49] Thomas Sutton prospered in Jamaica. By 1677, when he received his first appointment as one of the
two assemblymen chosen for Clarendon each year, he must have been
a well-respected and recognizable figure in the parish. Reappointed
as assemblyman in 1678, 1679, and 1686, Sutton rose to a position of
local political prominence and made close alliances with several of the
other leading planters in the region, including Henry Tennant, from
whom he had purchased his estate and who was married to Sutton's
niece; Edward Pennant, whose daughter, Elizabeth, was married to
Sutton's son John; and Francis Blackmore, a fellow resident of Clarendon Parish who shared a bookkeeper with Sutton, lived near the port
of Withywood, and owned two hundred and fifty slaves and two sugar
and indigo plantations.[50]

Although Sutton was a rising star, there were also one or two black
marks on his record. These chiefly stemmed from his involvement
with the interlopers. Many planters were dissatisfied with the Royal
African Company. Its prices were high, largely due to the expense of
maintaining a string of forts and factories on the West African coast;
the RAC favored Spanish buyers such as Castillo, whose seemingly
bottomless purse could cope with the agents' inflated demands; supply was irregular, especially in wartime; and the demand for slaves in
the Caribbean was considerably higher than the company could sat-
isfy. All this led to the rise of the interlopers: independent, monop-
oly-busting traders who sent small, swift vessels to the African coast
to purchase slaves who were sold directly to the planters in the West
Indies at low prices.[51] Due to the trade's illegality, evidence is sketchy.
Nevertheless, at the time of Inchiquin's arrival it is possible to identify
a few individuals involved in the trade. One was Oliver Cransborough, a Port Royal mariner who owned a part share in at least two of
the island's sloops and was also involved in shipping horses to Jamaica

from Rio de la Hacha on the Spanish Main. In 1687 Cransborough had embarked on a voyage to Southeast Africa and the Indian Ocean islands on board the *Margaret*. Having picked up 187 slaves, he returned to Jamaica on December 7 and sold the 128 who survived the voyage.[52] A second interloper recorded that year was an unnamed Dutchman who reached Jamaica with 477 slaves from Madagascar and West Central Africa,[53] and in 1686 a certain Captain Hawke arrived with "somewhat under a hundred" slaves. Landed on the sparsely populated north coast to avoid the attentions of the RAC's agents in Port Royal, the Africans were collected by two Jamaican merchants, Josiah Barry and a Mr. Waterhouse. The sick were left on nearby plantations to recover, while the rest were guided over the mountains by a hunter and sold directly to plantation owners in the savannahs in the south.[54]

Two possible references to the Suttons' involvement in interloping survive. The first is merely an allusion: in 1684 a certain John Sutton of Barbados (perhaps the same John Sutton who had financed Thomas Sutton's purchase of the Clarendon plantation in 1670 or perhaps a relative) had an unnamed ship seized by HMS *Diamond* for contravening the monopoly of the Royal African Company. The ship and its cargo of slaves were condemned and sold at Bridgetown by the governor, Sir Richard Dutton. According to protocol, the proceeds were divided into three shares: one for the crown, one for Captain Jones of the *Diamond*, and one for Dutton. Unsurprisingly for an age in which corruption was so commonplace as to be almost entirely unremarkable, Jones later complained that both he and the king had only received £100 while Dutton had taken £700.[55] The other reference is more concrete, though also lacking in detail. In September 1689 Thomas Sutton made a petition directly to King William calling for an enquiry to be made into his recent arrest by order of the RAC's agents at Port Royal "upon a charge of having traded to Guinea." According to the records of the Board of Trade, Sutton "entered into a recognisance of £2,000 not to trade on the coast of Africa without leave of the African company" in order "to avoid a heavy fine."[56] As mentions of interlopers are considerably more frequent in the Royal African Company's correspondence of the period than actual records of prosecution, it would seem plausible that Sutton considered the fine a reasonable outlay when weighed against the financial gains to be had when dealing with interlopers as opposed to relying on the intermittent offerings of slaves granted to planters by the RAC.

The majority of the slaves who arrived on Sutton's plantation, whether by way of the auctions of the Royal African Company at Port Royal or the shadowy dealings of the interlopers, would have undertaken the penultimate leg of their journey via coastal sloop—the roads of the Jamaican interior, even those of the relatively well-developed central-southern parishes, were poor in the late seventeenth century. Sutton's purchases would have disembarked at Carlisle Town, otherwise known as Withywood, the gateway to the interior of Clarendon Parish, where the estuary of the Minho River fed into the wide, sheltered reaches of Carlisle Bay. Called Port Emyas by the Spanish, the site was originally settled in 1660 by soldiers of Penn and Venables's expedition. By the last decade of the seventeenth century, it was a thriving community of one hundred houses with a "small well-built chapel," several "taverns and punch-houses," and a number of warehouses which bordered the sandy bay where "the neighbouring planters," Sutton not least among them, "lay up their commodoties . . . which they transport from hence to Port Royall." Withywood was also known for its community of "wealthy Jewes merchants" and a "biannual faire" which featured a horse race pitting the residents' best riders against those of the nearby town of Old Harbour. The winner received a silver cup.[57]

Chained together and supervised by Sutton's overseer, the slaves were marched inland across the flat, grassy expanses of Clarendon Plain. Thought by some of the English inhabitants to have been originally cleared by the indigenous Tainos for the cultivation of maize, by the late seventeenth century Jamaica's savannahs were home to the remains of once-mighty herds of feral cattle. Descendants of the animals which had been allowed to roam free by the Spanish, they had thrived on the thick grasses springing up from the rich, black alluvial soils washed down from the mountains to the north, but by the 1690s relatively few remained, the majority having fallen victim to the hunters who preyed on them in the aftermath of the English invasion.[58]

On arrival at Sutton's plantation, new slaves were rebranded. Silver branding irons were common artifacts in seventeenth-century Jamaican inventories, while Spanish owners preferred gold ones. It is known that Sutton used a distinctive mark. The initials "TS, with a heart" were burned into each of his purchases, normally on the shoulder.[59] The wound was then rubbed with palm oil to prevent infection.[60] Newcomers were also renamed. Slave nomenclature varied according to the whims of their owners, but many fell into one of four categories: Anglicized versions of their original names; those considered humorous; names with classical or historical allusions; and those more commonly associated to the modern mind with animals or children, the latter an interesting insight into how the slaves were viewed by their masters.[61] The only surviving references to the names of any slaves owned by Thomas Sutton are those recorded in his will of 1710. Among the thirteen men listed are Quashie, a corruption of an Akan or Coromantee "day name" suggesting its owner was born on a Sunday; Dick, Obee, Hector, Sambo, Yabboy, and Cromwell, the latter a hint that the Suttons may well have supported the crown during the Civil War. The children are unnamed, while the women included Nanny, Sukey, Daphne, Mulatta, Old Betty, Little Betty, Sox, Doll, and Daphne.[62]

During their first three months on the plantation, new arrivals underwent a period of "seasoning." Each was assigned to an old hand, either of the same nation as the newcomer or of a comparable language group, to be educated in the routine that would come to dominate the remains of their days. During this period, many succumbed to disease.[63] Although primarily concerned with the late eighteenth and early nineteenth centuries, research conducted into two Jamaican slave populations, those of Worthy Park and Mesopotamia, is revealing. Tuberculosis, the bloody flux, and diarrhea were the biggest killers. Although Europeans often remarked on Africans' propensity for personal hygiene, sanitation on board slave ships and in the squalid slave quarters of the plantations was appalling. The slaves drank contaminated water and ate half-rotten meat, while excrement and decomposing garbage littered the villages in which they lived. Dietary deficiencies were rife. In the West Indies slaves caught malaria and yellow fever. Others undergoing seasoning would have fallen victim to ailments they had acquired in Africa and harbored during the Middle Passage. These included yaws and parasitic infections such as hookworm. Entering the body via the feet, the hookworm burrowed into the intestine and sucked its victim's blood, leading to lethargy and ravenous hunger which compelled many slaves to eat dirt.[64] Suicide was common, especially among new arrivals. "[Slaves] believe in resurrection," explained Richard Ligon in his 1673 travelogue *A True & Exact History of the Island of Barbadoes*, "and [think] that they shall go into their own Countrey again, and have their youth renewed [upon their death]. And lodging this opinion in their hearts, they make it their ordinary practice, upon any great fright, or threatening of their masters, to hang themselves."[65]

Slaves who survived seasoning were assigned a specific role. The majority, 65 percent at Mesopotamia, became field workers. These were divided into work groups or "gangs." The first, or Great Gang, as it was known in Mesopotamia, was the largest and hardest working. Consisting of the strongest and healthiest males in their mid-to-late twenties and early thirties, the Great Gang was responsible for digging the deep, square holes in which the new cane shoots were planted, and for cutting the ripe stalks. Members of the second gang, also exclusively male at Mesopotamia, performed other hard labor such as weeding the cane fields, cleaning the pastures, and assisting the first gang at crop time. The third gang, consisting of weaker or older men, women, and older children, was responsible for relatively light tasks such as hoeing the cane shoots. The fourth, known as the "hogmeat gang" at Mesopotamia, consisted mainly of children between the ages of six and ten.[66] As Hans Sloane explained, they were given relatively light tasks, such as carrying fodder to the livestock, "clean[ing] the Paths, [and] bring[ing] Fire-wood to the kitchen."[67] Fieldwork was the most grueling of all occupations on a plantation. In Mesopotamia members of the gangs had an average working life of under twelve years during which they were in "able" health only 51 percent of the time.[68]

Each gang was governed by a number of drivers, one being typically assigned to every twenty field hands. Armed with a "Wand or white Rod" and a cowhide whip, they ensured their charges worked in unison and on schedule.[69] In the early days of the sugar plantations drivers were almost exclusively white, but by the late seventeenth century, as white workers grew increasingly scarce, slaves whom their masters deemed worthy of a modicum of trust were promoted into the role. Sloane mentions two such characters: The first was Henry, a "negro ... much given to Venery," who worked on Colonel Thomas Ballard's plantation in St. Catherine's Parish. Sloane treated Henry successfully for blindness thus allowing him to return to his former role. "[I] never heard he had a Relapse, which in all likelihood I should have done had his Distemper return'd," Sloane noted, "for Planters give a great deal of Money for good Servants, both black and white, and take great care of them for that Reason."[70] The second individual was "Hercules, a lusty black Negro . . . [driver], and Doctor." Hercules worked on Colonel Fuller's plantation, also in St. Catherine's, where he had acquired a certain fame for the treatment he gave to his patients—fellow slaves and white masters alike.[71]

Besides the role of driver, a number of other "skilled" or "craft" occupations existed to which slaves could "aspire." Roughly 10 percent of the population of a sugar estate were tasked with such roles. Millmen, boilers, distillers, clarifiers, clayers, potters, coopers, carpenters, and smiths were all required. Judging by the records of eighteenth-century estates, these positions were almost invariably filled by males who had worked in the field for some time before rising to their position of responsibility. Although such jobs were less taxing than field-work, with the working life of those holding such positions in Mesopotamia averaging seventeen years, some craft roles came with their own inherent risks.[72] A few other slaves would have been assigned to fish or hunt "wild hog and fowles" to supplement the diet of the masters and the white indentured servants on the estate. Indigenous slaves acquired from the Mosquito Coast (the eastern coast of present-day Nicaragua and the southern Caribbean coastline of Honduras), Florida, or the English colonies of North America were highly prized in such roles. "The [Indian] men we use for . . . killing of fish," Richard Ligon noted. "With their own bow and arrows they will go out; and in a dayes time, kill as much fish, as will serve a family of a dozen persons, two or three dayes."[73]

About 14 percent of Sutton's slaves worked as domestics.[74] This was almost exclusively a female role. Their tasks including washing, cooking, and cleaning as well as making and repairing clothes for the field workers. While domestics avoiding the backbreaking work of the cane fields, they were more exposed to the desires, cruelty, and culture of the whites. Field workers retained their African traditions; domestics lost their roots and acquired white cultural traits.[75] Mulatto offspring, the result of unions between white masters or indentured servants and slaves, became increasingly common. Born into slavery as the children of black mothers, some had their freedom purchased by guilt-ridden fathers. Others remained enslaved for life.[76] Thomas Thistlewood, the eighteenth-century overseer and diarist, left a comprehensive account of his sexual adventures while working as an employee on two different sugar estates in Westmoreland Parish (formed from the westernmost parts of St. Elizabeth's Parish in 1703) and as a self-employed farmer on the livestock pen he later owned on Breadnut Island. During his thirty-seven years in Jamaica, Thistlewood engaged in 3,852 sexual encounters with 138 different slave women.[77] Although most, if not all, of these acts were forcibly consummated, some master-slave relationships were mutually beneficial. After a particularly promiscuous period in his thirties, when he had as many as twenty-six different partners per year, in 1754 Thistlewood "settled down" with one particular favorite, a mulatto named Phibba, with whom he cohabited for most of his remaining thirty-two years. Phibba was emancipated by Thistlewood and became the de facto mistress of his livestock pen on Breadnut Island. The couple had one child, a son named John who died at the age of twenty, an event about which the normally loquacious Thistlewood was unusually reticent.[78]

The remainder of the four to five hundred slaves at Sutton's, some one hundred individuals, were nonworkers.[79] A small proportion would have been new mothers, whom Richard Ligon noted with begrudging respect were normally back in the fields just "a fortnight" after giving birth, a rare occurrence among the chronically overworked and malnourished slave women of the field gangs. A proportion of the rest were "pickaninnies"—young children under six years old among whom mortality rates were appallingly high. Principal among the causes were fatal blood infections caused when the umbilical cord was cut with unsanitary instruments. Up to the age of three, slave children would accompany their mothers in the fields. "As they work at weeding, which is a stooping work," Ligon noted, "[they will] suffer the hee Pickaninny, to sit a stride upon their backs, like St. George a Horse-back; and there hee Spur his mother with his heels, and sings and crows on her back, clapping his hands, as if he meant to flye; which the mother is so pleas'd with, as she continues her painful stooping posture, longer than she would do, rather than discompose her Jovial Pickaninny of his pleasure, so glad she is to see him merry."[80]

When old enough to walk, slave children roamed the plantation naked, playing or seeking out scraps to eat. They were excused from work until the age of six when they typically joined the fourth gang. The rest of the nonworkers were those too sick, old, or infirm to fulfill any useful role. These individuals would spend their days languishing in the slave villages which sprouted up beside the cane fields.[81] Although some estates employed a resident physician who would be tasked with maintaining their health, in the late seventeenth century medicine was a rudimentary blend of superstition, herbalism, and brutal practices which were often counterproductive. Many patients would eventually succumb to sickness or disease.

By one contemporary account, Thomas Sutton had just "six or seven" whites working on his sugar plantation.[82] When set beside the plantation's five hundred slaves, this gives a ratio of roughly one white to every ninety blacks. Contemporaries stipulated that a much higher proportion of whites was desirable. Richard Ligon recommended would-be sugar magnates begin their plantations with one hundred slaves, fifty of each sex, twenty white male servants, and ten white females—a ratio of one white to every three or four blacks, while the Council of Jamaica passed a law in 1689 stating that "all gentlemen, merchants, planters and other inhabitants . . . shall keep, have and mantaine one English servant in his house or plantation for every nine Negro slaves which he hath . . . and in default herein to forfeit one hundred dollars to ye king."[83] Considering the frequency of slave revolts on the island, this was a wise piece of legislation. The law, however, was difficult to enforce. Worthy Park, an estate in Lluidas Vale, St. John's Parish, operated with a similar ratio to Sutton's.[84] Also, the fact that the Council deemed it necessary to pass such a law in the first place suggests that planters generally had few whites on their estates. The reasons were numerous. The West Indies were increasingly unattractive for poor white settlers, hence the tendency to "spirit" or kidnap indentured servants in England. Disease was rife; the islands were far from home and unstable militarily and politically; they offered little opportunity for a social or family life; and, as the plantocracy bought up all available land, there were precious few opportunities for servants to establish a livelihood once their terms of indenture had expired.[85]

Free white workers were even harder to acquire. Notorious among employers for their nomadic nature, few lasted in any job more than a matter of months. One contemporary example was William Dampier, a curious young man who arrived in Port Royal in April 1679 to work at the previously mentioned Bybrook estate. Given a cordial welcome by William Whaley, the manager of Bybrook, Dampier was initially buoyant, believing his "future fortune" would soon be within his grasp. His relationship with Whaley deteriorated, however, when Dampier realized that he would not be employed as a bookkeeper as he had been led to believe back in England, but would instead be expected to indenture himself and learn one of the trades of the plantation. Dampier "thought it an under valuing of him to handle either skimmer or ladle." An impasse of four months ensued. Dampier neither worked nor was paid. Instead he spent his time with his neighbors, a certain Doctor Foster and his wife, whom Whaley damned as "the nastiest wasting slut as ever came into a House . . . and one fit to do nothing at all." Meanwhile, Dampier's relationship with Whaley reached new lows. On one occasion, the manager even gave his employee "a good box or two," which Dampier "returned" before he was finally released from his contract with six weeks' wages, most of which was promptly squandered on drinking binges with the doctor and his wife. Within six months, Dampier had left Jamaica.[86] In what proved the most unlikely of careers, Dampier worked for a time as a logwood cutter in Campeche and later became a pirate, botanist, and world explorer. He was the first person to circumnavigate the globe three times, landed in Australia eighty years before Captain Cook, visited the Galapagos one hundred and fifty years before Darwin, and wrote a series of best-selling travelogues which would inspire both Defoe's *Robinson Crusoe* and Swift's *Gulliver's Travels*.[87]

The principal white worker at Sutton's was the caretaker. Charged with managing the plantation during Sutton's frequent absences in

Port Royal and Spanish Town, he was responsible for supervising the daily running of the estate. His subordinates were the white overseers, each of which would have been given control of a field gang. Other whites may have included a doctor, and some skilled sugar workers, who toiled alongside similarly skilled slaves, such as the boilers, coopers, carpenters, distillers, and smiths. Judging by contemporary accounts, the caretaker would have been a free man and may have commanded a salary of around £50 per year.[88] He would also have been afforded considerable respect, "for he," as Ligon explained, "is a man that the master may allow sometimes to sit at his own Table, and therefore must be clad accordingly."[89] The overseers may have been free workers or indentured servants while all the other skilled workers would have invariably fallen into the latter category. One example was a certain Gilbert Milroy, a Scottish Covenanter transported to Jamaica in 1685 for refusing to bow to the authority of the Anglican Church. According to Robert Wodrow, author of *The History of the Sufferings of the Church of Scotland*, Milroy "suffered very hard things in Jamaica, after he was sold" at Port Royal.

His master would have him work on the Lord's day; this he peremptorily refused. After he had been beat several times, one day his master drew his sword, and had well nigh killed him; but afterwards finding him faithful, conscientious, and very diligent, he altered his way, and made him overseer of all his negroes. The blacks mortally hated him for his fidelity to his master, and made various attempts to murder him. One of them struck him on the head with a long pole, whereby he lay dead for some time, and lost a great deal of blood, so that ever since he was a little paralytic. At another time he was poisoned by another of the negroes, but was saved by timeous application of antidotes. In short he was continually in hazard of his life by those savages. Many of the . . . [transported Scottish Covenanters] died in their bondage, but Gilbert lived till the [Glorious] . . . revolution, and then was liberated, and came safe home to his wife and relations, and when my account was written December 1710, he was alive, a very useful member of the session of Kircowan; in the presbytery of Wigton.[90]

Being a transported prisoner, Milroy was not of the usual stock that made up indentured servants, a fact which his master soon realized, promoting him accordingly. Many of the transported Monmouth rebels were also of a better caliber and often did well in the West Indies as illustrated by a letter written by Governor Kendall of Barbados in 1690. "I have not announced the repeal of the Act concerning the Monmouth rebels to the Council and Assembly," Kendall informed his superiors at Whitehall. "When they arrived, the Lieutenant-Governor received positive orders from King James that their servitude should be fixed by Act at ten years. The planters accordingly bought them, and thinking themselves secure of them during that time, taught them to be boilers, distillers and refiners, and neglected to teach any other as they would otherwise have done."[91] As the first part of Milroy's account makes clear, conditions for white indentured servants on sugar plantations were harsh. Their diet was poor, their clothing allowance limited, and their housing was squalid. They were subject to a brutal legal code. They were forbidden to marry without their master's consent; females who fell pregnant were liable to be punished by the extension of their indenture, as were those who were caught attempting to flee. Servants were also subject to frequent physical punishment—whippings were commonplace, as was the use of the stocks, and they were obliged to serve in the militia during periods of conflict, a burden which could occasionally afford an unexpected reversal of fortune.[92] In 1673 the Jamaican Council passed a law stating that any individual who fought "manfully and like a true soldier" should be granted his immediate freedom.[93]

Life at Sutton's was dictated by the rhythms of the fourteen-to-eighteen-month sugar cycle. At the start of the wet season, which ran from June to November, the field workers dug a series of trenches six inches deep and six inches across into which they placed cane cuttings. In a ten-hour day, each slave was expected to dig between sixty and eighty trenches. Lightly covered with soil, the cuttings sprouted at each joint within a month, producing a sea of small plants "like a land of Green Wheat in England . . . high enough to hide a hare." In the first few months, the cane fields were weeded regularly by the second gang and manured with a mixture of cow dung and cane cuttings. More than disease or insect infestation, rats posed the principal danger. Once gnawed, the entire cane would rot. Some overseers deployed rat-catching gangs, but the only real deterrent was to burn infested fields from the outside in, thus wiping out the entire rodent population.[94]

The canes reached their full height of eight feet within twelve months. Two to six months later, the leaves turned from green to "a deep Popinjay," indicating the canes were ripe for harvesting. Typically, this occurred from January to May, an intensely busy period. Woken two hours before dawn by the shrill blast of a conch shell or hollowed animal horn or plantation bell, the Great Gang would cut the canes with "hand bills" three to six inches from the surface of the soil. "At [this] time," Ligon remarked, "they divide the tops from the Canes, which they do with the same bills, at one stroak; and then holding the Canes by the upper end, they strip off all the blades . . . which . . . are bound up in faggots . . . put into carts and carried home" for animal fodder. At noon, a further blast from the overseers indicated that the slaves were to stop for lunch. At two o'clock the work recommenced. The field slaves would not rest again until after dark.[95]

Once cut, the canes were carried to the millhouse, or ingenio, by mules. There, each was fed between triple brass and steel rollers powered by windmill, horse or cattle, or water wheel, as was the case at Sutton's. "A Negre puts in the Canes on one side," Ligon explained, "and the rollers draw them through to the other . . . where another Negre stands . . . receives them; and returns them back on the other side of the middle roller which draws the other way. . . . The Canes having past to and again . . . young Negre Girles . . . carry them away."[96] The process was a risky one. "If a Mill-feeder be catch't by the finger," Edward Littleton, a member of the Barbadian plantocracy and a contemporary of Sutton's, explained in a 1689 publication entitled *The Groans of the Plantations*, "his whole body is drawn in, and he is squeez'd to pieces."[97]

The dark-brown juice that issued forth when the canes were crushed was collected in a trough running beneath the rollers. Channeled into a pipe, it ran downhill to the boiling house where it was collected in a cistern. From there the juice was transferred to the largest of a series of four or five giant copper kettles suspended above a furnace fueled by the discarded cane cuttings. These boiling coppers, among the most valuable items in any planters' inventory, were used in descending order of size. In Bybrook, for example, they held 180, 120, 80, and 30 gallons, respectively. It was the job of the boiler, the most valued slave on the plantation, to ladle the juice into the first copper, skim off the impurities that arose, and transfer the remaining liquid into the next copper. The smaller the copper, the hotter the fire burning beneath it. As the juice progressed from one to the next, it reduced and purified, growing increasingly viscous and ever darker in color. In the final copper, known as the "tach," the boiler "tempered" the liquid with a few drops of lemon or lime juice to promote granulation. When the juice was deemed sufficiently tempered, a judgment perfected with experience, it was transferred to a cooling cistern. Boiling was even more hazardous than crushing the canes. "If a Boyler get any part into the scolding sugar," Littleton explained, "it sticks like Glew, or Birdlime, and 'tis hard to save either Limb or Life." The dangers were heightened by the need for haste. Once cut, the canes had to be crushed within a few hours to ensure the sugar content did not deteriorate, while the juice, once extracted, had to be boiled swiftly to avoid fermentation. During harvest time the slaves were required to work around the clock. Straw fires were lit in the mill and boiling houses to enable them to continue through the hours of darkness, while the overseers had to remain ever vigilant to ensure their charges did not doze off.[98]

The sugar was left to cool for twelve hours after boiling, then packed into earthenware pots and stored in the curing house. Each pot had a hole in the bottom which allowed the molasses to drain out onto a earthenware pan known as a drip. The pots were left draining for a month before the contents were knocked out. The top and bottom ends were then removed for reboiling, while the central two-thirds, which was now golden-brown muscovado, was broken up and spread out to dry in the sun. Packed into hogsheads for transfer to Port Royal, it would be stored at the quayside warehouses awaiting shipment to England there to be further refined to create clayed or white sugar. The molasses was transferred to the plantation's still. Mixed with a solution of inferior cane juice and skimmings from the boiling coppers, it was left to ferment for a week, before being boiled and condensed into a rough rum. Known locally as kill-devil, the drink was typically mixed with water, lime juice, sugar, and nutmeg to make

Sugar processing on a plantation. Sugar cultivation was a labor intensive and dangerous process. Brutalized by draconian punishments and barbaric working conditions, a third of all plantation slaves would die within three years of their arrival in Jamaica. (*Engraving, c.1749*)

punch. Again, the process was not without risk. "We lost an excellent Negro," Ligon recalled, "who bringing a Jar of this Spirit, from the Still-house . . . in the night . . . brought the candle somewhat nearer than he ought . . . the spirit being stirr'd by that motion, flew out, and got hold of the flame of the Candle, and so set all on fire, and burnt the poor Negro to death."[99]

When not required to work by the dictates of the sugar cycle, plantation slaves were afforded some free time, typically on Saturday afternoons and Sundays. Most spent their "leisure" time working private allotments at the plantation slave village.[100] A community of wooden shacks facing onto a central path to one side of the cane fields, the village was typically built in direct line of sight of the great house, thus allowing the master to keep an eye on his slaves from his shaded terrace. Slave dwellings excavated at Seville estate in northern Jamaica measured four by six meters and were divided into two or more rooms:

a living space and one or more areas for sleeping. The floors were lined with limestone cobbles, and the walls were constructed of a series of upright posts, between which wattle-and-daub was smeared to keep out the weather. The whole was covered by a thatch of interlocking palm fronds.[101] Slaves had few possessions. "They allow 'em neither coate, hatt, shirt, stockins or shoos," John Taylor noted, "only they allow to every man a linen arsclout or a paire of breaches, and to the women only an arsclout or line petticoat." Taylor, a visitor in the late 1680s, thought this only fair. "They deserve no better," he explained, "since they differ only from bruite beast only by their shape and speech."[102] Sloane added, "generally" each slave also had "a Mat to lie on, a Pot of Earth to boil their Victuals in . . . and a Calabash or two for Cups and Spoons."[103] Others used the red clay abundant in Jamaica to fashion pots and plates which they baked in the fire.[104]

Some slaves lived in family units. Polygamy, a widespread practice in West Africa, was commonly permitted by the planters who rewarded the hard-working or loyal with wives.[105] This Sloane noted, "is what keeps their plantations chiefly in good order." The masters "buy Wives in proportion to their Men, lest the Men should wander to neighbouring Plantations, and neglect to serve them."[106] Other houses were occupied exclusively by groups of young males or young females. Slaves were commonly allotted provision grounds to grow crops to supplement their rations. Sometimes these would have been in the same area as the village, but on other plantations the provision grounds were several miles away. On Sundays, their day of rest, or on the occasional feast days of Christmas, Whit Sunday, or the Crop Over Festival, the slaves tended to their yams, cassava, plantains, potatoes, and peppers.[107] Slave owners encouraged their charges to grow their own produce. As well as freeing them from the need to purchase extra supplies, the use of the provision grounds had a profound psychological effect on the slaves which lessened the possibility of their rising in revolt. By giving his charges a stake in the "society" of the plantation, albeit a very poor and insignificant one, the slave owner was encouraging them not to rebel. If they did so, they would lose even this small privilege.[108]

Slaves used the food grown at the provision grounds to add to their rations. Typically, this consisted of salt mackerel, occasionally supplemented by beans or flour in emergencies and the odd piece of salt beef or pork allowed them when a barrel was spoiled.[109] Rum was occasionally given to the slaves for good behavior. "Also," Taylor noted, "when a bullock or the like dies in the plantation, the carrion carcass . . . is given them, on which they will feed as hertyly as a plowman on bacon."[110] Another occasional source of protein were the rats roasted when the cane fields were burned to free them of infestation. As the vermin fed almost exclusively on the cane, the meat was sweet and highly regarded by blacks and whites alike.[111] Some slaves even had some livestock of their own: a pig or two or some chickens, which they acquired as presents from their masters or through trade at Sunday markets. These were commonplace throughout Jamaica and provided a means of social and economic interaction between slaves from different plantations and with the island's poorest whites. Surplus food, tools, and various craft items, such as necklaces, rings, horns, and drums, were bartered or occasionally exchanged for currency which the slaves used to purchase livestock or other goods.[112]

Sundays were for rest and socializing. "Then those pore slaves leave off work and repaire to their houses," Taylor recorded, "where they . . . make a great fier, and with a kitt (made of a gourd or calabash with one twine string) play, sing and daunce according to their country fashion, making themselves all mirth, men and women together in a confused manner; after they have thus sported as long as they thinck fit, they lay themselves naked on the ground all round their fier, the whole family together in a confused manner to sleep." On other occasions, slaves from different plantations would gather in "great companys . . . [to] feast, dance, and sing (or rather howle like beasts) in a anticque manner, as if they were madd."[113] Ligon wrote of slaves' wrestling matches, while Sloane described their music and dance.[114] "The Negroes are much given to Venery," the doctor began,

and although hard wrought, will at nights, or on Feast days Dance and Sing; their Songs are all bawdy, and leading that way. They have several sorts of instruments in imitation of Lutes, made of small Gourds fitted with Necks, strung with Horse hairs, or the peeled stalks of climbing Plants or Withs. These instruments are sometimes made of hollow'd Timber covered with Parchment or other Skin wetted, having a Bow for its Neck, the Strings ty'd longer or shorter, as they would alter their sounds. . . . They have likewise in their Dances Rattles ty'd to their Legs and Wrists, and in their Hands, with which they make a noise, keeping time with one who makes a sound answering it on the mouth of an empty Gourd or Jar with his Hand. Their Dances consist in great activity and strength of Body, and keeping time, if it can be. They very often tie Cow Tails to their Rumps, and add such other odd things to their Bodies in several places, as gives them a very extraordinary appearance.[115]

Another much-mentioned custom was the slaves' habit of celebrating funerals. These often paralleled West African ritual and were typically led by an obeah man. Part doctor, part spiritual leader, these figures were believed to have magical powers.[116] "When . . . slaves die," Taylor recorded,

they make a great adoe at their burials, for haveing caryed them to the grave in a verey mournfull manner, all both men and women which accompany the corpse sing and howle in a sorrowfull manner in their own language, 'till being come to the grave, into which they gently put the corpse, and with it casadar bread, roasted fowles, sugar, rum, tobacco, and pipes with fier to light his pipe withal, and this they doe (as they say and follishly imagine) in order to sustaine him in his journey beyond these plesant hills in their own country, whither they say he is now goeing to live at rest. After this they fill up the grave, and eat and drinck theron, singing in their own language verey dolefully, desiring the dead corpse (by ciseing the grave) to acquaint their father, mother, husband and other relations of their present condition and slavery, as he passeth thro' their country towards the plesant mountains.[117]

The whites believed the brutality inherent in chattel slavery was entirely necessary. They held that it was the only means they had of keeping their charges under control and lessening the threat of rebellion. "The unhappy condition of the Negro leads him naturally to detest us," explained Nicolas Lejeune, a French planter and slave owner of Santo Domingo.

It is only force and violence that restrains him; he is bound to harbour an implacable hatred in his heart, and if he does not visit upon us all the hurt of which he is capable it is only because his readiness to do so is chained down by terror; so, if we do not make his chains as proportionate to the dangers that we run with him, if we let loose this hatred from the present state in which it is stifled, what can prevent him from attempting to break the chains? The bird locked in his cage profits from the slightest negligence to escape. I dare to say that our negroes lack only sufficient courage or resolution to buy their freedom with the blood of their masters. Just one step can enlighten them about what they have the power to undertake. . . . It is not the fear and equity of the law that forbids the slave from stabbing his master, it is the consciousness of absolute power that he has over his person. Remove this bit, and he will dare everything.[118]

Flogging was the most common punishment. Although statistics from the late seventeenth century are not extant, the mid-eighteenth-century diaries of Thomas Thistlewood may cast some light on common practices. Over one eleven-month period, running from mid-1750 to mid-1751, Thistlewood whipped eighteen of the twenty-four male slaves under his supervision. Between them, they received thirty-one floggings, while seven of the eleven females received eleven. Thistlewood's floggings were a minimum of 50 lashes. Sometimes 100 or 150 were doled out. The maximum during the period was 250 lashes, administered to a stranger, presumably from a neighboring plantation, whom Thistlewood caught inside one of his animal pens. Other supposed crimes recorded in his diary included "being saucy" to a white supervisor, "carelessness," theft, "negligence," "stupidity," laziness, or *petit maroonage*, a term denoting the extremely common practice of fleeing from a plantation for a limited period with no intention of permanently escaping the system.[119] To intensify the pain inflicted, overseers often resorted to a practice known as "pickling." "After they are whip'd 'till they are Raw," as Sloane explained it, "some put on their Skins Pepper and Salt to make them smart; at other times their Masters will drop melted Wax on their Skins, and use several very exquisite Torments."[120]

Thistlewood also made much use of bilboes, or shackles, to punish transgressors for minor infractions. By forcing the slaves to lie down in the dirt with their legs hoisted up and their ankles shackled to an iron bar, the punishment was not only painful and degrading, but could also lead to permanent disability. Some malefactors were confined for three weeks at a time. An expert in degradation, Thistlewood also used punishments of his own invention. The most notable was administered to an unfortunate named Derby caught eating stolen sugarcane in January 1756. "Had Derby whipped," Thistlewood recorded in his diary, "and made Egypt shit in his face." Derby was caught eating cane a second time in May. Thistlewood "had him well flogged and pickled, then had Hector shit in his mouth." In July Thistlewood introduced new depths of depravity. After whipping and pickling a runaway named Port Royal, Thistlewood "made Hector shit in his mouth [and] immeadiately put in a gag while his mouth was full & made him wear it 4 or 5 hours."[121]

More serious crimes demanded more serious punishments. Repeat runaways were shackled with ankle rings of great weight. Others were given "Pottocks about their necks," Sloane noted, "which are iron rings with two long necks riveted to them, or a Spur in the mouth," a device designed to snag on branches and vegetation should the wearer flee again. Some were hamstrung or "gelded," a process by which half of one of the slave's feet was chopped off with an ax. Castration was another punishment.[122] Although slave owners were loath to kill their property, hanging or gibbeting were resorted to in the cases of those who dared strike their masters. After hanging a repeat runaway named Robin in 1751, Thistlewood mounted his head on a pole for four months to serve as a warning to his peers.[123] Rebels were also executed, but by far crueler methods, such as being torn apart by dogs or burned to death. "By nailing them down on the ground with crooked Sticks on every Limb, and then applying the fire by degrees from their Feet and Hands," Sloane recorded, "[they are] burn[t] . . . gradually up to the Head, where by their pains are extravagant."[124]

Eyewitnesses spoke of the stoicism of those punished in such ways. "Negroe slaves died . . . obstinately," Taylor noted,

not semeing in the least concern'd therat, for when they were burnning, or rather roasting at the stake (for the fier was made at some distance from the stake to which they were chained and all round soe that they roasted or burnt by degrees) they would sing and laugh and by noe tortur would they ever confes. . . . And soe their torment seem'd in vaine. And here 'tis worth observation to consider their undaunted resolutions . . . which I observed by a lusty Negro man executed at the Port while I was there, whoe being chained to ye stake, and the feir kindled about him, and seeing his master standing bie he said to him this: "Master why doe you burn me? Did I ever refuse to work? Or doe what you order'd me to doe? Or did I ever steal anything from you in all my life? Why therfore am I thus cruelly burnt?" His master answered him thus: "Samboo (for that was his name), I have done all I can to save thy life, and would now give a hundred pounds to save thee, but thou hast bin in the rebellion and therfor must die. . . ." "Well then (said hee), I thanck you good master, God for ever bless you, and now I will die."[125]

White residents rarely felt sympathy. "The corporal punishment of slaves is so common," explained an English doctor resident in Dutch Guiana in the 1790s, "that instead of exciting repugnant sensations, felt by Europeans on first witnessing it, scarcely does it produce, in the breasts of those accustomed to it in the West Indies, even the slightest glow of compassion."[126]

As slaves were considered property, owners could punish them with impunity. The only laws curtailing such behavior merely highlight the brutality of the system. Prior to 1688 the penalty for an owner killing one of his or her slaves "wantonly" was a fine of £25. Legislation brought in by the Lords of Trade raised this to a three-month prison sentence. Loopholes meant that these laws were rarely enforced: owners could simply claim that the slave had died while undergoing a severe beating, a punishment that was perfectly allowable by law.[127]

SLAVE RESISTANCE came in a variety of forms. Most were relatively trivial acts, but effective in terms of diminishing production and profitability. Theft of food or other property was common. Perpetrators targeted other slaves as well as whites, especially those from neighboring plantations. Another form of resistance was suicide. Sabotage was frequent: animals were wounded or poisoned, machinery was broken, and, occasionally, the canes were set on fire. It has been speculated that such acts were particularly appealing to the Akan, whose cultural legacy included tales of animal tricksters, such as the Anansesem, or spider stories. *Petit maroonage* was another common form of resistance.[128] Thomas Thistlewood noted that most slaves ran away alone, for personal reasons, and did not stray far or for very long. The plantation offered sustenance and shelter, and Jamaica was an extremely hostile place for slaves caught wandering off without written permission. Nevertheless, certain individuals appear to have become addicted to temporary escape. One example among Thistlewood's charges was a young Ebo named Coobah whom Thistlewood raped nine months after purchasing her as a fifteen-year-old. Coobah had a child with a free black man at the age of twenty. The child died at fifteen months old and from that point Coobah began to run. The first occasion was in August 1765; after a four-day absence, Coobah returned. She was flogged and had a collar and chain put round her neck. Three years passed before she ran again, but from then on her temporary absences became increasingly common. In 1770 Coobah ran eight times. She ran five times in 1771. She received severe floggings, was kept in the stocks, and was branded on the forehead as a repeat runaway. Coobah also indulged in other minor acts of resistance. She argued with other slaves about the amount of work she was expected to do and stole food from whites and blacks alike. In October 1770, Coobah stole Thistlewood's punch strainer "and shit in it, wrapping it up and covering it with a piece of board." Thistlewood had the excrement "rubbed all over her face and mouth," but noted that Coobah appeared oblivious to the punishment. In 1774 Thistlewood ran out of patience. He sold Coobah for £40 and she was transported to Georgia.[129]

Outright rebellion was an ever-present threat. Jamaica was ideally suited to the establishment of maroon communities. The sixty-degree forested slopes of the Blue Mountains rose 7,400 feet in the east while the 500-square mile expanse of the Cockpit Country to the west also provided a perfect environment. The region's nigh-on impenetrable undergrowth, deep canyons, abundant limestone sinkholes, and broken ground was far more akin to the West Africans' homelands than their masters' European habitats. Wild foodstuffs and medicinal plants that resembled West African equivalents were to be found, thus enabling runaways with some bush lore to survive indefinitely.[130] As these areas were also relatively close to the fertile savannah where most plantations were established, maroons could remain in contact with plantation slaves. The two communities bartered commodities and established communications. Maroons were thus able to encourage their enslaved brethren to join them. They would also launch raids against the plantations to capture weapons and ammunition and abduct young female slaves to enable their communities to be self-perpetuating. Another factor facilitating the establishment and success of maroon communities was Jamaica's indigenous heritage. Although most Tainos had died out by the time of the arrival of the English, it is believed that a few holdouts survived in the interior into the late seventeenth century. These individuals may well have mixed with the earliest maroon communities thus allowing a blending of indigenous and African culture, bush lore, and, perhaps most important, methods of guerrilla warfare, thus facilitating their continuing resistance.[131]

Lobby's Rebellion, the first recorded slave rebellion in English-held Jamaica, took place in 1673. Two hundred Coromantee slaves on Major Selby's plantation in St. Ann's Parish killed a dozen whites, including their master, seized arms, and fled into the mountains between Clarendon and St. Elizabeth's. Although they defeated the first militia detachment sent after them, the rebels were gradually reduced by subsequent attacks yet never entirely dislodged and went on to form one of the elements of the group which would later become known as the Leeward Maroons. The year 1676 saw a rash of defections from plantations in St. Mary's Parish which were deemed so serious by the authorities that martial law was declared and a permanent guard established in the outlying districts. In 1678 a rebellion broke out on Captain Edmund Duck's plantation near Spanish Town when the river that separated the property from the capital became impassable due to heavy rain. Duck was seriously wounded and his wife, Martha, was killed along with several other whites. One slave who remained loyal swam the river to raise the alarm in Spanish Town, and a troop of horse was sent out to attack the rebels. Some were killed, while the rest were captured and "put to exemplary violent deaths." In 1685 one hundred and fifty slaves revolted on Widow Grey's estate in Guanaboa Vale. The rebels laid siege to the great house on the neighboring plantation belonging to Major Francis Price but were forced to retreat when a detachment of militia infantry arrived from Spanish Town. After their leader, "one of their conjurors, on whom they chiefly depended," was killed, the survivors briefly held a limestone crag before dispersing into the interior. One of the resulting bands, led by a Cormantee named Cophy, terrorized St. Mary's Parish for several months afterward. A reward of £10 was offered for Cophy's head and £5 for those of each of his five lieutenants. Several bounty hunters took up the challenge. Bloodhounds were used and a group led by Captain Davis also employed "Indian" trackers from Central America. Cophy's death was reported soon afterward. Of the one hundred and fifty rebels in his band, seven were killed in battle, thirty were captured, and fifty surrendered. The rest remained at large. Escaping to the east of the island they merged with a shipload of Madagascan runaways who had been living in the woods ever since the slave vessel which had transported them had been wrecked near Point Morant sometime in 1669 or 1670. Bounty hunters continued to scour the area for the Widow Grey rebels until the middle of 1687, but by then the survivors were firmly established in several villages. Due to their position in the east of the island, they came to be known as the Windward Maroons.[132]

As the slaves came from several different, and linguistically distinct, areas of West Africa, the whites erroneously presumed that they could not understand one another and therefore would remain divided. "It has been accounted a strange thing," Richard Ligon wrote in 1673,

that the Negroes being more than double the numbers of the Christians that are there . . . should not commit some horrid massacre upon the Christians, thereby to enfranchise themselves, and become Masters of the Island. But there are three reasons that take away this wonder; the one is, They are not suffered to touch or handle any weapons: The other, That they are held in such awe and slavery, as they are fearful to appear in any daring act; and seeing the mustering of our men, and hearing their Gun-shot, (than which nothing is more terrible to them) their spirits are subjugated to so low a condition, as they dare not look up to any bold attempt—Besides these, there is a third reason, which stops all designs of that kind, and that is they are fetch'd from several parts of Africa, who speak several languages, and by that means, one of them understands not another.[133]

Ligon was wrong on at least two counts. Although it does seem that slaves lived in fear of the island militia, he was incorrect in his assertion that slaves were never allowed to handle weapons. Thistlewood makes several allusions to slaves carrying firearms when hunting, a practice encouraged by their owners to supplement their rations and thus reduce costs.[134] It also seems that language was not as much of a barrier as contemporaries believed. West African societies had significant linguistic similarities. Furthermore, bilingualism and multilingualism were commonplace. Jamaica was probably multilingual from the time of its colonization, and linguists argue that Twi-Asante, the dominant language of the Gold Coast, soon became the lingua franca of the plantations alongside an English-Akan patios, unintelligible to the early white settlers.[135]

Rebels were often led by obeah men. As well as being valued for the charms and spells they used to ward off bullets, they also orchestrated the blood pacts which bound rebels together.[136] One testimony, given after a failed revolt in Antigua in 1736 led by an individual named Secundi, provides some details as to how such ceremonies were performed.

[Quawcoo, the Obeah man,] took . . . [a] Cock[rel], cut open his Mouth, and one of his Toes, and so poured the Cocks blood Over all [himself]," the witness reported, "and then Rub'd Secundi's forehead with the Cocks bloody Toe, then took . . . [a] Bottle and poured Some Rum upon the Obey, Drank a Dram, and gave it to Secundi and made Secundi Sware not to Discover his name to any body. Secundi then Asked him when he must begin to Rise. Quawcoo took a String Ty'd knots in it, and told him not to be in a hurry, for that he would give him Notice when to Rise and all Should go well, and that as he ty'd those knots so the Bacarras [(the slaves' name for whites)] should become Arrant fools and have their Mouths Stoped, and their hands tyed that they should not Discover the Negro's Designs.[137]

PRIOR TO 1700 the great majority of maroon leaders across the Americas about whom information is available were African born.[138] Having grown up inside the plantation system, and having known (and perhaps played with) their white masters since birth, in contrast, creole slaves had mixed loyalties and were therefore considerably less likely to rebel.[139] Another pattern which emerges is that many rebel leaders had held positions of authority in Africa prior to their enslavement, with former royalty being particularly well-suited to the role, especially seeing as most such figures would have risen to their previous position due to military expertise. Indeed, four of the six most important early maroon leaders across the Americas claimed to have been kings in

Africa prior to enslavement: Ganga Zumba, a former Congolese
prince, was the first ruler of what was perhaps the most impressive of
all maroon settlements, Palamares in eastern Brazil, a fortified town
with a population of over 10,000 which existed for nearly ninety years
until finally reduced in 1694; Domingo Bioho, also known as King
Benkos, ruled a maroon settlement carved out of the forests and
marshes of Matuna in northern Colombia for close to two decades
until he was betrayed, captured, and hung; Gaspar Yanga, a slave who
established a community of maroons in the early seventeenth century
in the highlands of Veracruz in Mexico, was said to have been a former
prince of the "Bron" people (perhaps a reference to the Brong, an Akan
culture group from modern-day Ghana); while Bayano, a Mandinka
prince from modern-day Sierra Leone, set up a maroon kingdom in
the jungles of Darien in Panama in the mid-sixteenth century. Like
several of his peers, Bayano made treaties with the local governor, thus
establishing his community inside the legal framework of the colony
before he too was betrayed and sent to Spain for execution.[140] Aphra
Behn, the seventeenth-century English novelist, chose to make the
eponymous hero of her slave-rebel epic a former African prince:
Oroonoko was enslaved after being betrayed and later turned rebel in
the plantations of Surinam.[141]

To the list of royalty-turned-slave-rebel can be added the name of
Cudjoe, an obscure figure who is believed to have led the most significant slave rebellion in seventeenth-century Jamaica, which broke
out on Thomas Sutton's plantation on July 31, 1690. That Cudjoe was
Coromantee is apparent by his name. That he led the rebellion and
that he subsequently fathered a son, also named Cudjoe, who would
grow up to be the most significant figure in early Jamaican maroon
history, is all that is known about him.[142] It has been speculated, however, that he had been a warlord, aristocrat, prince, or king prior to
his capture. It is also likely that Cudjoe was a relatively recent arrival
in Jamaica. Typically, revolts were carried out by those who had not
long been in country. Once slaves had been institutionalized, their
moral as well as physical strength began to atrophy, while their fear
of retribution grew to such a point that rebellion became unthink-
able.[143] How exactly Cudjoe arrived at Sutton's plantation is unknown.
Although it is tempting to hypothesize that he may have arrived on

board the *Hannah*, the single largest shipment of slaves to arrive in the colony in the twelve months prior to the uprising, it seems more likely that he came on board one of the interlopers with whom it would appear Sutton habitually did business. Regardless as to how or exactly when Cudjoe arrived at Sutton's, what can be said is that he was a persuasive and charismatic individual. By late July, as the sugar manufacturing process was coming to a halt for the season, he had convinced the entire slave population of some four to five hundred individuals to rise up and kill their oppressors. Afterward, Cudjoe planned to move on to a neighboring estate. From the course of latter events it can be surmised that Cudjoe not only intended to secure his own freedom and that of his fellows at Sutton's, but also that he hoped that his rebellion would eventually engulf the entire island.

Exactly what triggered Cudjoe's rebellion is unclear. In a letter written a few weeks after the event, John Helyar, proprietor of the Bybrook plantation in St. Thomas in the Vale, mentioned that the slaves revolted "upon some disgust."[144] This could refer to a particularly harsh punishment meted out by an overseer, the rape of a slave girl, withheld rations, or perhaps the killing of a slave. The fact that the rebellion broke out five years to the day after the Guanaboa rising on Widow Grey's estate may have been significant: Were the instigators honoring their predecessors?[145] The end of July also signaled the end of the sugar cane harvest, an event celebrated throughout the plantations of the English West Indies with the Crop Over festival. According to Frederick Bayley, an Englishman who visited the islands for four years during the 1820s, flags were displayed in the fields "and all is merriment. . . . A quart of sugar and a quart of rum" were given out to "each negro . . . [and] all authority and distinction of color ceases; black and white, overseer and bookkeeper mingle together in dance." Another eyewitness, Robert Dirks, writing specifically on the Jamaican Crop Over celebration, added that the slaves gathered around the boiling house, dancing and roaring for joy as the overseer distributed saltfish and rum, and the "feast would be followed by a ball."[146] Such gatherings are known to have been exploited by slaves for political purposes. Crop Over would also have afforded the rebels at Sutton's time to gather their forces and prepare their arms as well as perhaps providing an opportunity for Cudjoe or one of his lieutenants to warn slaves from surrounding plantations to rise up in support once the rebellion broke out.

   Some details as to how slaves prepared for rebellions have survived. Oath-taking ceremonies were held at sites of cultural or religious significance such as burial grounds. The principal conspirators drank a glass of rum, grave dirt, and cock's blood. They pledged their willingness to kill all whites, follow their leaders without question, and stand alongside their fellow slaves. Another means of increasing solidarity among would-be Coromantee rebels was the Ikem, or shield dance. The particulars were recorded in a report compiled following an abortive rebellion in Antigua in 1736.

It is the Custom in Africa, when a Coromantee King has resolved upon a War with a Neighbouring State, to give Publick Notice among his Subjects, That the Ikem-dance will be performed at a Certain Time & Place; and there the Prince appears in Royal habit, under an Umbrella or Canopy of State, preceeded by his Officers, called Braffo & His Marshall, attended by his Asseng (or Chamberlain) & Guards, and the Musick of his Company; with his Generals & Chiefs about him. Then he places himself up an advanced Seat, his Generals setting behind him upon a Bench; His Guards on each Side; His Braffo and Marshall clearing the Circle, and his Asseng with an Elephants Tail keeping the flies from him; The Musick playing; and the People forming a Semicircle about him. After some Respite, the Prince arises, distributes Money to the People; Then the Drums beating to the Ikem-beat, he with an Ikem (i.e.) a Shield composed of wicker, Skins and two or three small pieces of thin board upon his left Arm, and a Lance, and the several gestures by them used in Battle. When the Prince begins to be fatigued, The Guards run in and Support him; he delivers the Ikem and Lance to the Person who next Dances; then is lead Supported to his Chair, and is seated again in State. . . . Then the Same Dance is performed by Several Others. . . . Then the Prince Stepping into the Area of the Semicircle, with his Chief General, and taking a Cutlass in his hand, moves with a Whirling motion of his Body round a Bout, but dancing and leaping up at the same time from one Horn or point of the Semicircle, quite to the other, so as to be distinctly viewed by all.[147]

PRIOR TO JULY 31, 1690, Thomas Sutton and his family left the plantation to travel to Port Royal or Spanish Town. Following their departure Cudjoe's plan was put into effect. Adorned with feathers, teeth necklaces, and charms and with their skins painted by the obeah men to ward off the whites' bullets, the five hundred conspirators rose up, perhaps on a signal given by the blast of an Akan horn and following a prayer to Onyame, the Creator. Having emerged from their quarters, the rebels converged upon the dwelling house. The caretaker was seized and killed and the arsenal broken open. "Fifty fuzees, blunderbusses and other arms, [a] great quantity of powder and ball" and "four small field pieces" were taken. The small arms and ammunition were distributed among the leading rebels while the cannon were loaded with nails. What became of the "six or seven" other whites who lived and worked on the estate is unclear. Although John Helyar's letter of August 7 reported that "some whites" were killed, it does not specify exactly how many or who they were. Perhaps all seven met the same fate as the caretaker or perhaps some fled before the rebels could seize them.[148]

Having secured Sutton's, Cudjoe led his men onto a neighboring estate. Exactly which is unclear, but judging by contemporary maps, it could well have been the plantation of Henry Rimes or either one of the two in the area belonging to Francis Watson, Inchiquin's self-appointed predecessor. Regardless of which it was, the neighboring plantation fell as swiftly as Sutton's had and the rebels set fire to the great house and killed the overseer. It was at this stage that Cudjoe's plan began to go awry. Rather than joining the rebels, the newly liberated slaves of the neighboring estate fled into some nearby woods and hid from their would-be liberators despite Cudjoe's pleas that they join him. Realizing that his hopes of an island-wide rebellion were rapidly slipping from his grasp, Cudjoe decided to return to Sutton's and prepare to receive the forces that he knew would soon be sent against him. A body of the rebels took up defensive positions inside the fortified great house, while another loaded the captured cannon with nails. The field pieces were hidden in "a skirt of wood" overlooking the track leading to the Great House, and the slaves took up positions to ambush the forces soon to be sent against them.[149]

"The alarm being given through the Quarters," the Clarendon Parish militia, based in nearby Old Harbour, were beginning to mobilize. The first to react were a squad of fifty cavalry and infantry led by a lieutenant of horse. Although outnumbered, the militia were heavily armed. "Each horseman [was] . . . well mounted with good furniture, . . . [had] a good sword and good case of pistols, and . . . a carbine well fixed." The infantry carried "a musket or fuse with high bore with a cartouch box . . . four pounds of good gunn powder & bullets proportionable." Advancing toward the great house, the red-coated troopers sprung Cudjoe's ambush. It seems the rebels may well have opened fire prematurely, and in their haste, the cannon shot were wasted. After "a small skirmish," the militia were forced to withdraw having suffered two wounded, including the lieutenant who had led them into action.[150]

By the morning of August 1, while the rebels marshaled their forces at Sutton's, the militia had regrouped. Headed by several parties of foot, they advanced once more and a firefight broke out around the great house. On the verge of being overrun, the rebels ransacked the building then retreated toward the mill house, dragging their four small field pieces behind them. They kept up a steady fire as they went and set fire to the canes, prompting the militia officers to order a company to outflank them. Guided by a compass, the company set out through the canes on a circuitous route, managing to elude discovery, before attacking the rebels' rear. Several rebels were killed in the rout that followed and others were wounded. The field pieces were recaptured along with some provisions and arms, while the survivors fled northward through the woods hoping to reach the safety of the mountains. Once the militia had regrouped, "thirty choice men fit for the woods" were sent off in pursuit. They caught up with their quarry after "several miles." Another skirmish followed in which twelve more rebels were killed. The rest fled into the mountains, leaving behind yet more looted provisions and "160 wt" of gunpowder.[151]

The hunt for the fugitives continued throughout August. Several companies of militia and bands of bounty hunters scoured the woods led by baying bloodhounds. By the end of the first week, the rebels were in dire straits. At least forty had been killed, and the survivors lacked provisions and medical supplies and were hampered in their

"A Rebel Negro armed & on his guard." By the end of the seventeenth century, the maroons—bands of escaped slaves—had become firmly established in the island's mountainous interior. (*Engraving by Bartolozzi based on John Stedman's original illustration, c.1796*)

flight by the women, children, and wounded. Faced with the imminent collapse of his command, Cudjoe allowed sixty women and children and ten men to surrender. "[They] related [that those remaining at large] had not above ten good arms," Inchiquin wrote to the Lords of Trade, "and that many [had] dyed of their wounds in the woods. Fresh parties are in pursuit of [the remainder] . . . who I doubt not will disperse them, but I am afraid that so many of them may remain that they will be very dangerous to the mountain plantations." In the next three weeks several bands of exhausted and dejected survivors handed themselves in, and by the end of the month two hundred of the five hundred who had rebelled had been taken prisoner. "[With] so many others killd and the rest so dispersed," Inchiquin reported on August 31, "we look upon this rebellion . . . which was the most dangerous one that ever was in this island . . . to be over." Although the governor's assessment would prove somewhat premature, the immediate danger had ceased.[152]   •

Edward Long, an eighteenth-century planter and Jamaica's first resident historian, provides the only information on the fate of the two hundred captured rebels from Sutton's: "[They] begged for mercy" and "the ringleaders . . . [were] hanged."[153] More details survive on the aftermath of a failed revolt in Barbados in 1692. There the ringleaders were tortured for several days until they gave up their fellow conspirators. "Many were [then] hang'd, and a great many burn'd. And (for a terror to others) . . . seven were hanging in chains alive, and so starving to death." In addition, a local resident by the name of Alice Mills was paid ten guineas "for castrating forty-two Negroes."[154] The authorities' reactions in the aftermath of other rebellions were equally brutal. Following the failed revolt in Antigua of 1736, forty-seven male slaves were banished, mostly to the Spanish colonies in America. Eighty-eight others were put to death. Of those executed, five were broken on the wheel, six were hung in gibbets and starved to death, some taking a week to expire, while the remaining seventy-seven were burned alive.[155] Public immolation, it seems, was a favorite with colonial courts in such cases. The spectacle served as a warning and perhaps also satisfied the whites' yearnings for revenge.

CHAPTER 5

No Peace Beyond the Line

Petit Guavos and the War with the French

1689–1691

I have by ye advice of ye Councill employed ye Swan Guernsey & Quaker
Ketch wth a hired merchant man & 5 privateer sloops of this island (whom
I have prevail'd wth to go upon their own accts.) to attempt yt destroying of
wt they can find of their shipping upon ye coast of Espanola from ye isle of
ash as farr as port de paix as well as their settlements on shour there is 900
good men gone upon this expedition under ye command of my son, from
whose prudence & courage I promise myself some good success.
—Inchiquin to William Blathwayt, Port Royal, April 3, 1691

WHILE THE LEEWARD ISLANDS remained the focus of Anglo-French
rivalry in the Caribbean during the Nine Years' War, Jamaica was also
subject to occasional French attacks. The principal threat emanated
from Petit Guavos, a haven for privateers situated on the west coast
of Hispaniola. At any one time during the late seventeenth century,
the settlement was home to as many as one thousand English, Scots,
Irish, French, Dutch, Spaniards, Portuguese, Native Americans, and
escaped African slaves. Willing to work for anyone who would grant
them a privateering license, they were heavily armed with cutlasses,
pistols, hatchets, knives, and long-barreled muskets and operated out
of large, heavily armed vessels and smaller, fast-sailing *barcolongos*,
Spanish fishing vessels equipped with oars and two or three masts
whose shallow drafts enabled them to evade pursuit by fleeing into
the mangrove swamps which hugged the coastline. When not at sea,

the privateers passed their time in drunken revelry, raising indigo and tobacco in nearby plantations or trekking into the interior to hunt the remnants of the once great herds of wild cattle which the Spanish had released whose hides remained valuable in trade.[1]

Perhaps the most notorious of all the privateers operating out of Petit Guavos at the turn of the seventeenth century was Laurens Cornelis Boudewijn de Graff. A tall, blond, moustachioed Dutchman, born in 1653, as a youth Laurens had gone to sea on merchant vessels, on one of which he had the misfortune to be captured by the Spanish. Enslaved, Laurens was sent to the Canary Islands, but later managed to escape and in 1674 he married his first wife, Petronilla de Guzman, before relocating to the Caribbean, where his career as a pirate in the pay of the French began. The Dutchman, who quickly earned a reputation as a fine "artillerist" and master swordsman as well as gaining notoriety for cruelty and womanizing, had his most notable early success in the autumn of 1679. Attacking the annual Spanish treasure fleet, Laurens captured a 24-gun frigate which he renamed the *Tigre*. Soon afterward he took the *Princesa*, a 50-gun vessel which had been ordered to hunt him down. On board was the payroll for the garrisons of Puerto Rico and Santo Domingo: 120,000 pesos in silver coin.

In 1683 Laurens joined forces with two fellow privateers, the Dutchman Nicholas van Hoorn and the Frenchman Michel de Gramont. Together they raided the Spanish port of Veracruz in modern-day Mexico. Although the town fell swiftly enough to their combined force of thirteen ships and 1,300 men, the unexpected arrival of a Spanish treasure fleet put the pirates on the defensive, while a disagreement as to the treatment of some prisoners led to Van Hoorn challenging Laurens to a duel. The former emerged worse off. Slashed across the wrist, Van Hoorn was dead within two weeks, his wound having turned gangrenous, while Laurens once again returned to Petit Guavos. Later that year, Laurens attacked Cartagena with a fleet of seven ships. Having defeated a hastily assembled force sent out to face him, he blockaded the town while ransoming off his prisoners before returning to Petit Guavos in early 1684. In June the following year, Laurens attacked the port of Campeche in Mexico. The garrison fought a rear-guard action, while the residents fled with their possessions into the jungle, leaving the pirates devoid of plunder. On his return to Petit Guavos, Laurens barely avoided capture when intercepted by a superior Spanish fleet. Only by tipping his cargo and cannon overboard was he able to escape. A lean few years followed. Although Laurens captured several Spanish vessels in the mid-to late 1680s, the period also saw him having to defend Petit Guavos against retaliatory raids launched from Cuba, and he was no doubt relieved when the outbreak of the Nine Years' War afforded him a new target: the English colony of Jamaica.[2]

Jamaica's northern shore was particularly vulnerable to attack. It lay dangerously close to Petit Guavos and several other French bases, including the island of Tortuga to the northeast of Hispaniola; the plantations which dotted the coastline were isolated, and, prior to the arrival of HMS *Swan*, their only protection, aside from the occasional private sloop fitted up as a man-of-war by the Council, was the sixteen-gun sixth-rate HMS *Drake*.[3] Having been on station since May 1686, the *Drake* was badly in need of repair and proved inadequate for the task, despite the energy and expertise of its captain, Thomas Spragge.[4] On July 26, 1689, a consortium of Jamaican merchants had expressed their fears in a letter to the Board of Trade: "The French are at present very near and powerful enemies, as they can sail . . . [to the north coast] in twenty-four hours from Petit Guavos or Tortugas, which are but thirty leagues away. The Island itself is long and the plantations being on the sea and far from one another are liable to be spoiled and burned by French pirates." English merchant vessels were also vulnerable. "All . . . bound [to Jamaica] . . . must pass by French ports," the merchants' letter went on, "as also by Point Anthony in Cuba on their return voyage, where French pirates . . . constantly lie in wait for them. We beg therefore for three frigates, good sailers, to ply to windward, one to secure the plantations on the seaboard, one to lie off Capa Altavoca for ships bound to the Island, and one to convoy homeward bound ships to the Gulf of Florida."[5]

In 1689, still awaiting reinforcement, the Jamaican Council took several temporary defensive measures. As well as prohibiting outbound ships from sailing unless in convoy, they purchased several old vessels to deploy as fireships in defense of Port Royal and occasionally hired one or more of the island's private sloops to undertake specific missions alongside the *Drake*. A new battery was built for Fort Charles at Port Royal under the supervision of the gout-ridden Colonel James Walker of the militia; a new fort of seventeen guns named after King William was erected at Port Morant; while several north coast planters were given permission to mount cannon and build earthworks on their properties to defend themselves against the French.[6]

Meanwhile, the privateering raids went on. In late October "Laurens with a ship and pirago, and about two hundred men . . . touched at Montego Bay" on the north coast of Jamaica. Although the pirate "did no harm," according to a letter from the-soon-to-be-disgraced Sir Francis Watson, "[he] gave out that he would sail up to Petit [Guavos] . . . and procure a commission from the governor, wherewith he will return with greater force, and plunder all the north side, killing man, woman, and child." The inhabitants were so "affrighted," the letter concluded, "[that] they have sent their wives and children to Port Royal."[7] Laurens proved as good as his word. At the beginning of December 1689, his ships surprised thirteen Jamaican sloops salvaging silver "dough boys . . . some broken plate and golden beads" from a sunken Spanish galleon wrecked several years before on the Serranillas Rocks "about forty leagues to the Southward from the west end of Jamaica." Laurens captured "eight or ten of them" before sailing on to St. James Parish on the north coast where he plundered a plantation belonging to the widow Mary Gavell, carrying away "several negroe slaves, household goods, plate, [and] ready money to the value of five hundred pounds."[8] Meanwhile, several other enemy privateers had launched a string of raids in St. Elizabeth's Parish. Anne Vassal, Sarah Flemming, and Richard Amrkes were robbed of slaves and property worth £800 per head, while William Rochester of nearby Alligator Pond had five slaves stolen for which he was compensated £98 by the island council.[9] The French returned to Petit Guavos with their prizes and prisoners, three of whom later managed "to make their escape . . . in a small canoe" and return to Jamaica. The Council responded by ordering all the island's armed sloops to Port Royal in anticipation of a counterstrike led by HMS *Drake*. The mission suffered interminable delays. As fear of the French grew, rumors of the Council's alleged collusion with the enemy gained currency, and on December 12, 1689, a certain Daniel Thornton was arrested "for saying that the Government was in correspondence with Laurens."[10]

Spragge and the *Drake* finally set sail on February 22, 1690.[11] Accompanying the sixth rate, whose crew had been bolstered by the impressment of fifty men, were "400 volunteers in small craft," twelve armed sloops, and the *Seahorse*, an armed merchantman of three hundred tons whose captain, John How, was noted for his "quarrelsome and abusive habits."[12] Having sailed for Port Royal from London, How had picked up a cargo of Madeira wine en route, but the presence of an outsized crew of ninety-two and the fact that the *Seahorse* was armed with thirty-six guns indicated that he had always intended to combine trade with privateering.[13] Indeed, such was How's confidence in the power of his ship that while the *Seahorse* and *Drake* were loading stores and ammunition at Port Royal, he had the audacity to quarrel with Spragge as to who should lead the expedition, "a dispute" which the Council minutes record was "amicably settled" prior to departure.[14]

By early May, having learned that Laurens was at the wreck at Serranillas, Spragge set sail in pursuit. Although the French fleet had departed by the time they arrived, Spragge, How, and the captains of the sloops decided to remain. Having located the exact position of the Spanish galleon's coral-encrusted hull, resting among several large rocks in three and a half fathoms, by the end of July they had succeeded in raising twenty-three lumps of silver, several gold beads, and some broken silver plate. Prevented from salvaging the ship's guns and ballast by the violence of the weather, the fleet was forced to abandon the venture and return to Port Royal at the beginning of June 1690.[15] On their arrival, the port captain, Reginald Wilson, duly logged the treasure they had salvaged and deducted the king's tenth, after which Spragge, How, and the others divided the remainder. With the port flush with silver and gold, no one thought to quiz Spragge too closely as to what had become of his original mission.

While Spragge had been wrecking, several other Jamaican ships, both privateers and a hired-government vessel, had been sent out on patrol. On March 13, two of the Jamaican privateers encountered the *Conssaint*, a French merchantman out of La Rochelle, near Port-de-Paix, another French privateers' lair on the north coast of Hispaniola. Carrying a cargo of wine, brandy, and flour, the *Conssaint* had a crew of twenty-eight men and was armed with twelve guns. "After 4 oures engagement . . . [the English] took her and brought her here where she was condemned," Reginald Wilson informed his patron William Blathwayt. "Their majesties 10th is about 260 l. . . . The French ship is flushing butt a good sailor and now fitted out [with the guns that they took her with] and six guns more put into her . . . [She is] now called the *Loyal Jamaica*," Wilson continued. "She departed out of Port Royal harbour yesterday with a man of warr sloope bound to windward."[16] Another Jamaican sloop, the *Calapatch*, which Wilson had fitted out for privateering in mid-May 1690 at a cost of £105, 9s had been less successful. Accompanying a flotilla of sloops sailing to the Caymans to gather turtles for the markets of Port Royal, one evening in early June the *Calapatch* was intercepted by a *barcolongo* commanded by Laurens himself. While the turtlers fled east for Jamaica, the crew of the *Calapatch* exchanged shots with the French. It was a brave stand, but with Laurens's men outnumbering them two to one, the Jamaicans were doomed. "The firing was heard continuing till eleven at night," a report later informed the Lords of Trade, "and as this was a month [ago] . . . and nothing has been heard of this sloop [since], we conclude that Laurens has taken her."[17]

Thus did matters stand at the start of Inchiquin's governorship. With the loss of the *Calapatch* and with the *Drake* "hardly able to float" since returning from the wreck at Serranillas, the earl found himself with just one functioning naval vessel rather than the three frigates Jamaica's merchants deemed necessary for the island's defense. The vessel in question was the much-maligned HMS *Swan*. "[She] is so bad a sailer," Inchiquin wrote to the Lords of Trade, "that she is little better than nothing. If she should fall ten leagues to leeward I never hope to see her again. . . . I must beg for a couple of prime sailers if they be only a fifth and sixth rate, or the North side of the island will inevitably be destroyed."[18]

The other defensive force at the governor's disposal was the militia. In the early 1690s legislation requiring all residents to serve meant that some five to six thousand foot and two thousand horse could be mustered at any given time.[19] Officers invariably came from the island's landowning class, with the higher ranks awarded almost exclusively to the plantocracy. Thomas Sutton was colonel of the regiment raised in Clarendon; Council member Nicholas Lawes was colonel at Liguanea; and Peter Beckford was colonel of the one thousand strong Port Royal regiment—the largest on the island. Opinions on the quality of the service varied. Numbering some three hundred horse and one thousand foot, the Clarendon militia had a reputation for being "sharp and stout soldiers," according to John Taylor, who also noted that they were known for practicing their marksmanship by shooting daily at targets.[20] Inchiquin, on the other hand, thought the militia "despicable," complaining in a letter to the Lords of Trade that as they were "much dispersed and divided . . . little . . . [wa]s to be expected from them."[21]

In mid-October Inchiquin received more bad news. The crew of the *Loyal Jamaica*, the French merchantman taken off Port-de-Paix in May and since converted into a privateer, had mutinied. "Throwing off all manner of obedience," they "did factiously . . . and Rebelliously depose their . . . Capt [John Harrison] from his lawful command and turned him on shoare" before "carry[ing] away the said Shipp with intent . . . to turne Pyrates," the Council notes surmised.[22] Inchiquin was determined to exact retribution. "For the prevention of such evill practices for the future," the governor's proclamation of October 15 announced, "[the Council] have commanded out the ship *Lyon* under the command of Coll Thomas Hewetson for this their Majesties special service."[23] Hewetson, it may be remembered, was the adventurer who had aided Coddrington's troops at St. Martin in February and had since been employed by the asiento agent, Santiago Castillo, to transship slaves from the Dutch colony of Curaçao to the Spanish Main. The mutineers of the *Loyal Jamaica* proved too wily for Hewetson. Having evaded their pursuer, they crossed the Atlantic, rounded the Cape of Good Hope, and sailed northward along the coast of East Africa into the Red Sea, a rich hunting ground for those of their profession. The next mention of the *Loyal Jamaica* comes in 1692 when the ship appeared off the coast of Virginia. Referred to locally as the "Red-Sea men," the former pirates were welcomed at Charles Town (now Charleston) where they used their ill-gotten gains to establish themselves as planters and escape prosecution for their crimes.[24]

THE FULL MOON that rose over Jamaica on the night of October 18, 1690, ushered in one of two annual rainy seasons. Continuing day and night "with great violence," a downpour which lasted a fortnight drenched the island.[25] In the Cockpit Country, whose tangled landscape provided Cudjoe and his maroons with refuge from the bounty hunters sent to search for them, torrential streams gouged the earth from the rock, carried it down the mountain sides, and deposited it in the plains below where it would sustain the following year's sugar crop. In Port Royal the rains brought sickness. Interned in one of the town's two jails, Gabriell Pitt, a mariner, composed his will. "Being sick and weak in body" but "of sound and perfect mind and memory," Pitt left half of his meager estate to his "loving wife" Anne, charged his friend Walter Earle with taking care of his burial, and left the rest to his "loving children."[26] On board HMS *Swan*, which had been at anchor in the roads ever since returning from Cartagena with a load of Spanish pieces of eight in mid-September, illness had also taken hold. Jonathon Rodgers was discharged from duty on October 26, able seaman Jonathon Anderson succumbed the next day, and on October 28, the frigate's captain, Thomas Johnson, died.[27] With Johnson's death, the *Swan* lost its greatest asset. A "diligent man of good carriage" and previous Caribbean experience, the captain had been popular with the island's Council.[28] His replacement was anything but. The younger son of Baron Bergavenny, the Honourable Edward Neville was a "lazy" wastrel, prone to "idleing on shore."[29]

In November the rains ceased and the island's social season began. A period of feasting and heavy drinking continued until December. Balls, parties, and horse races were held in Spanish Town, Port Royal, Old Harbour, and Withywood.[30] On December 4, the *Betty* slaver arrived at Port Royal. Its captain, James Tucker, brought one hundred and fifty slaves from Old Calabar on the West African Coast for auction.[31] Two weeks later, anxious to avoid a repeat of the recent upheavals at Sutton's, Inchiquin and the Council passed an act with "orders for measures to keep the negroes quiet at Christmas."[32] January brought yet more rain, though without the violence of that of October. Several even complained that the rains were insufficient and the indigo harvest suffered as a result.[33] January also ushered in the new harvesting cycle in the plantations, a period which would last until June.

On the night of January 16, Phineas Bowjer of HMS *Swan*'s carpenter's crew deserted.[34] Another of the Royal African Company's slavers, the *Benjamin*, arrived four nights later with "2 tons of elephants' teeth" and one hundred and twenty-nine more slaves for the plantations.[35] Meanwhile, Governor Inchiquin had also grown sick. Fearing the worst, the fifty-one-year-old composed his will. At the end of the month, as the governor was showing signs of recovery, the roads at Port Royal reverberated to the thunder of multiple salutes as the merchantmen and shore batteries commemorated the forty-first anniversary of the "horrid murder of our blessed sovereign Charles the First."[36]

February 1691 saw royal dispatches arrive from England on board the *King William* yacht.[37] Among the orders was a warrant for the suspension of Sir Francis Watson from Council duties. On February 9, the Council noted that Inchiquin "thought fit" to appoint his son, James O'Bryan, in Watson's stead. The governor also issued a proclamation that day. "If any person will advance money towards the maintenance of two sloops to cruise round the island for the protection of the inhabitants," it began, "his excellency and the Council do promise that they will doe their utmost endeavours to see them reimbursed by the Assembly." It was decreed that any seaman volunteering for service would "be paid at the rate of two pounds five shillings pr. Month," while those impressed would receive "one pound fifteen shillings." All would be compensated with a share of any plunder taken "above the Gunn deck" from enemy vessels. Furthermore, Inchiquin promised that any man wounded in action would be "cured at the Country's charge and if a limb be lost to be further considered proportional to the damage."[38]

February saw the arrival of an eleven-strong merchant fleet from London. Ranging in size from the 30-ton *Madeira Merchant* to the 190-ton *Joseph*, a broad stern captained by an old hand in the Jamaica trade named John Brooks who was to play a leading role in the war against the French, the fleet brought some much-needed "provisions and stores for ye *Swan* friggat," hundreds of barrels of beer, Rhine wine, Madeira, cherry brandy, spirits, cider, mum, and port, and over seven hundred tons of manufactured goods to sell on the island and in the wider Caribbean beyond.[39] The long-awaited naval reinforcement was also accompanying the fleet. HMS *Guernsey* was a 255 ton sixth rate of one hundred and ten men, built in 1654 at the cost of £1,592. Following a major refit in 1660, the *Guernsey* had seen action at the battles of Lowestoft and Vågen in the Second Anglo-Dutch War and the Battle of Texel in the third, before stints in Iceland, Tangiers, and the West Indies in the late 1670s and early 1680s. The *Guernsey* was heavily armed. As well as a main battery of sixteen demiculverins on the lower gun deck, the frigate carried twelve sakers and four saker cuts on the upper gun deck, and had two 3-pounders hoisted up into the tops.[40] The second of the two naval vessels to arrive in Jamaica with the London fleet, the *Quaker* ketch, was significantly smaller. A sixth rate purchased by the navy in 1671, the *Quaker* had a crew of forty men, was armed with ten guns, measured fifty-four feet along its gun deck and had a displacement of just eighty tons. It had served in the Leeward Islands in the late 1670s and off the coast of Virginia in the mid-1680s.[41]

Both the *Guernsey* and *Quaker* had been part of the fleet commanded by Admiral Wright which had escorted Inchiquin and the *Swan* to Barbados. Both had taken part in the campaigns against St. Martin, St. Bartholomew, and St. Kitts, and would have remained under Wright's command had the admiral not received orders from London to dispatch two vessels for the defense of Jamaica.[42] Unwilling to part with any of his prime sailing vessels, Wright had chosen the worst of his fleet. After inspecting the ships at Port Royal, Inchiquin expressed his disgust in a letter to William Blathwayt, the Secretary of Trade: "Its no small mortification to me after ye hopes I had . . . that such tubs should be sent," he fumed.[43] Despite Inchiquin's reservations, the ships did have some redeeming features: the *Quaker*'s shallow draft would allow it to pursue enemy vessels close in shore; while the *Guernsey*'s captain, Edward Oakley, was a seasoned professional of thirty years' service.[44] Furthermore, in Lieutenant Edward Moses, the frigate was blessed with a first-rate junior officer who was brave to the point of recklessness and would go on to have a distinguished career.

With the arrival of HMS *Guernsey*, Inchiquin decided to take the fight to the French. On March 10, 1691, having spent most of the morning reorganizing the island militia, he announced his plan to the

Council. As all three of the naval vessels at his disposal were too slow to catch the enemy at sea, Inchiquin proposed a combined operation against "[French] shipping upon ye coast of Espanola from ye Isle of Ash [Isle de Vache, or Cow Island] as farr as Port de Paix as well as [against] their settlements on shour."[45] Although Inchiquin did not make the correlation clear in his correspondence, the move was no doubt prompted by recent French reverses in the region. Stung into action by corsair attacks the previous year, the Spanish had landed two thousand six hundred men at Cape François in January 1691. After rendezvousing with seven hundred more who had marched overland from Spanish Hispaniola, the combined force had descended on the plain of Limonade, where the French had gathered to confront them. Outnumbered three to one, at first the French held their own, but when a hidden detachment of three hundred Spanish cavalry suddenly burst upon their flank, they were routed. The French commanders, along with four to five hundred of their men, were killed on the field, leaving the Spanish free to pillage the settlements of Cape François before retiring to their bases to the north.[46]

Besides allocating the *Swan*, *Guernsey*, and *Quaker* to the expedition, Inchiquin hired five privateer sloops and the *Joseph*, the 28-gun merchantman which had recently arrived from London under Captain John Brooks.[47] The crews of the chartered vessels were to be compensated for their efforts with a share of the prize money taken. One of the sloops appears to have been the *Marlin*, whose captain, George Carew, was given a further £240 "for expenses of wages and vicutalling."[48] Besides their standard complements—one hundred and fifteen men for the *Swan*, one hundred and ten for the *Guernsey*, forty for the *Quaker*, thirty-eight for the *Joseph*, and an average of just under twenty for each of the sloops, amounting to a total of four hundred "good men"—the ships were to carry five hundred militia for shore operations. Command was given to Colonel James O'Bryan, the governor's son, who was granted the brevet rank of major general for the duration.[49] Having fought alongside his son in Ireland during the Glorious Revolution, Inchiquin was confident James's "prudence and courage" would carry the mission through.[50]

The fleet spent the better part of March in preparation. Canoes were pressed to ferry water from the Rock to fill the ships' butts, while the port captain, Reginald Wilson, supplied provisions from the government's stores, a task costing £700, 17s. 9d.[51] Captain Oakley of the *Guernsey* unloaded his ballast and guns and careened his ship alongside one of the wharfs at Port Royal. The frigate was then reloaded and the rigging repaired while new cables were spliced for the bower anchors and fresh sails were cut and hoisted. Finally, the provisions were loaded and the sails bent in preparation for departure.[52] All the while, the ships were busy recruiting and pressing crew to make up for the constant drain in manpower brought about by disease, accident, and desertion. On March 13, Emmanuel Castle, an ordinary seaman, ran from the *Guernsey*; the following day two more, Febulon Carter and Peter Gozden, followed suit, and two others fled on March 15.[53] To compensate, Oakley had fifteen men pressed the following morning while a heavy rain fell across the roads and lightning flashed overhead.[54] Captain Neville of the *Swan* was also busy. One hundred and fifty-one of the two hundred and fourteen names which had been entered in the frigate's muster between August 1689 and March 4, 1691, had been struck out. Thirty-five had died on board, forty had deserted, and seventy-seven had been discharged, mostly due to sickness. Among the sixty-three recruited in England still present as of March 1691 were the Hodge brothers, Jonathon and Andrew, both of whom had been pressed on December 28, 1689, at the Nore. To make up the shortfall, as the *Swan* provisioned and watered at Port Royal between March 11 and 26, fifty new names were added to the muster.[55] The expedition's officers took advantage of the delay to sample the delights of Port Royal, none more so than Captain John Brooks of the *Joseph*. "[He did] not behave . . . too discretely toward the town," Inchiquin noted. "[He] has been tried and fined for riot, but I hope that at his next coming his manner will be a little mended."[56]

On March 20, the Council reconvened at Port Royal. As well as reviewing the preparations for the expedition, they interviewed an officer lately escaped from the French. While sailing near Cow Island off the southern shore of Santo Domingo, Captain Thomas Addison, the commander of an English merchantman, had been taken by a *barcolongo* of twenty-two cannon packed with over one hundred armed men. The vessel had been commanded by none other than Laurens himself. With little choice but to surrender, Addison was taken ashore as a captive where he learned that the privateers had a fleet of eleven vessels and over one thousand men, all ably commanded by the newly appointed French governor, the former privateer and slaver Jean-Baptiste du Casse. Addison also discovered that the French had recently taken a Spanish vessel and that their flagship, a ship of fifty guns, had captured a Dutchman of thirty-six cannon within sight of Caracas on the Spanish Main. Accordingly, Inchiquin and his councilors "resolved that the sloops be sent out with all Expedition to cruise between Cape Tiburon till ye Frigates are ready to join ... them."[57] As it transpired, such a move would prove unnecessary. The *Guernsey* and *Swan* were ready to sail.

On the morning of March 25, 1691, the fleet at Port Royal took on board the five hundred militiamen who were to act as Major General O'Bryan's marines.[58] Dressed in scarlet coats lined with blue and armed with "fuzze, sword and ammunition," the men crowded aboard alongside several horses which would serve as mounts for their officers.[59] That afternoon Captain Oakley of the *Guernsey* ordered the boats hoisted up to the waist and a signal gun fired to alert any malingerers of the frigate's imminent departure. The next morning the *Guernsey*, *Swan*, and *Joseph* and the five hired sloops stood out to sea with a "fine land breeze." Sailing past Fort Charles, each fired a salute which was returned by the gunners on the battlements before coming to anchor two miles to the west-northwest, where Oakley ordered the *Guernsey*'s flag raised at the main mast as Governor Inchiquin was rowed out from shore. The earl spent the whole day on board, finalizing the plan of attack and wishing his commanders well. The next day the fleet sailed east, and on March 31, rounded Point Morant, the eastern extremity of Jamaica. That afternoon a lookout posted in the *Guernsey*'s maintop spotted a strange sail in the offing. Oakley ordered his men to put on all sail, but the stranger escaped as night came on.[60]

On April 2, the English had more luck. "We saw a ship att 9 of ye clock this morning," the *Guernsey*'s master noted in his log, "& ... gave him chase." The pursuit lasted all day. "Clappd upon a wind," the English vessels became strung out over several miles and at 8 P.M. the swiftest of the sloops began exchanging fire with the stranger. Three hours later, with the *Guernsey* rapidly gaining, the chased ship realized the game was up. "She fired never a gun [at us]," the frigate's log recorded triumphantly, "but struck to us so we lay by her til 2 of ye clock this morning then we made saile & stood in for Port Morant."[61] The stranger proved to be a French privateer of ten guns and one hundred men. Under interrogation the crew revealed they were part of a flotilla of four ships out of Cow Island which was planning to lie in wait off Cape San Antonio for a convoy of English merchantmen due to set out from Port Royal for Bristol on April 10. The next day O'Bryan landed a rider with a message for his father detailing his recent success and the French fleet's plans. Arriving at Port Royal the same day, the news caused the merchantmen to delay their departure until an escort could be arranged, while several of the island's armed sloops were prevailed upon to venture out in search of the three French vessels lying in ambush.[62]

Back at Port Morant, the crew of the *Guernsey* hoisted two guns out of the prize to add to their own armament and transferred a prize crew aboard. The captured privateer was sent back to Port Royal escorted by a single sloop while the rest of the fleet continued their patrol. On April 5, another sail was spotted. "We gave her chase & she stood to ye ESE," the *Guernsey's* log recorded. Running through the night, the stranger managed to elude all pursuit.[63] The next day, while the *Guernsey* remained out on patrol, the *Swan* anchored in Morant Bay to take on water. The process took until April 9, during which time no less than fifteen of the frigate's crew, mostly men pressed in March at Port Royal, deserted.[64] With the frigates resupplied and the *Guernsey* having received a pilot aboard, on April 9, the fleet set sail on the second leg of its cruise. Although bound for Santiago on the south coast of Cuba, O'Bryan had arranged a prior rendezvous at Cape Mayo, Cuba's easternmost promontory. That afternoon the *Guernsey* came across a shoal in open water. With an able seaman playing out the sounding line at the frigate's bow, it inched onward, but when four and a half fathoms was recorded the whole fleet tacked and stood back the way they had come. "A sloop went ahead of us," the *Guernsey's* log noted, "& in a small time she had but 16 feet water." Desperate to avoid running aground in open sea, Captain Oakley tacked again and managed to find a channel of deep water leading out to the southwest. By nightfall the fleet were clear of the shallows. The

Guernsey tacked to the north once more and made all sail for Cuba through the night.[65]

At dawn the *Guernsey's* lookouts sighted the Cuban coastline. With no sign of the *Swan*, the *Joseph*, or the hired sloops, Captain Oakley pushed on alone to the east, hoping to rejoin the fleet at their rendezvous. On the afternoon of April 11, a packet ship arrived with a letter bearing Inchiquin's congratulations for the capture of the privateer and by noon on April 13, the *Guernsey* was within eight leagues of Cape Mayo. At 6 p.m. the following evening, with the *Joseph* and three sloops having rejoined, the *Guernsey* arrived off Santiago.[66] The island's second biggest city, Santiago boasted Cuba's finest natural harbor: a wide bay beyond narrow headlands guarded by the magnificent Morro castle and framed to the northwest by hills honeycombed with copper mines, the mainstay of the region's economy.[67] The next afternoon, having been denied access to the bay by the Spanish authorities, captains Oakley and Brooks sailed to Machanan, a sheltered and uninhabited inlet a few miles away. On April 22, the *Swan* rejoined and that afternoon the *Lion*, the free-ranging English privateer which had served Coddrington at Barbados and transported slaves for the asiento agent Santiago Castillo from Curaçao, also arrived. Saluting the fleet with eleven guns, Captain Hewetson had himself rowed aboard the *Guernsey* to present his letter of marque before sailing on again, presumably still in search of the mutineers on the *Loyal Jamaica*. The fleet spent three more days at anchor filling their water butts from a nearby stream.[68] On board the *Swan* the mortality rate remained high. On April 27, a "cloudy [day] with raine," able seaman Jason Owenton died. His clothes and other possessions were auctioned off at the main mast, and his body was "committed to the deep."[69]

The next morning, the fleet, now consisting of three ships and seven sloops, "waied anchors" and stood to the westward "being bound to Petit Guavos." While still within sight of Cuba's Cape Mayo, a stranger was spotted. The fleet gave chase and caught the prize that afternoon. Armed with six guns and with a crew of sixty-five men, it was identified as a French privateer out of Petit Guavos. On May 5, the ships sighted Cape Saint Nicolas, the northwesternmost point of Hispaniola, and the next morning, as the fleet sailed southward down the coast of Hispaniola, a strange bark was spotted. O'Bryan ordered the ships' boats lowered to pursue it as it fled toward land. "Before the ... [boats] could cum up with [the bark]," the *Guernsey's* log recorded, "[the crew] ran her ashore" and fled into the jungle, leaving a single Portuguese man behind who was taken prisoner. The new capture was originally an English vessel, laden with tobacco and cocoa which the privateers had recently captured and were in the process of taking back to Petit Guavos when the fleet had intercepted them. O'Bryan added the bark to the fleet and sailed on southward. On May 7, another stranger was spotted, a 20-gun ship one-quarter laden with tobacco, which also ran in shore in an attempt to evade the English. The French beached the vessel, hoisted out its guns, and constructed a battery on the beach to protect it. Not to be outdone, Colonel O'Bryan ordered the fleet to bombard the enemy then landed his soldiers the next day under a flag of truce hoping to negotiate the ship's surrender. The enemy refused and a skirmish ensued. Although the enemy captain and seven of his men were killed, the survivors managed to hold their position and on May 9, O'Bryan reembarked his troops and sailed on.[70]

On May 12, O'Bryan called a council of war, and the next few days were spent reprovisioning around a lagoon. While the ships were wooded and watered, the militia killed and butchered several wild hogs and bullocks. On May 19, O'Bryan called another council of war. Having learned that a French fleet had recently sailed from Petit Guavos for Saint Malo leaving the expedition's principal target all but deserted, the officers decided to attack the nearby settlement of Nipo instead.[71] On the face of it, this appears a rather bizarre decision: as every Jamaican resident well-knew, Petit Guavos was the chief privateering port in the entire region. Considering the morale climate of the time, it seems not beyond the realm of possibility that bribery was involved. Did Governor du Casse convince O'Bryan to change his objective? The Frenchman was certainly a most able and unscrupulous operator. Born into a Huguenot family, du Casse had renounced his faith in 1685 to retain the favor of Louis XIV. He had prospered in the West African slave trade in the late 1680s and used the money to set himself up as a privateer in the Caribbean. Du Casse then purchased a commission in the French navy and was later appointed governor of Hispaniola following the death of his predecessor at the hands of the Spanish in January 1691.[72] Regardless of such speculation, what is known is that O'Bryan's fleet set sail for Nipo on the afternoon of May 19 and the following day, to the blare of trumpet and bang of drum, the troops were landed. After a brief skirmish, during which "4 or 5" of O'Bryan's militia were killed and several more wounded, the French fled with their possessions into the jungle, leaving the English to put the settlement to the torch. The next four days were spent in the vicinity with O'Bryan hoping to ambush any French vessels which might arrive. None came, and on May 24 the fleet set sail for Port Royal, arriving to a blaze of salutary cannon fire from the forts the following day.[73]

THE EXPEDITION RECEIVED mixed reviews. Inchiquin's official version of events, relayed to William Blathwayt in a letter dated August 12, 1691, was decidedly upbeat. "Ye expedition my son was gone upon . . . was attended wth . . . good fortune," he began. "Tho they came a day or two too late to overtake two of ye French Kings men of warr & 2 or three St. Malos men homeward bound yet were they time enough to meet wth three of their small men of warr a mercht man of 22 guns & two other small ones wch they have all brought into this place after landing at Nipo & destroying that settlement . . . wth little opposition."[74] Others viewed the expedition with more skepticism. "They did nothing there but got broken hands for there paynes," remarked the planter John Helyar in a letter written that July, while Walter Ruding, the resident factor for the Royal African Company, noted that "the ships had not the hoped for success on Hispanola."[75] Another indicator of the expedition's relative fortunes is the amount of prize money awarded. Once the captured ships had been condemned and auctioned by the Admiralty Court overseen by Reginald Wilson, captains Oakley and Neville were awarded £150 each to split among themselves and their crews. Although the precise division of prize money had not yet been formalized, the captains would have received roughly £36 each. Each man aboard received a diminishing portion according to rank, with able seamen Jonathon and Andrew Hodge of the *Swan* awarded about ten shillings. Lieutenant Moses of the *Guernsey* did significantly better. Singled out for special praise for the part he played in the capture of one of the prizes, Moses was awarded "the sume of fifty pounds as a gratuity over & above his share in the one hundred and fifty pounds given to his capt and ships company for his good service."[76]

On July 11, more good news reached Port Royal. While the *Swan* and *Guernsey* were provisioning for their next cruise, the sloops Inchiquin had sent out in search of the French vessels lying in wait for the Bristol-bound convoy returned. To "ye great satisfaction of this island," the governor recorded, "[they had] all ye success I could reasonably expect having brought wth them ye sd *Calapache* ... that being ye vessel [whose loss] ... gall'd [us] most of any, they have likewise brought another man of warr sloop ... & three prizes they had taken." The only downside was that the *barcolongo* that had taken the *Calapatch* when it had been out turtling off the Caymans in June 1690 had escaped due to "her prime sailing" though only after "a short recounter in wch the ... [sloops] killed her Capt & seven of her men." The news prompted Inchiquin to claim that his recent successes "[had] been almost incredible ... having not left our neghbors ye French of St Domingo any more than one embarcation from Port du Paix to ye Isle of Ash [Vache]."[77] Simon Musgrave, the island's attorney general, was equally ebullient. In a letter of January 31, 1692, he went so far as to claim that all ye "Peace & quiet we have enjoyed ever since" was owed to Inchiquin's successes in mid-1691.[78]

The true cause of Musgrave's half year of stability may have had more to do with events in the Leeward Islands. One thousand miles to the east of Jamaica, the combined English forces under Governor-General Coddrington and Admiral Wright had continued their campaigns against the French. In mid-April the tiny enclave of Marie Galante had been captured with relative ease after "sundry skirmishes" and "hunting-work" had put paid to the defensive efforts of the island's governor and his garrison of three hundred men. Having forcibly deported the entire population, Coddrington had moved on to Guadeloupe where the 1,400 soldiers and militia under his command, boosted by four hundred sailors from Wright's fleet, landed unopposed on April 22, advanced inland, and captured a series of breastworks and redoubts which the enemy abandoned as soon as each was outflanked. On April 23, fearing its spirit cellars would prove too great a distraction, Coddrington set fire to the capital of Basse-terre, which was utterly destroyed, before besieging the garrison of three to four hundred which had withdrawn to a series of fortifications built on an overlooking height. With the French well dug in behind stone emplacements and supported by a further eight hundred men, half of whom were encamped in the island's mountainous interior while the rest were dispersed in small parties to "annoy" the English, the siege proved protracted: by the end of April, having lost two hundred men to enemy action and disease, Coddrington dispatched a subordinate to Barbados to request reinforcements. Before Governor Kendall could react, a French fleet, which had retaken Marie Galante en route from Martinique, arrived off Basse-Terre. Admiral Wright insisted on the return of his sailors, thereby forcing Coddrington to abandon the siege, while simultaneously balking at the chance of a decisive naval engagement with the enemy. Coddrington was furious. "I was an eye-witness of the whole action," he wrote, "and never saw such cowardice and treachery in any man as in . . . Wright." At the end of May the admiral sailed for Barbados, his last act in what would prove a career-ending campaign, while Coddrington and the army made for Antigua on board two converted merchantmen which Wright had begrudgingly provided.[79] As attorney general Musgrave would rightly remark the following January, with both parties having retained the possessions they had held before the outbreak of hostilities and with the war in the Caribbean at an impasse, matters were to remain thus for the better part of the next year.

ALTHOUGH INCHIQUIN would not have to worry about the French for several months, domestic issues now came to the fore. In mid-May 1691, a convoy of two hundred French women and children arrived at Port Royal. Prisoners of war deported from St. Kitts by Christopher Coddrington following his successful invasion of the island in late 1690, these refugees had originally been destined for the French colony of St. Croix, but as the island's governor had refused to take them, they had continued to Jamaica. The refugees had run out of provisions en route and were "in a miserable starving condition." The island Council provided shelter, medicine, and food and by May 29, as the residents of Port Royal celebrated Restoration Day in honor of the return from exile of Charles II thirty-one years earlier, the refugees had "pretty well recovered theire health."[80] Inchiquin hired a sloop and packed them off to Petit Guavos on June 7, escorted by the *Swan*. The next day Captain Oakley had the *Guernsey* "cleared . . . to sail" for Central America. Despite a chorus of protest from the island's planters, who held that the principal purpose of Jamaica's naval provision was to protect the coast, the frigate was bound for Portobelo on asiento business with Santiago Castillo aboard.[81] Such issues would prove the least of the governor's worries. The general meeting of the island Assembly was to be held that afternoon. The event, which occurred once every two years, was notoriously divisive. The year 1691 was to prove particularly controversial.

CHAPTER 6

The Decline and Fall of the Earl of Inchiquin

THE ASSEMBLY, THE WRECKERS, AND THE DEATH OF A GOVERNOR

June 1691–June 1692

People die here very fast & suddenly, I do not know how soon it may be my turn . . . I find I decay apace, insomuch that I must desire His Majesties leave to recruit my self with a little English aire if I do not mend, and hope your lords will favour me with ye obtaining of it.
—Governor Inchiquin to the Lords of Trade, August 12, 1691

By MID-1691 Governor Inchiquin was beginning to loathe Jamaica. The searing heat and enervating humidity was only broken by torrential downpours; the clouds of "stinging and tormenting" muscatas, merrywigs, botleears, galanippers, and chegars "miserably plagued" the island's residents after dusk;[1] there was a constant threat of French attack and slave rebellion; moral and physical decay abounded; and the inhumanity and cruelty which punctuated daily life was shocking even for one hardened by the brutalities frequently committed in seventeenth-century Ireland. Jamaica's infamous insalubrity was another concern. Inchiquin had suffered "twelve days" of "violent fever" in August 1690, and a virulent illness in the new year had led him to contemplate the possibility that he would never set foot on home soil again.[2] "People die here very fast & suddenly," he wrote to the Lords of Trade on August 12, 1691, "[and] I do not know how soon it may be my turn . . . I find I decay apace, insomuch that I must desire His Majesties leave to recruit my self with a little English aire if I do not mend, and hope your Lords will favour me with ye obtaining of it." In a letter to William Blathwayt written on the same date Inchiquin added that he found himself "much weakened, particularly in my right arm."[3]

If there was one thing that aggravated the irascible Inchiquin even more than his health, it was the inhabitants of Jamaica. The slaves were little better than beasts; the poor whites were degenerates— the sweepings of English, Scottish, and Irish society; while the plantocracy and governing elite were the worst of all. Factionalism, corruption, and infighting were endemic, there was no sense of the common good, and private interest and the accumulation of wealth ruled above all. Nevertheless, the governor felt he had made much progress since his arrival. The "unquencionable flame" of animosity he had noted within days of stepping off the *Swan* had been "much allayed," both by the suspension of Sir Francis Watson and his supporters and by Inchiquin's own wise governance.[4] This, at least, is what the governor told his superiors. It also seems to have been what Inchiquin himself believed, as evidenced by his decision to reconvene the Assembly on June 9, 1691. That such divisions were merely awaiting the appropriate time to resurface would soon become abundantly clear.

The Assembly was Jamaica's equivalent of England's House of Commons. It had the power to challenge the authority of the Council and the governor himself. As no bills could be passed on to the king for ratification without the approval of all three parties, it was essential they work together. Things did not always proceed so smoothly, as Edward Long, a historian, resident planter, and one-time speaker of the Assembly explained in his three-volume *History of Jamaica*, published in 1774: "The Assembly consider[ed] their privileges as derived to them from their constituents; and that they are not concessions from the crown, but the right and inheritance of the people; and that the privileges which they claim are absolutely necessary to support their own proper authority, and to give the people of the colony that protection against arbitrary power, which nothing but a free and independent Assembly can give."[5] While some may have maintained such high ideals, the plantocracy also used their dominance of the Assembly to force the governor to implement bills which went against not only his own interests, but also those of the crown. The Assembly of 1691 would prove no different.

In the first week of June the elections were held. In thirteen of Jamaica's fifteen parishes two assemblymen were chosen, while Port Royal and St. Catherine's, in recognition of their larger populations, elected three. Only freeholders who could demonstrate a minimum annual income of £10 "arising from lands, tenements, or hereditaments" could vote, while those who stood for office, ostensibly "the fittest and discreetest" of all freeholders in the parish, were required to prove "possess[ion] of 300 l. per annum, or 3000 l. in gross, over and above what is sufficient to pay his debts."[6] Such, at least, was the theory. While those elected were invariably from the propertied elite, the rules governing those who were allowed to vote were frequently twisted. The most common way was for candidates to grant parcels of land to their tenants, thus making them eligible, in return for their promise to elect them. Intimidation and physical force were also employed. In Sir Francis Watson's time such practices had been widespread.[7] Although the use of physical threats seems to have diminished following his dismissal, the creation of new freeholders for electoral purposes was still relatively commonplace.

Among those elected that year were several of the island's leading lights. James Banister, son of the former governor of Suriname, was chosen to represent St. Dorothy's; Thomas Ballard, one of the few surviving veterans of the 1655 invasion and the owner of a 2,391-acre estate, was elected in St. Catherine's; John White, Jamaica's longest serving Council member, was chosen for the much-ravaged northern parish of St. Ann's; respected physician and long-standing plantocrat Fulke Rose was elected in St. John's; attorney general Simon Musgrave was chosen in both St. Thomas's and Port Royal; while Thomas Sutton was chosen in Clarendon.[8] The other assemblyman in Sutton's parish, Charles Boucher, was a creature of Inchiquin's.[9] No doubt placed in the role as a result of the machinations of the governor, Boucher was a former Council clerk who had been excused from his duties in February to care for his sick mother.[10] A keen astronomer, Boucher was the proud owner of what was perhaps Jamaica's only astronomical telescope and maintained a lively transatlantic correspondence with fellow Oxford graduate and heavenly enthusiast Edmund Halley, of comet fame.[11]

Several other Assembly members elected that June were firmly placed in the planters' camp and opposed to the governor's interests. Chief among them were Richard Lloyd, the third candidate elected for St. Catherine's, and Edward Harrison of St. Andrew's.[12] The former was a "wealthy lawyer" and a major of horse in the militia who had registered a claim for a 1,370-acre estate in St. David's Parish in 1670. More recently Lloyd had cemented his position among the plantocracy by obtaining the post of Clerk of the Crown and Peace of Jamaica and by marrying the wealthy heiress Mary Guy, the daughter of the deceased invasion veteran Richard Guy, who had earned a fortune as a privateer in the early 1660s and gone on to become one of the island's leading planters.[13] Edward Harrison, for his part, was chief judge of St. Andrew's parish court.[14] He also owned a plantation in St. Andrew's which Hans Sloane noted was "the best furnished of any in the island with European Garden plants" due to its "lofty situation" in the foothills of the Blue Mountains.[15] Both Lloyd and Harrison were close associates of Peter Beckford, Samuel Bernard, and Nicholas Lawes, planters and Council members who sought greater independence for Jamaica's leading businessmen.[16] While Inchiquin was concerned with raising money, either via direct taxation or by selling goods, principally slaves, to the Spaniards via the asiento, the planters' focus was ensuring the Royal African Company delivered sufficient slaves to run their plantations. They also sought to secure lower tariffs and the abolishment of restrictions on trade. To Inchiquin's frustration, the two positions would prove incompatible.[17]

The Assembly first convened at Spanish Town on June 9, 1691. The presence of so many wealthy and influential men would transform the capital for the next ten weeks. As the islands' planters flocked to town in their carriages, accompanied by their families and troops of liveried domestic slaves (for whom the occasion was of equal social importance), the population swelled with salesmen and other opportunists keen to profit from the new arrivals, while local businesses thrived on the extra income. Others profited by renting out properties, and lodging houses did good business, as did the capital's "ordinaries," the restaurants of the day. The hub of all this activity was the old

Spanish Market Place, the square that stood at the heart of town at the junction of the capital's principal commercial thoroughfares: White Church Street and Barrett Street both of which were lined with shops and overlooked by the Brick Red Church. A residence for Dominican friars under Spanish rule, the building had been turned into an Anglican cathedral by the English in 1655. It is also believed that it housed the Assembly meetings that June.[18]

Besides the Assembly, Spanish Town would also play host to a series of events timed to coincide with the gathering. Horse races were held on the outskirts of town; plays were put on in the theater; banquets, feasts, and dances were given in the major houses; and the capital's taverns did a roaring business.[19] Other visitors may have had more high-minded pursuits. Boucher perhaps took the opportunity of conversing with others who shared his interest in astronomy and swapped a book or two, while Harrison may have met with some fellow horticulturalists. Perhaps James Harlow, the Irish botanist who had sailed to Jamaica with Inchiquin, was also present. Harlow had been busy touring the length and breadth of the island collecting a dizzying array of specimens. By the time he returned to the Carrick-fergus home of his sponsor, Lord Rawdon, in April 1692, Harlow would have gathered one thousand live shrubs and trees, a number of dried plants, including a large selection of ferns, and well over one hundred live seeds—many of which had never been catalogued by scientists before.[20]

On the morning of June 9, the thirty-four Assembly members swore allegiance to William and Mary and took "the oath of qualification."[21] A welcome message from Inchiquin was then read which "recommended to them amongst other things the Lamentable Condition of some of our settled planters who have been plundered & undone by the Invasion of the french."[22] Chosen as the Assembly's speaker, Thomas Sutton of Clarendon Parish proceeded to the Council chamber to inform Inchiquin of his selection. According to the Council minutes, Sutton was a picture of modesty. At first he "endeavoured to excuse himself," but Inchiquin announced his approval and "told him he was Glad the . . . [Assembly] had made choice of so worthy a man."[23] Sutton then made claim, "in the name of the house, [for] their ancient rights and privileges, freedom of debate, liberty of access to his excellency's person, and exemption from arrests during the sitting." The formalities concluded, all returned to the meeting room where two further appointments were made: Modyford Freeman, a planter and lieutenant colonel in St. David's Parish militia, was chosen as officer for the Assembly, while John Gay was appointed clerk. The "standing rules" were then read and, with that, the first session broke up. Some headed for the races held on the outskirts of town, but "at least two thirds," according to a scandalized Inchiquin, made directly for the capital's taverns, where they "s[at] . . . up drinking all night." It was during such informal reunions that Richard Lloyd and Edward Harrison began to sow the seeds of discontent which would later enable them to use the Assembly to further the interests of the island's plantocracy. Considered by Inchiquin as "heroes of faction . . . whose advice tends to the destruction of all government," over the next few weeks Lloyd and Harrison would convince their fellow assemblymen that their interests and those of England were diametrically opposed.[24]

At the Assembly's next meeting, Sutton introduced the first vote: what allowances were to be made for fighting the French. "We were at first soe sensible of the suffering of our neighbours & soe desirous to secure our selves agt. the like attempts," Musgrave recorded, "that it was resolved to Raise the Sume of £4700 for fitting out one man of warr sloope or vessell with 60 men besides 3 officers, & to turne the *Quaker* Ketch into a three mast vessel to mend her Saileing & to add tenn supernumerary men on board her at the Countrys Charge for Six months."[25] The bill was drawn up, read aloud three times, and approved by the majority. "The very next thing done by the Assembly," Inchiquin later informed the Board of Trade, "was a bill repealing all laws made in the last Assembly [held under Albemarle's governorship], which are still under the King's consideration."[26] According to a letter written by several Assembly members, the reason for such a sweeping proposal was the widespread corruption that had characterized the final period of the duke's governance and Sir Francis Watson's brief period in charge.[27] While such logic appears reasonable, the real motive behind the Assembly's decision was more controversial. Included in the bills they proposed to strike from the record was one stipulating a perpetual revenue for the king. As it, in its turn, had replaced a prior bill concerning taxation, its repeal would have left William and Mary without so much as a "farthing" from Jamaica, something which no doubt held strong appeal for the plantocracy, who would have had to pay the lion's share. When first read out, the proposal proved divisive. On one side were those who curried Inchiquin's favor; on the other were those more concerned with their own financial interest. Leading the latter, on behalf of their masters in the Council—Bernard, Beckford, and Lawes—were Harrison and Lloyd. Their late-night campaigning now proved invaluable. Having "violently pressed the passing of this bill," they persuaded their supporters to back them. "The only opposers," according to Inchiquin, "were Judge [John] White, my son, Peter Heywood and Charles Knight, on the ground that it was disrespectful to the King, destroyed the whole revenue, and tended to destruction of the Government." Nevertheless, the bill was passed.[28]

As June turned to July, three more acts were debated. First came a proposal for three new taxes: ten shillings to be charged on each pipe of wine imported; forty shillings on each slave exported; and an extraordinary tax to be imposed on Port Royal's Jews. While the first was sure to upset the island's merchants, it would leave the plantocracy relatively unaffected while perhaps also acting as a sop to the governor. The second tax, on the other hand, was a direct attack on the much-hated asiento. By discouraging Walter Ruding and Charles Penhallow from selling their cargoes to the Spanish, the planters hoped to ensure themselves a better supply of slaves. As Inchiquin profited personally from the Spanish trade, the bill was sure to prove controversial despite the addition of a placatory clause granting the governor £2,000 per year from the money raised, a figure which gives some indication of just how much money Inchiquin was making from his dealings with the Spanish. The second bill debated by the Assembly was a proposal for an allowance to be paid to agents in England to solicit Parliament for the furtherance of Jamaica's affairs. Between £300 and £800 per year was deemed sufficient for the task. The money was to be paid to a seven-man committee, later to be known as the Sugar Lobby, which would be selected by Beckford, Bernard, and Lawes. The final and least controversial bill was a proposal to build a road along the undeveloped north coast of the island, linking St. George's Parish to St.

Mary's and St. Ann's, thus not only facilitating the transport of the region's sugar to market, but also allowing the rapid movement of troops to areas threatened by seaborne raiders.[29]

On July 16, the Assembly's five bills were brought before the Council. Those concerning the defense of the island and the road-building project were soon accepted. The remaining bills proved more controversial. Inchiquin thought the proposed taxes on imports of wine and exports of negroes would have a disastrous effect on the economy. "Trade and the Assiento . . . are the life of th[is] . . . place," he explained, "and ye encouragement of which . . . were specially recommended to my care. The last fleet carried home £100,000 in bullion, thanks to the Assiento, but the Assembly are bent on destroying it just when the Dutch are longing to get it." The proposal to instigate an extraordinary tax on the Jews was also dismissed, perhaps in part due to the bribe they had given Inchiquin on his arrival in May 1690. The governor thought the two final bills the worst of all. "Besides the disrespect of it," he explained in reference to the act proposing the abolishment of all bills passed under the Duke of Albemarle's governance, "[it would also] take . . . away the last farthing of the King's revenue." The bill proposing a fund for solicitation of the island's affairs was deemed "equal[ly] insolen[t]." Taking personal offense at the fact that he was not to be included among the commissioners charged with spending the funds, "as if . . . [I] were a Judas, not to be trusted with the other seven apostles," the governor refused to allow the bill to be read aloud.[30]

On July 24, the road bill was passed while the defense bill was returned with the Council's amendments for the Assembly's final approval. The three remaining acts were rejected. Rather than being cowed into compliance as Inchiquin had hoped, on receiving word of the Council's decision the assemblymen dug their heels in. By refusing to ratify the defense bill unless the Council reconsidered, they hoped to blackmail the governor into changing his mind. By July 29, Inchiquin was growing desperate. He insisted that the Assembly ratify the defense bill immediately so that a request for the funds required could be dispatched with the *Quaker* ketch which was soon to depart for England. The Assembly proved equally stubborn. They sent a message imploring the governor to approve the other bills so they could comply with his request. Inchiquin had had enough. First he asked the Council to refuse to acknowledge the Assembly's message. When they balked, he summoned the entire Assembly to the council chamber "in some passion," accused them of showing disrespect to himself and the king, and claimed their proposals were "an indignity and an affront." With that he tore up the Assembly's final message, threw it down among them, and announced that the body was to be dissolved immediately.[31]

Although Inchiquin's decision was seen as scandalous by some, the controversy soon died down. Such were Jamaican politics in the seventeenth century. It was not the first time an Assembly had been dissolved, and by mid-July rumors of an even more newsworthy event had reached Port Royal.[32] Three Spanish ships had been wrecked at Point Pedro Cays, an archipelago of sand spits and half-submerged coral islets sitting astride the sea-lanes linking Cuba and the Spanish Main some fifty miles southwest of the westernmost point of Jamaica. The vessels in question had been part of a fleet of four galleons commanded by the Marquis de Bao. Said to be "floor'd with silver," they had been sailing from Cartagena to Havana when they had run aground on the shoals due to an error of navigation. At least one of the ships had subsequently caught fire: "all her upper parts were burnt" and quantities of the silver plate loaded into her hold had melted. Fortunately for the marquis and his men, several Jamaican sloops had been in the area at the time. Although the governor of Portobelo— one of several distinguished passengers on board—was "cast away & . . . drown'd," the sloops were able to rescue 776 men, women, and children as well as salvaging part of the treasure and other cargo.[33]

News of the wrecks sparked gold fever at Port Royal. By mid-August over one thousand of the town's mariners had sailed for Point Pedro Cays in at least thirty-seven vessels, prompting the attorney general to complain that Port Royal was dangerously exposed to attack by the French.[34] Among the first to react was Peter Bratelier, the Huguenot sloop captain who had fled France in 1685 following the revocation of the Edict of Nantes. On hearing the news from Point Pedro Cays, Bratelier recruited thirty "English saylors" from Port Royal and paid a visit to the port captain, Reginald Wilson, to put down a deposit of £2,000.[35] Each captain to sail for the wreck would be obliged to do the same to ensure that they would return with their treasure and pay the king's tenth.[36] Around August 1, Bratelier set sail in the *Newcastle*, a 20-ton sloop of 4 guns. Joshua Leake, another of Port Royal's resident mariners, sailed soon afterward in the *Elizabeth*, having recently returned from a voyage to Carolina with a cargo of salt pork and beef and staves and hoops for constructing barrels.[37] Another to leave in August was Robert Scroope. One of Port Royal's leading wreckers, Scroope had a quarter share in at least two of the vessels that would fish the hulks off Point Pedro Cays that August: the *Diligence*, which Scroope himself commanded, and the *Dragon*, a 30-tonner which would sail at the end of the month under his associate, Robert Glover.[38]

On August 7, a Council meeting was held at Spanish Town. Besides Governor Inchiquin and the usual members of the island's plantocracy, Captain Hugh Gaines of the *Seahorse* was present. A gentleman adventurer in the mold of Captain Hewetson of the *Lion* or Captain Brooks of the *Joseph*, Gaines had been granted by William and Mary exclusive wrecking privileges on all vessels found within seventy leagues of Jamaica. Although the Council deemed that the Point Pedro Cays wreck did not fall under Gaines's exclusive remit, as it had been discovered since their majesties' order had been written, he was, nevertheless, allowed to take part. The size and power of the *Seahorse*, a 300-tonner armed with 36 guns and with a crew of seventy, would give him a distinct advantage over the majority of those who would fish the wreck that August.[39]

UNDERSEA TREASURE SALVAGE, or "wrecking" as it was known, was big business in the Caribbean in the late seventeenth century. Initiated by the Spaniards not long after Columbus's landing in the Americas, the practice had developed in response to the frequent loss of Spanish treasure galleons. At first, indigenous divers had been employed. The Arawak and Caribs had both engaged in pearl diving prior to European arrival—the latter on a surprisingly large scale at several locations, notably the island of Cubagua off the coast of modern-day Venezuela—but it was the Lucayans of the Bahamas that the early Spanish colonial historian Oviedo considered the masters of the trade.

Allegedly able to dive to depths of one hundred feet by using stone weights tied to their backs and remain submerged for an incredible fifteen minutes, the Lucayans became victims of their own success: they were enslaved by the Spaniards and wiped out by European diseases. Subsequently, the Spaniards used African slaves. They also became adept and their role was soon diversified: as well as pearl fishing (which had by then spread to the Pacific as well as the Caribbean), the divers were tasked with locating and sealing underwater leaks on ships' hulls; salvaging treasure and supplies from submerged wrecks; and even preventing unscrupulous masters from smuggling goods attached to the undersides of their ships.

In the early seventeenth century, the English muscled their way into the business. When raiding the Spanish pearl fisheries of Cubagua and the nearby island of Margarita, privateers from Bermuda carried off several African divers whom they put to work salvaging Spanish wrecks. So lucrative did the business prove, that it soon became the principal industry of the island. Bermuda's hegemony did not last long. Due to its strategic location near the principal sea-lanes frequented annually by the Spanish treasure fleets, Jamaica had eclipsed Bermuda as the hub of wreck salvaging in the Caribbean by the 1660s. With a sizable population of unscrupulous mariners, Port Royal was ideally suited and by 1673 as many as fifty of the town's burgeoning fleet of sloops and schooners were dedicated to the trade.[40]

The Caribbean's greatest salvaging success story came in 1687. The man primarily responsible was a former shepherd boy from the frontier outpost of Nequasset in Massachusetts named William Phips. After completing a four-year apprenticeship in carpentry, Phips had moved to Boston to set himself up as a shipbuilder, but had later turned his hand to wreck salvaging in the Caribbean after his yard was destroyed by a Wabanaki raiding party during King Phillip's War. Phips's initial attempts at salvage, though small scale, proved profitable. His ambition grew and in the mid-1680s Phips set his sights on the long-lost wreck of *Nuestra Señora de la Concepción*, a Spanish galleon shipwrecked in 1641 on the Ambrosia Bank, a reef off the north coast of Hispaniola. The expedition was financed by a London-based consortium which included James II and Christopher Monck, the second Duke of Albemarle and future governor of Jamaica. After stopping at Port Royal to pick up twenty-four African divers, Phips spent March and April 1687 working the site with a flotilla of three ships and returned to London in mid-1687 with thirty-four tons of treasure worth £205,536 in contemporary currency or over $3 million today. Albemarle received a quarter and the king got a tenth. Phips received £19,000 as his share, out of which he awarded his crew £8,000 including bonuses for each of the Port Royal divers.[41] At least twenty-three Jamaican sloops spent time salvaging the wreck in the months that followed Phips's departure, and a further £10,000 worth of treasure was raised. Among those to profit were William Diggins of the *Phenix* and James Wetherill of the *Mary,* both of whom were among the sloop captains to fish the wreck at Point Pedro Cays three years later. Phips's success also sparked wrecking fever in London.[42] For the next two decades, the crown was petitioned by numerous consortiums seeking to secure exclusive "fishing" rights to one section of the Caribbean or another, the latest example being Captain Gaines of the *Seahorse.*

A variety of methods were used to locate the treasure at Point Pedro Cays and haul it up from the seabed. On arrival, the ships would anchor some way off the reef and wait for good weather. Once the waves were calm and the wind had died, the captains lowered their boats—better suited for working the shallows—and rowed out to the site, leaving the remains of the crew to man the sloop's cannon in case other opportunists should venture too near. The boats' crews would then spread oil over the surface of the water to calm it and better enable them to see beneath the surface. If any irregularities were detected on the seabed, African or indigenous divers were dispatched to perform an underwater reconnaissance. Attached by lines to the boats and carrying net bags in which to place any artifacts they might recover, some divers held oil-soaked sponges in their mouths from which they could extract an extra lungful of oxygen thus maximizing their dive time.[43]

Such a task was not without its dangers. "The exertion undergone during [the dive]," one observer noted, "is so violent, that upon being brought into the boat, the divers discharge water from their mouths, ears and nostrils, and frequently even blood . . . [and] quite often . . . [they] will suddenly drop dead from haemorrhaging or congestion."

A diving bell used to salvage on the seabed. Wrecking (salvaging the cargoes of sunken galleons) was such a profitable business in the seventeenth century Caribbean, that some of the age's greatest minds, including Edmund Halley of comet fame, had turned their hands to designing the latest technological innovations. (Etching, Halley's Diving Bell, *Universal Magazine*, 1754)

The bends was not the only risk. "The divers have more to fear from sharks, manta rays, and poisonous sea snakes," noted another writer. The former could grow to "a monsterous size," were "very fierce and voracious and . . . often devour[ed] the poor divers," while the manta rays could "embrace the diver so strongly that they squeeze him to death, or else by falling on them with their whole weight . . . crush them to death against the bottom." The divers carried knives to "wound . . . the fishes and put . . . them to flight," while one man kept a lookout for their approach from the boat "and when he sees any . . . making towards . . . [the divers], gives them notice by pulling on the line."[44]

Various devices were employed for fishing for treasure. The most frequently used were hooks and trawling grapples lowered on chains and dragged along the sea bottom. More innovative was the diving bell. The first recorded use of such a device in the waters of the New World was in 1612 by an Englishman. A former pirate turned wrecker, Richard Norwood lowered himself to a wreck site on the sea bottom off Bermuda inside an inverted wine barrel to which he had attached several weights. In 1616 a German named Franz Kessler improved the design by covering the bell with watertight leather and cutting two windows in its side. In 1677 a wooden bell thirteen feet in height and nine feet in diameter was constructed in Spain to salvage two shipwrecks off the port of Cadaqués. Its Moorish pilots were able to remain submerged for an hour, and the bell proved a huge success. In 1689 a French scientist, Dr. Denis Papin, took the design a step further. By incorporating a large bellows which pumped fresh air into the bell, he was able to increase the time the pilots could remain beneath the surface while also equalizing the water pressure to some extent, thus allowing the device to reach depths of up to seventy feet. Although Papin's bell would not get beyond the theoretical stage for another century, a contemporary who turned his attention to the quandary would have more practical success. The astronomer Edmund Halley built a diving bell at the same time as Papin which was supplied with air via a valve attached to a tube installed in a lead cask, thus providing the pilots with as much air as they required. At sixty cubic feet, Halley's bell was larger than Papin's and had glass viewing ports and an exhaust system via which the pilots' breath could be expelled.[45]

Which, if any, of these devices was employed at Point Pedro Cays is unclear. What is known, at least in part, is the amount of treasure recovered. While it seems the Spaniards themselves, as the first on the scene, hauled away the majority, several Jamaican sloops also made considerable profits. By the end of 1691, after six months working the site, over one and a half tons of broken silver and silver plate, 137 pieces of eight, ten ounces of gold, a few hundred old pieces of iron, and a waterlogged parcel of logwood had been raised from the wreck, taken back to Port Royal, and entered into the shipping accounts by Reginald Wilson, who deducted one tenth for the king. Some individuals did considerably better than others. The Huguenot Peter Bratelier brought home just twenty-five pieces of eight (the equivalent of £6, or four shillings a head when divided among the *Newcastle*'s crew of thirty); Joshua Leake salvaged ten pieces of eight and one hundred pieces of "old iron"; James Wetherill hauled up twenty-five pounds in weight of coinage and broken plate; while Robert Scrope of the *Diligence*, one of several sloops to make multiple trips to the site, returned to Port Royal with 120 pieces of eight after his first voyage alone. This was the equivalent of twenty shillings per head when divided among his crew of thirty—a not unreasonable wage for a seaman for a few weeks' work.[46]

The figures above are unlikely to be comprehensive. The wreckers no doubt attempted to smuggle several valuable trinkets past Reginald Wilson, while some of the ships involved, notably Gaines's 300-ton *Seahorse*, were not required to enter their finds into Wilson's records. Another potential measure of the success of the Point Pedro Cays salvaging operation was the amount of attention it received from official sources. William Blathwayt was kept well-informed of developments by Reginald Wilson and Simon Musgrave, among others, while HMS *Guernsey* and *Swan* also visited the site.[47] The former was there for several days in mid-September, while the latter set sail from Port Royal for Point Pedro on October 12, and returned nine days later.[48] As the relevant page in the *Guernsey*'s logbook is missing and the *Swan*'s log would be lost at sea the following year, what exactly the Royal Navy vessels were doing is open to speculation. Previously, such ships had been used to provide protection from enemy vessels and police the area (it was not unknown for wreckers to turn their guns on one another in their rush to be the first to access the choicest sites), but it also seems likely that they may have been involved in raising the treasure. If so, how much they salvaged or what became of it is unknown.

AT THE END OF September 1691, a fleet of thirteen sail departed Port Royal for England under convoy of the *Quaker* ketch. Among them were the *Warrington*, a Royal African Company slaver which had arrived from Angola with five hundred slaves in July, and the *Grayhound*, a small armed merchantman captained by John Finch. The *Warrington* carried 200 hundredweight and sixty barrels of sugar, fifty barrels of indigo, six barrels of pimento, twenty tons of logwood, and fifteen bags of cotton; the *Grayhound* was loaded with sugar, fustic, and sarsaparilla.[49] The flagship of the fleet was the *Lion*, commanded by John Hewetson, the privateer-cum-wrecker-cum-asiento-enabler who had spent the previous three years adventuring in the Caribbean. A rebel to the last, Hewetson left without informing Reginald Wilson of the cargo he was carrying. "Six hundred hog sugar at least might be on board," the port captain recorded soon after the *Lion*'s departure, "but what other goods of ye Growth of this island I had no account of."[50] Among Hewetson's passengers was Lady Inchiquin. Sick of island life and finding the tropical heat every bit as unhealthy as her husband, the most honorable Elizabeth Herbert was to return home alone. Inchiquin was dismayed to see her go. The earl delayed their parting until the last moment by sailing aboard HMS *Guernsey* in company with the *Lion* and the rest of the fleet as far as Port Morant. On September 27, having spent his final night with his wife on board the *Lion* as Hewetson's guest, the governor bade Elizabeth farewell and returned to Port Royal on the *Guernsey*. The couple would never set eyes on one another again.[51]

The last three months of 1691 passed with relatively little incident. In October the annual social season kicked off once more in Spanish Town,[52] and King William's birthday was celebrated on November 4. A dozen of the island's sloops arrived at Port Royal from the wreck, each carrying a little less broken silver plate and pieces of eight than the one before.[53] Four Royal African Company slavers—the *Bonaventure*, the *Ann*, the *East India Merchant*, and the *Mediterranean*—reached Port Royal with 59, 65, 570, and 430 surviving slaves, respectively.[54] The RAC's resident agent, Walter Ruding, reported that no less than five interlopers were busy fitting out for Gambia. The disgraced and suspended Sir Francis Watson died, his passing going all but unnoticed in the extant documentation aside from a single line in a letter written on November 17.[55] Meanwhile, with the French still recovering from Colonel James O'Bryan's raid on Hispaniola, the *Swan* and *Guernsey* divided their time between convoying the asiento's ships to Havana and Portobelo, bringing home ever more profit for Castilo and Inchiquin, cutting and fitting new masts and other routine repairs, pressing recruits from visiting merchantmen, and watching over the sloops fishing the wreck.[56]

The year 1692 began inauspiciously. "Very dry and hot weather" settled over Jamaica like a suffocating quilt.[57] Depressed at his wife's departure, Inchiquin had not attended a Council meeting since December 19, and his health had been failing ever since.[58] George Reeve, the governor's personal secretary, noted that his master was indisposed with "fever" and "ague," a reference to either malaria or yellow fever, diseases which were as little understood as they were deadly.[59] As many of "a third part of" the population "were taken ill" at any one time with such ailments, according to Hans Sloane. Symptoms included splitting headaches, burning fever, jaundice, a falling pulse, nausea, and delirium. As bad air, or miasma, thought to arise from swampy ground at night, was held to be the chief cause, treatment consisted of shutting out the night air by enveloping the patient's bed with curtains and closing all windows in their quarters, a practice which could only have added to the patient's discomfort. Others held that purging or bleeding by means of cupping and scarification were effective, although both only reduced the sufferer's ability to resist, while the African cures—"Country Simples" according to a scoffing Hans Sloane—which some slave owners turned to as a last resort were of equally dubious benefit.[60]

On January 12, Inchiquin made a partial recovery. Following a visit to the governor that morning, Reginald Wilson noted that although the earl had "been very ill," he was then "sumthing better." It proved only a temporary reprieve. Within the next few days Inchiquin relapsed. Dysentery, or the bloody flux as it was known, was added to his woes. Weakened by the fevers he had been suffering since December, Inchiquin deteriorated rapidly. On January 14, "being sicke and weake in body but of sound mind and memory," he composed his will. Among the signatories were George Reeve, Simon Musgrave, and Emmanuel Heath, the newly appointed rector of St. Paul's Church in Port Royal. Inchiquin left most of his estate to his family: his eldest son, William, received the manor house of O'Bryan's Bridge in Clare County; James, the earl's second son and the commander of the expedition to Petit Guavos, was bequeathed "all [the governor's] American interests," including all the "money and other effects and revenues whatsoever in the Asiento"; a thousand pounds was left to Lady Inchiquin to redeem the jewels she had been obliged to pawn in London before the couple had set sail for Jamaica; and £50 was donated "to the poore of the Parish of Saint Catherine's." On January 15, Inchiquin's condition deteriorated and he died at 8 A.M. the next morning. That night his body was carried to the cathedral in Spanish Town and buried alongside Governor Modyford. No expense was spared, Inchiquin himself having designated £600 for his funeral in his will.[61]

WAS INCHIQUIN'S governorship a success? During his period in office trade had fallen, French attacks on the north coast had caused considerable financial damage, political in-fighting remained rife, and the largest slave rebellion in the island's history had taken place. Although it is difficult to apportion blame to Inchiquin for such occurrences, especially as the latter happened a mere two months after his arrival, the responsibility was surely his. Judged by Inchiquin's own priorities, however, the answer to the question above is a resounding yes. In a state of bankruptcy when he took office, Inchiquin made a fortune during the nineteen months he spent in Jamaica. "No Governor had ever so much money in so short a time,—£15,000 is well within compass,—nor strove so earnestly to get it," opined Samuel Bernard in a letter written three months following Inchiquin's demise.[62] As the earl had always viewed the governorship as little more than an unpleasant yet highly lucrative posting, the profits he passed on to his descendants indicate that his time in Jamaica was most successful indeed.[63]

Few mourned the Inchiquin's passing. While Reginald Wilson, Simon Musgrave, and George Reeve wrote glowing accounts of the governor's time in office and dismissed any dissent as being born of jealousy and personal interest, those with whom the earl had shared the council chamber were considerably less ebullient.[64] In two separate letters sent to the Lords of Trade less than two weeks after Inchiquin's death, each of which was signed by all the councilors remaining, they complained that he had restricted freedom of debate and allowed his own private interests, principally his stake in the asiento, to take precedence over the needs of the colony. The latter bias, so the councilors claimed, not only resulted in Inchiquin's refusal to pass the Assembly's bill proposing a tax on the exportation of slaves—thereby starving the plantocracy of the workers essential to maintain their businesses—but it also deprived the island of the use of the two Royal Navy frigates supposedly intended for defense just at the time when the warships were most needed. As James O'Bryan had resigned his post as councilor and commandant of the island's defenses shortly after his father's death, the body was unanimous in its condemnation of its former leader. While Inchiquin would no doubt have been entirely unsurprised to find the signatures of those "ambitious . . . [and] insolent . . . incendiaries"—Beckford, Bernard, and Lawes—at the foot of such a damning document, he would probably also have been annoyed to see those of Peter Heywood and that "honest gentleman" John White, the very man whom the earl had recommended as "the fittest" candidate to replace him.[65]

The new acting governor was an obscure character. Nothing is known of White's origins aside from the fact that he had been in Jamaica since at least 1670, when he was granted two relatively small parcels of land: 259 acres in St. John's Parish and thirty in St. David's. By the following year, however, White appears to have risen considerably in his peers' esteem: he had been appointed to the twin roles of councilor and chief justice of the colony. Although he later rescinded the latter post, White also served as a judge in Jamaica's High Court of the Admiralty and remained a near permanent fixture on the Council for the following twenty years, all this despite the occasional whiff of corruption and persistent claims that he was in the pay of the asiento agent Santiago Castillo. It would appear that White was somewhat of a chameleon. Able to be all things to all people, he barely ruffled feathers, maintained a low profile in times of crisis, and chose his enemies wisely, punishing severely those who could not oppose him, such as an attorney named Thomas Bromhall whom White had gagged and pilloried on the parades of Spanish Town and Port Royal for daring to accuse him of bribery, while pandering to those who could. All the while White was busy accumulating power and wealth through occasionally shadowy business dealings. By January 1692, he had risen to the pinnacle of the island's government. As head of the Council, White suddenly found himself in a position to dictate policy. Whatever his faults, he was undoubtedly an intelligent and able man. Unfortunately for Jamaica, he would not remain in his post for long.[66]

White's period as the island's principal administrator began with an emergency meeting of the Council held at Spanish Town on the morning of January 16, a few hours after Inchiquin's death. As his first act, White had the final clause of his predecessor's Royal Commission read aloud, thus placing the governance of the colony solely in the hands of the Council with himself at its head. Warrants were then issued for the appointment of Samuel Bernard, John Towers, Nicholas Lawes, Francis Blackmore, and Andrew Orgill to sit alongside him. Two days later a second meeting was held. In response to rumors suggesting that Hispaniola's privateers would soon resume their offensive, White instigated a reshuffling of the island militia intended to resolve the "constant disputes as to seniority" and proposed the Council reconvene at Port Royal on January 21, to inspect the town's fortifications and the colony's military stores. The results were far from satisfactory: the barrels of eight of Fort Charles's thirty-eight cannon were "honeycombed with age . . . the walls [were] out of repair owing to the shortness of the guns and some of the carriages [were] decayed"; several of the carriages of Fort James' twenty-six guns were rotten and the site's "walls and platforms [were deemed] out of repair"; Fort Rupert was found to be "in good order" with only "one [gun] carriage and some trucks wanting"; while forts Carlisle and Walker were "in good condition" and Fort Morgan had "five [of its twenty-six gun] carriages decayed, but all else in good order." Most worryingly, the stores were found to be "much diminished. . . . There is little powder and few small arms, most of which are useless." White's report continued, "the fort at Point Morant is in a ruinous state . . . [and] we beg that we may be furnished with ordnance and ammunition."[67]

The councilors also took advantage of Inchiquin's demise to relaunch their attack against Jamaica's Jews. As a wealthy minority in direct competition with the island's English merchants, the Jewish community attracted considerable resentment. Their skill in working gold and silver led many to accuse them of coin clipping, a common crime of the period punishable by death. Several worked as moneylenders, including the aforementioned Rodriguez de Sousa, a resident of Port Royal whose assets were worth over £9,000, a fact which did little to improve his and his coreligionists' reputation; while the Jewish practice of presenting newly arrived governors with a barely disguised bribe also raised hackles. The Jews were to some extent victims of their own success. Due to frequent persecutions and expulsions from their adopted homelands, by the turn of the seventeenth century the diaspora had spread across the globe. This, combined with the fact that the community remained relatively close-knit despite its geographical distribution, afforded them considerable advantages in international trade, yet provided another cause for the ire they provoked from their gentile competitors.[68]

The Council began their attack with a letter addressed to the Lords of Trade on January 28, 1692. "The Jews eat us and our children out of all trade," they complained. "We did not want them at Port Royal, a place populous and strong without them; and though told that the whole country lay open to them they have made Port Royal their Goshen, and will do nothing but trade. When the Assembly tries to tax them more heavily than Christians, who are subject to public duties from which they are exempt, they contrive to evade it by special favors. This is a great and growing evil, and had we not warning from other Colonies we should see our streets filled and the ships hither crowded with them. This means taking our children's bread and giving it to Jews."[69]

In response, Port Royal's Jewish community solicited the help of the attorney general Simon Musgrave, who wrote to William Blathwayt in their defense. "The Jews . . . [,] who have always behaved themselves very quietly to the Governmt[,] have reasons to fear some trouble . . . [from] other merchants . . . who Envy their frugality & gaine," the letter, which was dispatched to London a week after the Council's complaint, began. "[Their enemies] Intend . . . by some distinct tax . . . to oppress and discourage them even to forsaking the Place in this time of Warr . . . & yett I am satisfied . . . that such as have letters of Denization—under the Great Seale of England or Naturalized here According to our law are as well qualified to trade . . . as those that clamour against them. . . . [I] Most humbly pray you to stand their friend & procure a letter or order . . . from their Majesties in their favour." Musgrave's motivations were far from high-minded. "I dare undertake the . . . [Jews of Port Royal] will not be wanting in all manner of thankfulness . . . to acknowledge your Paines & friendship," he assured Blathwayt with his closing line.[70]

The attorney general was right in his assumption that recent English policy afforded the Jews protection. In 1655 Cromwell had encouraged Jewish immigration into England from the Dutch provinces with which the country was then at war. As well as sharing the admiration felt by some Puritans for the Jews as practitioners of the most ancient form of the worship of God, by overturning the edict by which Edward I had ordered their expulsion from England in 1290, the Lord Protector hoped to strip the Dutch of some of their trade with the Americas, much of which was engendered by Amsterdam's Jewish community. Although the law remained ill-defined, Charles II, himself a beneficiary of Jewish financial support during his exile on the Continent, continued Cromwell's policy of encouraging Jewish settlement in both England and the colonies despite the opposition of economic heavyweights such as the East India Company, who painted the Jews as alien infidels and perpetual enemies of the crown. William and Mary continued their predecessors' policy. Rumored to have been loaned two million guilders on the eve of the Glorious Revolution by two Jewish merchants, Antonio Lopes Suasso and Baron Avernes de Gras, the king was happy to dismiss the Jamaican petition out of hand.[71]

On February 4, the Jamaican councilors turned their attention back to the French. Following ten months of "a quiet and flourishing condition" in the aftermath of the raid on Hispaniola, the island was once more under threat.[72] After swearing in Thomas Sutton as its latest member, the Council held an Assembly of War to which all sixteen of the most senior militia officers were summoned. The points addressed were mainly disciplinary. Commanders were given the power to court-martial their subordinates should they "use any unlawful oath or exercration"; capital punishment was prescribed for deserters, traitors, cowards, looters, and anyone caught uttering "tratorious words against William & Mary"; while those caught killing an enemy who had yielded, would be dealt with by "arbitrary punishment." Over the next two weeks the Council also awarded several privateering commissions. As well as offering some protection to the settlements of the remote north coast, the policy was intended to discourage the captains and crews of Port Royal's sloops from accepting similar offers from the French. With the wreck at Point Pedro Cays fished dry of treasure there were plenty of takers. Captain John Griffin of the *True Love* sloop signed up on February 4, while Robert Scroope of the *Diligence* took a commission four days later. The following day martial law was declared. All merchant ships were banned from leaving port; fifteen cannon were requisitioned from HMS *Drake* and *Swan* to set up shore batteries at Mantinaneal Bay, Withywood, Morant Bay, and Port Maria; payments were authorized for the improvement of the fortifications at Port Morant, the erection of a new battery "behinde the Church on Port Royal," and the construction of a breastwork at Negroe's River in St. Mary's Parish; guards were posted to Three Rivers in St. Andrew's; and Captain Gaines of the *Seahorse* was charged with organizing the thirty or so merchantmen interned in Port Royal "in[to] a posture of defence." Aided by his Council-appointed deputies—Thomas Shirley of the 30-gun RAC slaver *East India Merchant* and Daniel Updick of the *Caesar* broad stern—Gaines ordered his charges to anchor their ships in line across the mouth of the bay, thus presenting their broadsides to any Frenchman who dared to approach.[73]

On March 2, news arrived of the first French attacks on the north coast since mid-1691. The man responsible was Nathaniel Grubbing, an Englishman born in Jamaica who had sided with the French at Petit Guavos following the Glorious Revolution. Whether this was due to religious considerations (Grubbing was rumored to be a Papist) or opportunism is unclear. What is apparent is that his raids were extremely well executed. Captaining a small sloop, Grubbing used his intimate knowledge of Jamaica's backwaters to make a nighttime descent on the small holdings of Spanish River in St. George's Parish. Before the militia could react, he made off with twenty-two slaves and a quantity of plunder. Determined to make an example of him lest his success inspire others, the Council commissioned Matthew Want, commander of the *Grayhound* sloop, and John Harris of the *Thomas and Elizabeth* to hunt Grubbing down. Want and Harris were ordered to cruise to the windward of Hispaniola and were allocated three barrels of gunpowder, "one seane of match . . . [,] a quire of cartridge paper," and two dozen "hand granadoes" to aid them in their task. In compensation, as well as being allowed to keep all prize money including the tenth typically awarded to the crown, Want and Harris were promised a reward of £100 should they bring Grubbing back to Port Royal alive.[74]

On April 4, sixty-four English prisoners ransomed by the French arrived in Port Royal from Petit Guavos. "[They reported] that there is ten or twelve privateers cruising to windward between Cape Altevel and Cape Tiburon," the Council minutes recorded, "and . . . that six days before their departure . . . Nathaniell Grubbing was sailed for this island in order to attack and doe some mischief on the remote parts thereof." The Council was swift to react. The sloop *Pembroke*, then at anchor in Port Royal roads, was requisitioned for government service, crewed with ten pressed men and a detachment of sixty sailors from HMS *Guernsey* under the command of Lieutenant Edward Moses (the hero of the previous year's expedition to Petit Guavos), and sent to intercept Grubbing in company with the *Grayhound* sloop. Moses set sail at 10 A.M. on April 8. Three days later the Council ordered Captain Neville of HMS *Swan*, recently arrived from Portobelo with the *Inchiquin*, an English merchantman in service with the asiento, to press yet another of the island's sloops into service to be dispatched to the north coast to join Moses's flotilla. Further defensive measures taken included a prohibition on the firing of the morning and evening guns at Port Royal so as to preserve the town's powder store, and the establishment of beacon fires along the coast "for giving alarms."[75]

On April 15, a terrible accident occurred. At 3 P.M., as the crew of HMS *Guernsey* were unloading their ballast in anticipation of yet another cruise to the Spanish Main, the *Inchiquin*, the London-built broad stern of one hundred tons and twenty-four men captained by William Martin which had recently returned from Portobelo with HMS *Swan*, "was blown up all to pieces." The cause of the explosion was unknown. Twenty of the crew were killed along with the captain. The four survivors were blown clear. Among those most affected by the loss was Joseph Norris, the London-born Quaker who had worked as a merchant in Port Royal since 1678. Along with several unnamed associates, Norris had had a financial interest in the *Inchiquin*, which had arrived from London in December 1691 laden with beer, Spanish wine, flour, and bread for the Jamaican market and sixty tons of manufactured goods to sell on the Spanish Main. In a letter to his brother and business partner, Isaac, then in Pennsylvania overseeing the delivery of a load of Jamaican dyewood, Joseph explained that the ship's mate, despite having been back in Port Royal for nearly a week, had failed to unload his cargo prior to the explosion resulting in a loss to the brothers of £50 worth of Spanish pieces of eight.[76]

The loss of the *Inchiquin* was not the only bad news suffered by Port Royal's Quaker community that April. "The measles runs through all the country," Joseph Norris informed his brother, "seizing both young and old . . . I think Wm Pike is dead . . . [and] we have also lately buried honest Mary Green, who died of a violent flux and fever, leaving behind her a husband void of any sense of his loss, having kept to his old strain of drinking, not only while she was sick, but at the very time of her burial." The most tragic news of all came in a footnote. "Since this writing our d[ea]r baby is taken from us," Norris concluded, "being violently seized and carried off in 24 hours to the great sorrow of my dr. wife, who is deprived of her pretty companion." Such was the strength of Joseph's faith that he could take solace in the belief that even this loss was somehow in keeping with the workings of the Almighty.[77]

At the end of April 1692 a convoy was preparing to sail from Port Royal for London. At its head was the *Seahorse* under Captain Gaines. Having laden his vessel with over £2,000 worth of currency acquired through a typically Jamaican conglomeration of asiento business, privateering, and wreck fishing, Gaines was heading for home. "She is the richest ship that ever went out of this town," Simon Musgrave opined. The voyage was not without mishap. "Going out [of the harbor] they run upon Smith Key," one of a dozen small islets scattered across the bay. With help from the crew of HMS *Guernsey*, Gaines lightened his ship sufficiently to get off with the land breeze the following day. Among the *Seahorse*'s passengers was the last of the Inchiquins remaining in Jamaica. Following his mother's departure and his father's death, the twenty-six-year-old James O'Bryan had decided to go home.[78]

As April turned to May the weather took a turn for the worse. The "hot and dry" conditions which had characterized the opening five months of 1692 gave way to strong winds "and much rain."[79] It was an inauspicious portent. Along with "black streaks under the sun, springs and fountains [becoming] trobled and unholsome, a strange calmness of the air, and [when] birds forebear to warble forth their pleasant tones," such circumstances were held to presage an earthquake. Many residents believed such a disaster was long overdue. Six years previously "a certain astrologer" had arrived in Port Royal, predicting that an earthquake would soon strike the island and "the Point [on which the town was built] should be swallowed up by the sea." The prediction had caused widespread panic. "Many for fear removed themselves from off the Point, but the . . . time being come, their hap'ned noe such earthquack as was foretold" and "soe it past off," John Taylor noted. Nevertheless, a residual fear remained. When the rains came that May the doomsayers took to the streets, begging the residents of the wickedest town in the English Empire to ask forgiveness for their sins before God struck the colony from the face of the earth. Such harbingers were commonplace in the seventeenth century. This time, however, their apocalyptic predictions were to come true.[80]

CHAPTER 7

A Dismal Calamity

THE EARTHQUAKE

June 7, 1692

Sir . . . give me leave to present you with an Account of a late dismal Calamity and Judgement, which hath befallen us here . . . by a Terrible Earthquake, which a just God hath sent upon us on Tuesday the 7th, of June.
—Account of the Late Earthquake, 1693

LYING ONE HUNDRED MILES south of the junction of the North American and Caribbean tectonic plates and directly on top of the Walton and Enriquillo-Plantain Garden fault lines, Jamaica is prone to seismic activity. It was a danger of which the Spanish colonists were fully aware. In their century and a half as masters of the island, they had learned to construct their homes low to the ground with deep, central foundations and to avoid building on the shifting soils and loose sand masses which characterized many of Jamaica's coastal areas, notably Point Cagway, the site on which Port Royal was built. In geological terms, this area is a disaster waiting to happen. Made up of a number of independent coral cays or islets linked by a hundred-foot-deep layer of sand, silt, gravel, and sediment deposited by the waves and tides over the previous four hundred years, the spit was extremely unstable, particularly as the water surrounding it deepened rapidly only a few feet from shore. Exposed to earthquake, the areas of sand, silt, and gravel were prone to liquefaction, a phenomenon associated with landslides where a layer fluidizes causing a general collapse. It was a lesson that the English, with their contempt for foreign know-how and propensity for building precarious multi-story brick edifices in the northern European style, had failed to appreciate.[1] In 1688 Hans Sloane noted that major seismic events were expected each year, yet only two, those of 1673 and 1684, had occurred during English governance.[2] By 1692 a cataclysmic earthquake was long overdue.

In Port Royal the morning of Tuesday, June 7, began much like any other. Following the strong winds and heavy rains of May, the weather had turned "excessive hot, calm and dry."[3] The sky was beautifully clear. As the sun climbed over the hills of Port Morant, the temperature increased steadily to a debilitating eighty-six degrees. On the battlements of the town's five forts, dozens of scarlet-coated militia kept a watchful eye on the signal pyres to the east and on the southern sea approaches for any sign of French invasion. Due to the Council's prohibition on merchantmen leaving the port unescorted, the roads were particularly busy with shipping. Although HMS *Guernsey*, Captain Updick's *Caesar* broad stern, John Griffin's *True Love* sloop, the hired sloop *Pembroke*, and the *San Antonio*, a Spanish vessel of twenty-two guns which had previously been involved in the asiento, had set sail for the north coast some five days earlier to protect the plantations of St. Mary's and St. Ann's from a rumored descent by dozens of French privateers, HMS *Swan* had remained behind to be careened.[4] With one side of its hull hard up against the wharf, the keel lay exposed. Captain Neville and most of the crew, as was their custom, were sleeping off the previous night's excesses in town, while a few stalwarts, mercifully cooled by the sea breeze which had sprung up from the south at 8 A.M., scraped away the sea life that had accumulated over the past two years that the frigate had been engaged on its Caribbean sojourn.[5] At anchor nearby were dozens of merchantmen. Amid numerous island sloops of twenty to fifty tons were Captain Richard Conning's 150-ton *Richard and Sarah* broad stern of twenty-two guns, the 200-ton *Syam Merchant*, heavily laden with sugar belonging to the Royal African Company, the *Mainyard* broad stern, and the swift-sailing *Barclay* frigate.[6] There were also at least two foreign ships in Port Royal that June. As well as a French prize recently captured off Hispaniola, there was a Spanish merchantman, presumably in town to purchase slaves for the asiento.[7]

At 9 A.M. the Council met at Port Royal. Having made their way through the crowds heading for the morning markets, John White, Peter Beckford, Nicholas Lawes, Andrew Orgill, and Charles Knight were all present, each no doubt accompanied by a gang of liveried slaves. The order of business that morning was routine. First, it was decided that the embargo on ships leaving port unescorted should be lifted for "sloops and boats which trade about this island and noe other." All vessels bound for England would have to wait until June 10 before being convoyed home. The second point raised that morning concerned the cargo of the recently departed *Seahorse*. According to the minutes, Captain Gaines had failed to pay duty on a number of barrels of wine and brandy which he had imported from Carolina. It was decided that a letter should be sent to Governor Phillip Ludwell in Charles Town to find out more details about the affair. The final order of business concerned a new protocol imposed on every ship arriving at the harbor. In future none was to be permitted to pass Fort Charles between sunset and sunrise without sending a boat ashore announcing its arrival, "from whence they came and who they are." By 10 A.M., the Council's business had concluded. John White adjourned the meeting and the members dispersed around town.[8]

Several other residents were also on the move that morning. Keen to take care of business on his estate, Chief Justice Samuel Bernard had risen early to take a boat with his son to Liguanea on the far side of the bay. Leaving his wife and five servants at their home, a towering townhouse built on the quayside, Bernard had finished his business by mid-morning and had boarded a boat with his boy to return.[9] Other residents were engaged in less businesslike pursuits. The merchant John Uffgress had left his wife and domestic slaves at home to enjoy a morning drink in one of Port Royal's many taverns.[10] June 7 also saw the Quakers' monthly meeting held at Spanish Town. Dozens of Port Royal's Friends traveled across the bay as a result. The merchant Joseph Norris and his wife were among those who made the journey, while the joiner, John Pike, his wife, Ann, and their seven children, the shopkeeper Thomas Hillyard, and Joseph Norris's wife's sister and his aging father, Thomas, had chosen to stay at home.[11]

In St. Paul's Church, the newly appointed Anglican minister, Dr. Emmanuel Heath, was preoccupied with religious matters. "I had been at church reading prayers," the rector recalled, "to keep some shew of religion among a most ungodly debauched people." Afterward, Heath retired to the covered stone walkway nearby where the town's merchants habitually congregated. Having caught his breath, Heath was about to press on to the Thames Street house of Walter Ruding, where the Royal African Company factor was hosting a lunch with his wife and family for several friends. Heath's departure was providentially delayed, however, by the arrival of John White, who had adjourned that morning's Council meeting a few moments before. "He being my very great friend, I staid with him," Heath explained. The friends had a glass or two of "wormwood wine . . . as a whet before dinner." Subsequently White lit his pipe and was enjoying a leisurely smoke when, at roughly 11:30 A.M., the ground began "rolling and moving under [their] . . . feet." Unfamiliar with Jamaica's frequent seismic rumblings as a recent arrival, Heath was inclined to panic. "Lord, sir, what is this?" he asked, jumping to his feet. "It is an earthquake," White announced with the composure of one accustomed to such things. "Be not afraid, it will soon be over." The acting governor could not have been more wrong.

Rather than subsiding as White had assured Heath it would, the earthquake intensified. Accompanied by an eerie rumbling sound, compared by one witness to that made by "a rustling wind, or . . . a hollow . . . thunder" with "puffing blasts . . . like those of a match made of brimstone," the initial tremor built in magnitude and was followed by a series of terrific shocks. The ground shuddered and rose in waves, hurling the steeple of St. Paul's Church to the ground in a cloud of choking brick dust. Landing amid a crowd of fifteen people whose last act was to gawp upward at their impending doom, the steeple shattered on impact, its bell making an ominous metallic clang as it skittered crazily across the street. Seconds later the rest of St. Paul's crashed to the ground. Panic ensued. Hundreds of men, women, and children, merchants, sailors, shopkeepers, slaves, servants, militiamen, and councilors alike, took to the streets and ran in all directions. Others stood rooted to the spot. The air filled with wailing, crying, and sobbing, and a terrifying splintering sound emanated from the heaving ground. In the chaos, Heath and White were soon separated.[12]

At the waterfront to the north of town, all hell was breaking loose. In an instant the earthquake liquefied the layer of sand and shingle upon which Thames Street was built. The quayside collapsed. With an awful cracking sound, it slid into the sea and sank thirty or forty feet. The water surged forward in a spitting mass of foam. The merchants' three-and four-story houses and the warehouses on the north side of Thames Street bubbled into the ocean along with King's House and Forts James and Carlisle. Bizarrely, as the buildings moved with the earth beneath them and their foundations more or less intact, most remained upright. Several roofs remained visible above the water. Others were swallowed entirely by the brine. The forts' cannon, torn from their carriages by the shuddering of the earth, rolled wildly along the battlements, causing carnage amid the fleeing scarlet-coated militiamen assigned to man them as the low-lying forts boiled out of sight.[13]

Among the houses first affected were many belonging to Port Royal's elite. Samuel Bernard's wife was "in her closet, two pairs of stairs high" with her daughter and white maid. Feeling the ground lurching beneath them, Mrs. Bernard ordered her maid upstairs to the garret where another of the family's domestics, "Mrs. B," was trapped with her child. The maid complied, but as she came running back downstairs to where she had last seen her mistress, the sea came rushing upward to meet her. Somehow the maid survived. The rest of the residents, including Bernard's wife and daughter, Mrs. B and her child, and two men employed by Bernard, were drowned.[14] Walter Ruding was preparing for the dinner to which Reverend Heath had been invited along with his family and friends when his house collapsed about him.[15] Aside from a single "negroe man," all inside lost their lives. Reginald Wilson, the port captain of Port Royal, was killed in his house with his only son, while the councilor and planter Peter Beckford, his two daughters, and a grandchild were buried alive.[16]

One or two minutes after the earthquake had started, the sea had advanced five hundred feet into town from the northern shore. As well as Thames Street, Queen Street and the High Street and parts of New Street and Common Street had sunk as the sand slid away beneath them. In the interior of town most of the houses "were shaken down, save only eight or ten that remained from the balcony upwards above water."[17] The residence of the Quaker joiner John Pike sunk four fathoms under water. "I lost my wife, my son, a 'prentice, a white-maid, and 6 slaves and all that ever I had in the world," Pike recalled. Pike's neighbor and fellow Quaker George Phillips was also killed, but his house, a dwelling made entirely out of timber, survived.[18] Another of the houses to remain standing belonged to the physician Thomas Trapham. As the building subsided and the water flooded in, drowning his wife and several of his children, Trapham and his youngest daughter, Elizabeth, ran upstairs and leaped out of the garret window. "Hanging by his hands upon the rack of a chimney" with Elizabeth clinging to his neck, Trapham struggled to maintain his grip as Port Royal collapsed about him.[19]

At the junction of New Street and Common Street, the Norris's house and adjacent shop where they did business sank into the ocean. Joseph's wife's sister, his partner, Thomas Hillyard, and his family, and the majority of the Norris's black and white domestics were killed. Another of the household slaves, who had been out on an errand at the time, ran toward the shop to save his masters, "but by mistake seized in his arms the captain of a vessel and escaped with him" instead. Realizing his error, the slave returned to the property and dove into the water. He found Thomas Norris in his counting house, but with the building sinking ever farther and the sea rushing in, he was unable to save him. The two men perished side by side.[20]

To the east, the area known as the Pallisadoes was also badly affected. The land at the narrowest point of the sand spit liquefied and sank and a wall of water surged across the gap, cutting Port Royal off from the mainland. The wooden palisade was "utterly ruined"; Fort Rupert was entirely submerged; and the graveyard was destroyed. The tombstones were uprooted and dashed to pieces, hundreds of buried corpses were unearthed as the ground yawned open, and the sea washed the coffins and decomposing bodies around the ruins of the town. The rest of Port Royal's forts suffered similar fates. Forts James and Carlisle had sunk forty feet under the water with the initial shock. To the southeast Morgan's Line was severely damaged, while Walker's Fort and Fort Charles on the southwestern corner of the sand spit, although largely intact, were "sorely shaken and rent, and so sunk" as not to "be tenable." Somehow, the town's magazine, housed in a tower in the courtyard of Fort Charles, was entirely unscathed—the powder remained dry and the cartridges ready.[21]

Outside St. Paul's Church, Emmanuel Heath was running for his life. Reasoning that he would be safest in an open space, the rector decided to make for the parade ground next to Morgan's Line. As he sprinted down Church Street, houses and walls collapsed on either side. "Some bricks came rolling over my shoes," he recalled, "but none hurt me." On reaching the battery, Heath "saw the earth swallow up a multitude of people" who had gathered there, "and the sea mounting in upon . . . [them] over the fortifications." Resigning himself to his fate, Heath determined to return to his "own lodging [in the center of town], there to meet death in as good a posture as . . . [he] could."[22] Nearby, the merchant John Uffgress had fled the tavern where he had been enjoying an early morning drink and was also running for his life. "On either side" he recalled, he "saw . . . houses . . . swallowed up [by the earth, while] . . . others [were] thrown on heaps . . . [He felt] the sand in the street [beneath his feet] rise like the waves of the sea, lifting up all persons that stood upon it, and immediately dropping [them] down into pits."[23]

"The shake was so violent," another who witnessed events in the center of town recalled,

that it threw people down on their knees, and sometimes on their faces, as they ran along. . . . It was a very difficult matter to keep one's legs. The ground heaved and swelled like a rolling sea . . . by which means several houses . . . were shuffled and moved some yards from their places . . . [and the streets] crack[ed] and open[ed, then] shut quick and fast . . . in some . . . many people were swallowed up; some the earth caught by the middle, and squeezed to death; the heads of others only appeared above ground: Some were swallowed quite down, and cast up again by great quantities of water; others went down, and never more were seen. . . . Other [openings] . . . swallowed up great houses; and out of some . . . issue[d] whole rivers of water, sprouted up a great height into the air, which seemed to threaten a deluge to [the center] . . . of Port Royal . . . [these water spouts were] accompanied with ill stenches and offensive smells, by means of which openings, and the vapours at that time, belched forth from the earth. . . . The sky . . . was in a minute's time . . . dull and reddish . . . like a . . . oven.[24]

Amid the chaos, some were miraculously saved. The Huguenot merchant Lewis Galdy fell into a chasm which opened beneath his feet only to be thrown into the sea by a subsequent tremor and picked up by a passing boat. Mordecai Lloyd, a twenty-three-year-old Quaker merchant who traded with the North American colonies, found himself in his shop when the earthquake struck. "On a sudden the earth opened and let me in," he later informed his father, a native of Wales who had immigrated to Philadelphia in 1683. "Then was I carried under earth and water," Mordecai continued, "until at last I got upon a floor of boards where multitudes lay about me most of them mortally wounded and I amongst them very little hurt."[25] A certain Mrs. Akers lost consciousness for "the tenth part of a minute" that she and several others alongside her were swallowed up by the earth, before being "vomited" forth into the water. She emerged unscathed, aside from a small scratch on one cheek "that did but just draw blood." Those buried beside her were less fortunate. Held fast "in dismal torture" by earth locked around their legs, arms, or bodies, they were pulled underwater and drowned. In "the moment before the Earth swallowed her . . . [Akers] imagin[ed] . . . herself upon the brink of a boundless Eternity. . . . [I] put up a short ejaculation to Almighty God," she later recalled, "begging him to pardon . . . [my] Sins, and . . . receive . . . [my] Soul."[26]

The merchant John Uffgress survived along with "sixteen or eighteen" others by alighting upon "a small piece of ground" which lay upon solid substrata. "Praised be God . . . [it] did not sink," he recalled.[27] Reverend Heath was another recipient of good fortune. Having reached his home, he "found there all things in the same order I left them; not a picture . . . being out of place. I went to the balcony," he continued, "and saw never a house down there, not the ground so much as cracked."[28] Uffgress's wife and slave also survived. Having run out of their house as the earthquake started, "the sand lifted up [around Uffgress's wife], and [with] her negro woman grasping about her, both dropped into the earth together." Seconds later the sea rushed in on top of them and "rolled them over and over, till at length they caught hold of a beam" and were swept out into Kingston Bay.[29]

The ships moored in the harbor also suffered. As the earthquake began, the sea "suddenly . . . swelled as in a storm" and a monstrous wave swept across the roads. With their cables snapping under the strain, the ships were tossed about like driftwood. A few crashed into one another; several were damaged by timbers, roofs, and other debris from town; others were carried over some of the survivors who were clinging to the debris, killing them instantly. The *Syam Merchant* sprang a leak which would trouble her for several months; the French prize was driven into one of the quayside markets and wrecked; and HMS *Swan* was driven across the half-submerged rooftops of Thames Street.[30] Crashing into the remains of King's House, where former governor Inchiquin's reception had taken place over two years before, the frigate demolished the upper story, "part of . . . [which] fell upon her and beat in her round-house."[31] Although the *Swan* remained afloat, it lost its rigging, guns, anchors, and cables, and twelve of the crew were killed. Among the casualties were the ship's cooper, Phillip Bryan, the purser, Joshua Nash, the cook's mate, John Harris, and Able Seaman Andrew Hodge. His sibling, Jonathon, survived.[32]

After Port Royal roads, the tidal wave swept across Kingston Bay. Samuel Bernard and his son, returning home by boat from their early morning visit to Liguanea, met it midway. "We were near being over-whelmed by a swift rolling sea, six feet above the surface, without any wind," the chief justice recalled, "but it pleased God to save us." The Bernard's boat was forced back to Liguanea by the swell. "I found all the houses even with the ground," he related, "[and there was] not a place to put one's head in, but in negro houses." A certain Captain Phipps had been standing by the seaside at Liguanea with a friend at the time of the earthquake. "The sea [had] retired from the land in such sort," he related, "that for two or three hundred yards, the bottom . . . appeared dry." Spotting several fish which had been grounded, Phipps's friend "ran and took them up, and in a minute or two's time, the sea returned again, and overflowed [a] great part of the shore."[33]

The rest of the island suffered in kind. "[The earthquake threw] down almost all of the houses, churches, sugar works, mills, and bridges through the whole country," Reverend Heath reported. "It tore the rocks and mountains, [and] destroyed some whole planta-tions, and threw them into the sea."[34] On the north coast "about 1000 acres of land sunk, and thirteen people with it," one witness noted, while another added that "the planters' houses, with the greatest part of their plantations . . . were swallowed, houses, people, trees, all up in one gape; instead of which, appeared for some time after, a great pool, or lake of water."[35] A few miles off the northern shore, the crew of HMS *Guernsey* also felt the effects. "All ye forenoon we had a fine gael of wind," the logbook recorded, "[and] at noon we had a great Earthquake which lasted 4 minutes."[36]

In Sixteen Mile Walk between the parishes of St. Thomas in the Vale and St. Catherine, "two great mountains . . . fell and met, and stopped the [Cobre] river, [so] that it was dry from that place to the Ferry" at Kingston harbor "for a whole day." The water "forced its passage out from [Salt-panns] hill, in . . . twenty or thirty . . . places . . . most of them, six or seven yards high from the foot of the hill," thereby flooding the salt pans to the northwest of Kingston harbor. In a nearby plantation, the ground opened, swallowed and smothered two cows belonging to a certain Mr. Bosby, while only one of Passage Fort's "thirty houses, ten taverns, and as many storehouses" survived.[37]

At Yallahs in St. David's, the sea retired "above a mile from the shore, while inland "a great mountain split." Carrying a wave of uprooted trees before it, the land slid into the valley below, "covered several settlements, and destroyed nineteen white people." Among the dead was a man named Hopkins, who "had his plantation moved half a mile from the place it formerly stood." To the east, in St. Thomas's, "a large and high mountain, near Port Morant" was swallowed up by the earth, leaving "a great lake or four or five leagues over." In Clarendon Parish, "about twelve miles from the sea" in the vicinity of Thomas Sutton's plantation, "the earth gaped, and . . . great quantities of water . . . sprouted up with a prodigious force," while in the neighboring parish of Vere "all the Brick and Stone buildings . . . [were] levelled with the ground" and left "shattered and torn . . . [and] irrepairable. While they were tumbling," the reverend of Withywood wrote, "the Earth opened in multitudes of places, and . . . spew'd out Water to a considerable heighth above ground, in such quantities in some places, that it made our Gullies run on a suddain, tho' before [they had been] exceeding dry."[38]

At Spanish Town the death toll was comparatively light. Most of the houses built by the English were destroyed, the cathedral was "devoured in the same Ruines," while "the low houses built by the wary

A London broadsheet announcing the June 7, 1692, earthquake at Port Royal. The destruction of Port Royal made news around the trans-Atlantic world. Doctor Thomas Trapham can be seen clinging to the sill of his gable-window in the bottom-left-hand corner, while the rector of Saint Paul's, Emmanuel Heath, is leading a group of survivors in prayer in the centre of the image. (*Printed by R. Smith, London, c. July 1692*)

Spaniards" survived. The Quaker Joseph Norris and several other Friends were at their meetinghouse at the time. "[We] ran outside," Norris related, "where the ground waving like to a sea, we could not stand." Norris "beheld the walls and houses shake, as a man would shake a twig, till they were laid flat around us, and we persevered in the middle within a small spot." After "a quarter of an hour," with the tremors "somewhat ceasing . . . we walked about the town," Norris continued, "and glutted our eyes with the dreadful desolation of the houses." Despite the damage, Norris noted that there were only "about 4 persons killed."[39]

In the wilds of the Blue Mountains and the Cockpit Country, which none but the maroons called home, there was considerable devastation. From the high slopes "came . . . dreadful roarings," one contemporary source related. The noises were "terrible and amazing to all that heard them." The "tops of the great mountains" collapsed in an avalanche of rock and earth. "Sweeping down all the trees, and everything in . . . [their] way" they made "quite a path from top to bottom." Afterward, the mountaintops had a "miserable shattered appearance" and seemed "half naked," stripped of their "large aspiring trees." Other peaks fell "in a huddled and confused manner, [and] stopped up . . . the rivers for about twenty-four hours." What damage and how many casualties such destruction caused in the rudimentary settlements of the maroons is unknown.[40]

After three to four minutes, the earthquake abated. In Port Royal, which was to be plagued by a series of aftershocks of diminishing frequency and intensity that would last until mid-September, the survivors began to take stock. Having reached the safety of his lodgings in the center of town, Reverend Heath surveyed the destruction from his balcony. One third of the point was under water. The buildings on the wharf and on Thames Street, Queen Street, and the High Street were all submerged, save "eight or ten that remained from the balcony upwards above water." The area where St. Paul's Church had once stood was now covered by a large lagoon, and the "once brave streets of stately houses" had disappeared save "here and there a chimney, and some parts and pieces of houses."[41] To the south, Fort Charles had been inundated and even in the area least affected, from New Street to the great seaside on the southern edge of town, there was considerable flooding and several buildings lay in ruins. In the areas still above water, hundreds of chasms had opened up in the streets. Everywhere were the dead and dying. Many had fallen into the chasms only for them to close up again, trapping their victims and squeezing them to death. Some had been buried up to their waists, others were caught up to their necks with only their heads remaining above ground. Many more corpses were floating on the ocean amid a bobbing carpet of debris. Timbers, with survivors still clinging to them, partially destroyed roofs, broken furniture, and the coffins and decomposed corpses disgorged from the burial place at the Pallisadoes were being washed back and forth along with casks, crates, barrels, and bales of goods which had risen from the warehouses on the wharf. Death proved a great leveler. "Great men . . . and women whose top-knots seemed to reach the clouds, now [lay] . . . stinking upon the water," alongside the corpses of indentured servants and African slaves.[42]

The survivors gathered on the ground that remained above water. One group, having noticed Emmanuel Heath looking down from his balcony, called the rector to join them in prayer. "When I came into the street every one laid hold on my clothes and embraced me," Heath recalled, "that with their fear and kindness I was almost stifled. I persuaded them at last to kneel down and make a large ring. . . . I prayed with them near an hour, when I was almost spent with the heat of the sun, and the exercise. They then brought me a chair, the earth working all the while with new motions, and tremblings, like the rollings of the sea; insomuch that sometimes when I was at prayer I could hardly keep my self upon my knees." Among Heath's mostly Protestant congregation "were several Jews that kneeled, and answered as the . . . [others] did. They were heard to call upon Jesus Christ: A thing worth observation."[43]

Other survivors began to search for missing family and friends. "I endeavoured to go towards my house," John Uffgress recalled, "upon the ruins of the houses that were floating upon the water, but could not: At length, I got a canoe, and rowed up the great sea-side towards my house, where I saw several men and women floating upon the wreck[age] out to sea." Uffgress rescued "as many of them as I could" and rowed on "till I came where I thought my house had stood, but could not hear of neither my wife nor family, so returned again to that little part remaining above water." By now a considerable crowd had gathered, but none had any news of Uffgress's family.[44]

At about 1 P.M., having urged his congregation to repent the "heinous provocations" which had brought the Lord's wrath upon them, the Reverend Heath was approached by several merchants. "[They] desired me to go aboard some ship in the harbour and refresh myself," he recalled. Clambering across the rooftops which remained above water, Heath was led to a canoe and rowed out to a long boat which took him aboard the *Syam Merchant*. Despite having sprung a serious leak, Master Charles Guy's 200-tonner had survived and was now a floating refuge for grateful survivors, a fate it shared with several other merchantmen in the roads. Among those on board was John White, whom Heath had last seen when the earthquake had begun two hours before. The president was "overjoyed to see me," Heath recalled. Both men spent the night aboard the *Syam Merchant* "but could not sleep," due to "the returns of the earthquake almost every hour, which made all the guns in the ship . . . jar and rattle."[45]

In the immediate aftermath of the earthquake, several of the sailors aboard the ships in the roads, including a number of Spaniards, began scavenging the ruins. Taking to their boats, they picked up any boxes and chests they found floating on the surface.[46] Others began to dredge the ruined houses, and after sunset "a company of lewd rogues, whom they call privateers, fell to breaking open ware-houses, and houses deserted, to rob and rifle their neighbours." As a result of the continuing aftershocks, several looters were killed when damaged properties collapsed about them.[47] "Even the very slaves thought it their time of liberty," one witness recalled, "wherein they committed many barbarous insolences and robberies." The dead were also looted. "Some [were] stripped, others searched, their pockets picked, their fingers cut off for their rings, their gold buttons taken off their shirts." Other survivors, busy trying to salvage their own goods, were robbed, while some of the looters fought over the choicest pickings. Elsewhere, dogs feasted on the dead, chewing the heads and limbs of those who had been partially buried, while several "audacious whores who remain still upon the place" drank themselves into oblivion after finding bottles and barrels of booze floating amid the wreckage.[48]

ALTHOUGH THE exact death toll of the earthquake of June 7 is unknown, by correlating contemporary accounts it can be surmised that somewhere between 1,000 and 2,000 of Port Royal's 6,500 inhabitants were killed. Of the victims, it is possible to identify 121 individuals. At least thirty-eight of Port Royal's community of Quakers were among the dead; as were twelve of the crew of HMS *Swan*. No less than two of the most prominent members of the town's Jewish community also perished: Moises de Lucena, the moneylender and merchant who left behind property and debts worth over £2,000, and his fellow merchant Isaac Gonsales. Other victims of note included two merchant ship captains: Richard Conning of the *Richard and Sarah*, who was on shore at the time of the earthquake and "buried in the ruins," and a certain Captain Martin who was said to have been "swallowed" up by a chasm in the ground. The most prominent residents to perish were the port captain, Reginald Wilson; the Royal African Company agent, Walter Ruding; the disgraced provost marshal, Thomas Ryves; and the attorney general, Simon Musgrave, about whose death no particulars survive. Initially, Peter Beckford, the prominent planter and Council member who had attended the meeting held at Port Royal that morning, was also thought to have died following the collapse of his wharfside home. Buried in the ruins along with his two daughters, seventeen-year-old Priscilla and fourteen-year-old Elizabeth, and a grandchild, all three of whom were killed, Beckford was later dragged from the rubble "wounded and badly bruised."[49]

Outside of Port Royal, the death toll was relatively light. Four people had been killed in Spanish Town; thirteen had been swallowed up on the north coast; and nineteen "white people" were killed in Yallahs.[50] Presumably, other casualties went unreported, while slave deaths barely warranted a mention. Similarly, fatalities among the maroons are impossible to assess. The financial cost of the earthquake was extreme. "'Tis not to be computed what is lost," the Reverend of Withywood opined in a letter to England, "but many People think [that goods] at least to the Value of 400,000 l. [were lost] at Port Royal only, of which the Merchants at home will bear the greatest share."[51] Joseph Norris lost assets "being as near as I can compute to the value of £3000, for I saved not more than what I had on, of all that I had on Port Royal, not so much as a bond, bill, or book."[52] Property loss was also extreme. As many as half of Port Royal's two thousand buildings were destroyed or damaged beyond repair. Given the value of the town's real estate, compared by numerous contemporaries to that of the properties in the street of Cheapside in London, it can be estimated that property losses may have amounted to £300,000. Combined with the material losses mentioned by the Reverend of

Withywood and the property damage caused elsewhere on the island, the total cost of the earthquake may have been somewhere in the region of £1,000,000 in contemporary money.

Rising after a sleepless night on the *Syam Merchant*, Reverend Heath spent June 8 tending to the spiritual needs of his flock. "I went from ship to ship," he recalled, "to visit those who were bruised, and dying; likewise to do the last office at the sinking of several corps which came floating from the point. This indeed hath been my sorrowful employment ever since I came aboard this ship," he continued, "we have had nothing but shakings of the earth, with thunder and lightning, and foul weather ever since."[53] The merchant John Uffgress also spent the morning of June 8 rowing between the ships in the roads in search of his family. "At length," Uffgress recorded, "it pleased God that I met with my wife, and two of my Negroes. I then asked her, how she had escaped? She told me, when she felt the house shake, she run out, and called all within to do the same: She was no sooner out, but the sand lifted her up, and her Negro woman grasping about her, they both dropt into the earth together; and, at the same instant the water coming in, rolled them over and over, till, at length, they catched hold of a beam, where they hung, till a boat came from a Spanish vessel, and took them up."[54]

In the immediate aftermath of the earthquake, Port Royal was lawless. Chaos ensued. Hundreds of dead remained unburied, and sanitation became a serious issue. The treatment of the wounded was pressing, while the looters, emboldened by the authorities' failure to react, grew ever more violent. Several "negroes" were arrested under suspicion of "murder and felony" and many survivors abandoned town. Some, like Heath and Uffgress, were accommodated on board the ships in the roads "where many continued about two months after."[55] The majority headed north across Kingston harbor to the mainland. Those unable to find accommodation with family or friends elsewhere on the island set up a refugee camp on the shore opposite Port Royal at a site known as Kingston, or Killclown, where the new capital would later be built. Conditions in the camp were appalling. Some survivors huddled together in "little hovels" and "huts built with boughs, and not sufficient to keep out the rain." The Norrises spent the first few nights after the earthquake sleeping "in carts covered with sheets and blankets" and later rented a slave cabin, a temporary solution that many of the better-off survivors resorted to in the first few days. The irony was not lost on John Pike, the Quaker joiner who had lost his wife and son, his apprentice, a white maid, and six slaves in the earthquake, along with "all that [he] ever . . . had in the world." "All those it has pleased the Almighty to save . . . do now think a Negro's house that is daubed with mortar and thatched, the eves hanging down almost to the ground, a pleasant house," he noted in a letter to his brother written on June 19. "Here you may see colonels and great men bowing their bodies to creep into this little hutch, who before had houses fit not only to receive but to feast in an extraordinary manner a prince or King, as great as England's monarch upon occasion, and now by this sad disaster have hardly bread to eat and never a house to be in."[56]

"Lying wet, and wanting medicines, and all conveniences," many died of exposure or disease in the days and weeks that followed. A plague of mosquitoes, brought out by damp weather, tormented them, while clouds of flies, feasting on the bodies washed up on the shore, "sometimes a hundred or two hundred in a heap," spread diseases. By one account the "general sickness" that ensued "all over the island . . . swept away . . . three thousand souls." The illness was exacerbated by a lack of supplies. With the Rio Cobre blocked by the landslide triggered by the earthquake, fresh water was hard to come by and little food was available.[57] "I must live now in a hut, eat yams and plantans for bread, which I could never endure; drink rum-punch and water, which were never pleasing to me," one survivor complained.[58] Among those who died of disease were Judith de Lucena, widow of the Jewish merchant Moises who had died during the earthquake, and Joseph Norris's sister, Weamouth.[59]

On June 14, the Council reconvened. As most of Port Royal remained underwater and the frequent aftershocks, as many as twenty per day according to various accounts, meant that further damage was likely, the meeting was held aboard the *Richard and Sarah*, the 150-ton merchantman formerly commanded by Captain Conning. The first order of business was to formally requisition the ship as the Council's floating headquarters and as a guardship for Port Royal in case of attack by the French. Next, a successor for Reginald Wilson, the port captain, was chosen. John White nominated Thomas Lamb, "collector of the outbound customs," as "a fit person for the execution thereof" and, with his nomination approved by the other eight councilors to attend that morning, Lamb was sworn in. The councilors then turned their attention to the looting and general disorder that continued in Port Royal and around the island as a whole. A proclamation was drawn up warning that any person "privately to hide detaine or secretly convey away any goods moneys negroes plate and gold shall be deemed and taken as thieves . . . and shall be prosecuted with all imaginable severity." Assemblymen and councilors were appointed to each parish to act as adjudicators in the many cases of disputed ownership of salvaged property which had already arisen, while others were charged with organizing for "ten half barrels of flower, four barrels of beefe and six hundred weight of biscuit . . . to be distributed amongst the poor and necessitious people occasioned by the late dreadful calamity."[60]

The Council convened on a further three occasions on the *Richard and Sarah* in the following week. On June 16, the *Swan* was surveyed and was found to be so badly damaged that it was laid up and all its crew transferred to other vessels. Among them was the *Neptune* sloop, pressed into service to carry word of the recent disaster to London along with a request for reinforcements to help defend the island from the French. "We have in the midst of this confusion applied ourselves with all vigour to the restoring of things," the letter informed the Lords of Trade. As well as "protecting the merchants in their fishing on the ruins of their owne houses," the Council assured the Lords that they had been busy "preventing robberies and stealing amongst the ruins, deciding controversies and punishing quarrels . . . sinking floating carcasses . . . takeing care of the sick and wounded . . . [and] feeding and sustaining the necessitious." The Council also ordered the masters of the merchant ships remaining in the roads to sound out a channel from the open sea to the harbor as the earthquake had transformed the underwater geography of the bay. Blame for the loss of the *Swan* was placed on Captain Neville. "We must inform their lordships that could repeated persuasions and even threats have prevailed on . . . [him] to any degree of diligence the Swan . . . [would have] long before been refitted and at Sea against their majesties enemies."

The letter ended with a warning that the island was particularly vulnerable to slave uprisings as well as foreign attack. As "many of the
great gunns of the fortifications are two fathoms under water and . . .
the small arms of the country are generally broake by the fallen
houses," a request was made for at least "three fifth rates with one or
two good forth rates . . . together with four or five hundred land soldiers and all sorts of arms and ammunition."[61]

THERE WAS ONE PIECE of good news for the Jamaicans that June. The
mission to intercept the French privateers who had landed on the
north coast in May had been a resounding success. On June 21, the
five-ship flotilla, led by Captain Oakley of HMS *Guernsey* who had
set out on his mission sixteen days before, returned to Port Royal. The
Guernsey and the hired sloop *Pembroke*, under command of Oakley's
former second, the heroic lieutenant Edward Moses, were laden with
prisoners. Most were French privateers, but there was also a smattering of English turncoats. Former residents of Jamaica who had sided
with the French on the outbreak of war, in some cases due to their
mutual "Papism," they were destined for a brief trial before being hung
at Gallows Point. Their former comrades in arms were to be repatri-
ated. The *San Antonio*, the Spanish ship which had accompanied the
expedition, was filled with wounded, both French and English, a testament to the hard fighting that Oakley's command had endured. Also
present were the *Caesar* and *True Love* sloops. Both bore the scars of
a severe ship-to-ship engagement which had cost them at least sixteen
dead. Topping the butcher's bill was Captain John Griffin. A part-
time wrecker and the *True Love*'s commander, Griffin had received a
mortal wound in the fight.

Captain Oakley's report, delivered to the Council on board the
Richard and Sarah the morning after his arrival, began with the events
of June 6. Having "spied" a strange sail fleeing into the shallows off
Galina Point in St. Mary's Parish, he had ordered Captain Updick of
the *Caesar*, Captain Griffin of the *True Love*, and Lieutenant Moses
commanding the *Pembroke* sloop into shore in pursuit. Although the
stranger had evaded them, Updick, Griffin, and Moses learned from
a resident named Clarke that eighty-five of the enemy had recently

landed in Saint Ann's Parish from a 12-gun ship which had then sailed for Cape Cruz in Cuba to lie in ambush near the shipping lanes for any wayward English merchantmen who happened to pass that way. Oakley arrived at St. Ann's Bay two days later, the master of the *Guernsey* having noted the reverberations of the earthquake of June 7 had lasted a full four minutes before subsiding. Landing a party of armed men equipped with a number of small cannon to deal with the invaders, Oakley dispatched captains Griffin and Updick of the *True Love* and *Caesar* to pursue the French ship to the north, while remaining offshore with Moses and the *Pembroke*.

At dawn on June 11, Oakley's landing party came up with the enemy in the hills above St. Ann's Bay. At anchor offshore, the crews of the *Guernsey* and *Pembroke* watched as cannon and small arms fire were exchanged. Oakley and Moses "made all ye saile . . . [they] could," but before they were able to arrive, the French had surrendered. Seven of the enemy had been killed and seventy-eight captured. The prisoners were taken aboard the *Guernsey* and *Pembroke* for transportation to the jails of Port Royal. The next day, while Oakley and Moses were watering their ships in preparation for departure, the *True Love* and *Caesar* sloops rejoined them. "At 12 of ye clock they came to an anchor and came a bord of us & gave us an account of thaire meeting with the French ship," the *Guernsey's* master recorded. As it transpired, the sloops had endured a "hot ingagement" with the French ship off the southern shore of Cuba. Despite being outgunned, the French commander refused to surrender. After a furious exchange of broadsides which saw sixteen Englishmen killed and Captain Griffin receive a "mortal wound," the French ship caught on fire. The survivors were unable to douse the flames and all eighty-five men aboard were killed. Oakley spent the next six days off St. Ann's Bay while Lieutenant Moses searched the mountains inland for French stragglers. On June 18, Moses returned with eight more prisoners, and the next day the fleet had set sail for Port Royal.[62]

OVER THE NEXT FEW MONTHS, several salvage operations got under way at Port Royal. On June 28, part of the long-awaited naval reinforcement arrived in the shape of HMS *Mordaunt*, a 46-gun fourth

rate. Her captain, Francis Maynard, was put to work raising "six of
the guns that was sunke in Walker's Forth."[63] Elsewhere, the Reverend
Thomas Scrambler, "a beneficed minister" who had been arrested in
May for refusing to swear allegiance to William and Mary, had hired
a diver "to take up Money and Goods he had lost in the great earthquake." Among the objects Scrambler's man salvaged was "a common
glass bottle" covered in seaweed, which eventually made its way into
the possession of Doctor Hans Sloane.[64] The merchant James Wale
was also engaged in a salvaging operation. Fishing the ruins of the
house that had previously belonged to his "Dear bro."-in-law, neighbor, and former business associate, the recently deceased RAC factor
Walter Ruding, Wale snagged an iron chest in a fathom of water and
hauled it to the surface. Inside was "some gould and some broken plate
. . . to ye value of about 200s." Wale was soon to be disappointed.
Rather than being allowed to keep the chest and its contents as well
as a number of Ruding's domestic slaves whom he had rounded up in
the aftermath of the earthquake, all were confiscated by the chief justice Samuel Bernard to cover the debts that Ruding had left behind
him. Whether or not Wale was legally entitled to the goods is unclear
from the surviving documentation. What is apparent is that Wale believed that Bernard, whom he referred to as "a very cunning man," was
less interested in justice than feathering his own nest.[65]

One of the consequences of the earthquake was a resurgence in religious devotion. In an attempt to make sense of the tragedy, a widespread belief arose that the disaster had been inflicted by a wrathful
God intent on punishing the sinners of Port Royal. On June 28, the
Council issued the following proclamation.

Nothing but a generall reformation of manners will stop . . . God
Almightys . . . avenging hand, and make us fitt for the divine pardon and
blessing . . . we doe therefore strictly command & require all military officers
vigorously and impartially to put in execution all those articles of warr that
relates to piety to almighty god or to the preventing the dishonouring him,
either by comon swearing prophanety blashphemey or otherwise and we doe
hereby declare we will severly punish all contempters of this proclomation
and will hereafter heartily endeavour that no person shall have any commission civil or military that shall so little regard the welfaire of this island as to
live in the open habit of any known sin.

The Council also ordered that July 13 was to be "a day of publick fast and humiliation throughout the whole island in respect of God almightys severe judgement." The highest-ranking militia officers in each parish were charged with ensuring that the fast "was strictly observed."[66]

The Quakers were also moved to contemplate the religious significance of the earthquake. Joseph Norris was profoundly affected. Having spent the second half of June attempting to converse with the Lord but finding himself unable, Norris began an extreme fast, "not suffering meat or drink to go into [his] body," and "went forth into the fields to pour out . . . [his] spirit." Eventually, the Lord broke his silence and commanded Norris to go to Port Royal "and in three several places to warn those people to repentance, and to show them the Lord was yet angry and his hand was stretched forth still to destroy all those who would not repent." On July 13, Norris preached at Halfway Tree on the road to Spanish Town where he came to the following conclusion. "I believe and am assured," he wrote to his brother Isaac, then on his way to Port Royal from Philadelphia, "the Lord hath a very large controversy with this island, which a short time may manifest. For he must and will be feared and acknowledged by the whole creation and happy will they be who find a place in him, to hide them in this day of his wrath, be not thou troubled at anything that may happen, but learn to be truly quieted and resigned up to the blessed will of God. Prize his judgments and fly not from them, they are sweet to all those that love and fear him, and only terrible to the wicked and rebellious." By this stage, Norris was dying. Whether this was as a result of an illness or as a consequence of his fast is unclear. "Farewell (but not forever)," he ended his letter, "for I hope in the Lord we may and shall meet in the everlasting Kingdom of righteousness where our love will be much more abound." As it transpired, Joseph was to see his brother one last time. Isaac arrived in Jamaica on September 13. Joseph died the next day.[67]

CHAPTER 8

Inhuman Barbarities

THE FRENCH INVASION OF 1694

June 1692–August 1694

Some of the straggling people that were left behind they tortured, some, and in particular two, they murdered in cold blood, some women they suffered the negroes to violate, some they dug out of their graves, so that more inhuman barbarities were never committed by Turk or infidel.
—Governor Beeston to the Duke of Shrewsbury, August 18, 1694

ALTHOUGH THE EARTHQUAKE of June 1692 did not signal the end of Port Royal's history, the town was never to regain its former glory. As early as June 28, 1692, a proposal put before the Council to replace Port Royal with a new town to be built on the far side of Kingston Bay was approved, and £1,000 was allocated for the purchase of a plot of two hundred acres of land.[1] The site belonged to Colonel William Beeston, a planter, former speaker of the Assembly, judge of the court of common pleas, and militia officer, who had been resident in Jamaica for nineteen years before being exiled to England by Governor Carlisle in 1679 for leading the Assembly's refusal to vote for a bill to grant perpetual revenue to the crown. Beeston had remained in correspondence with his friends and allies in Jamaica over the next fourteen years and had used his wealth and influence to lobby for the plantocracies' interests in Westminster. In 1692, this led to his appointment as Inchiquin's successor as governor of Jamaica. Beeston's commission was passed before Queen Mary in August and approved that September. On March 9, 1693, he returned to Jamaica.[2]

On his arrival, Beeston found that little had been done to develop the land the Council had purchased from him. Although John Goffe had drafted a street layout in August 1692, few residents had taken up the Council's offer to buy lots of land on the coastal strip at a rent of 10 shillings per year. The site remained little more than a refugee camp, diminishing in size as many of those who had fled Port Royal in the immediate aftermath of the earthquake returned home.[3] "The Island is in a ruinous condition," Beeston reported to the Lords of Trade two weeks after taking up his new post; "the people have been very sickly, but health is perfectly recovered, and our arrival has put new life into them."[4] Beeston proved an energetic and dynamic leader: Fort Charles was rebuilt, plans for a new tower to replace Fort Rupert were approved, the embargo on outgoing vessels was lifted, trade revived, and the merchants who had been the lifeblood of the old town returned to construct new houses. Perched on the ruins, the new builds were crammed precariously onto the twenty-five acres of the spit which remained above water—now separated from the mainland by a channel which cut across the area formerly known as the Pallisadoes. The arrival at Barbados of a new fleet from England under Rear Admiral Francis Wheeler, on March 10, 1693, further boosted the islanders' morale. Although Wheeler's attack on Martinique that April ended in failure and a thousand of his men died of sickness and disease, the threat of an immediate assault on Jamaica by the French appeared to have diminished.[5]

In May 1693 the *Mordaunt* raised the wreck of HMS *Swan* from the sunken ruins of old Port Royal. Little remained to salvage. A few guns were hauled up and transferred to the battlements of the town's forts. The frigate's crew had long since dispersed. Most had ended up on HMS *Mordaunt* or *Guernsey*; a lucky few had sailed for London soon after the earthquake in a fast yacht named the *Neptune*, their mission to bring word of the disaster home.[6] On October 8, 1692, they were discharged and paid off at Broadstreet. Among the fortunate was Able Seaman Jonathon Hodge, one of the two brothers pressed aboard the *Swan* at the Nore in December 1689—the genesis of the frigate's ill-fated Caribbean adventure. While Jonathon's brother, Andrew, had been killed in the earthquake along with eleven other crew members, Jonathon had survived. At Broadstreet, he received over £70: the £36,

11s. he was due for two and a half years' service once deductions had been made for the food, clothes, and tobacco he had purchased from the purser, and the £34, 13s. owed to his brother.[7]

Despite being blamed for the loss of the *Swan* by the island Council, the Hodges' former captain, Edward Neville, was cleared of responsibility in February 1694 and awarded the back pay he had accumulated.[8] Nevertheless, Neville spent the next six years out of the Admiralty's favor, until being given the captaincy of HMS *Lincoln* in 1700. A 50-gun fourth rate built at Woolwich five years earlier, the *Lincoln* was being fitted out for a voyage to Virginia. The transatlantic crossing was a difficult one. Having lost one of its masts in a storm on the high seas, it limped into the Bermudas in May 1701, there to refit for several months before pushing on to Williamsburg, where it arrived on September 14. According to a deposition later penned by Captain James Moodie of HMS *Southampton*, also on the North American station, Captain Neville had died four days before the *Lincoln* arrived. The thirty-six-year-old's funeral, held at York on September 15, was attended by a "a great Concourse of people, and a great many of the Militia, on horse and foot." It was somewhat more, perhaps, than the high-born idler deserved.[9]

THE LONG-ANTICIPATED French invasion of Jamaica finally occurred in 1694.[10] The war in the Caribbean had been simmering ever since Rear Admiral Wheeler's departure the year before: French raids against Jamaica had continued, principally against the north coast parishes of St. Ann's and St. Mary's, and the sparsely populated St. Elizabeth's to the southwest. Turncoats continued to play a leading role. Nathaniel Grubbing remained active, as did two others named Lynch and Stapleton. The latter, whom Beeston identified as a Roman Catholic, stole £1,000 and an island sloop one night in March 1694 and sailed off to join the French. In April, Grubbing attacked the plantation of Mrs. Barrow, a minister's widow, in St. Elizabeth's. Not content with plundering "all her negroes, household goods, and all she had," Grubbing tortured Barrow to ensure she was not hiding anything, then sailed back to Petit Guavos with the widow's "maiden daughter, Miss Rachael Barrow, of about fourteen years old." Meanwhile, other privateers led by Lynch and Stapleton raided the north coast. As well as capturing two sloops at anchor, they kidnapped the wife of a local planter named Major Terry and stripped and beat her until Terry agreed to pay a ransom. Several other Jamaican sloops were captured at sea, among them the *Pembroke*, then under the command of Captain Stephen Elliot. Taken while conducting illegal trade with the Spanish in a small bay near Portobelo, the *Pembroke* was carried back to Petit Guavos with a cargo of manufactured goods worth £10,000.[11]

The security situation deteriorated further in May. While cruising eight leagues off Jamaica's easternmost point, HMS *Falcon*, a 36-gun fifth rate sent to Jamaica to replace the *Guernsey* and *Mordaunt*, was attacked by four French men-of-war, three of which—the 44-gun *Hasardeux*, the 50-gun *Envieux*, and the 54-gun *Téméraire*—had recently arrived at Petit Guavos with a merchant convoy from France. Despite being heavily outgunned, the *Falcon's* captain, Mr. Bryan, "fought until many of his men were killed and wounded and the rest forced into the hold. . . . When he yielded the ship," Governor Beeston reported, "there were but two men left on deck besides himself." The *Falcon* was taken back to Petit Guavos, where Bryan was treated with the utmost respect. Having learned of his valiant stand from Rear Admiral Rollon, the commander of the newly arrived French men-of-war, Governor du Casse, presented the Englishman with "a silver-hilted sword and belt . . . and lodged him in one of the best houses in town."[12]

By late May 1694 Governor Beeston was growing increasingly worried. With no sign of the *Falcon*, Jamaica was now reliant on a single aging frigate, HMS *Advice* of 48 guns, and two hired sloops for coastal defense. To make matters worse, earlier that month Beeston had received a letter from a stranger in Curaçao, warning that the French "were preparing a great strength to take Jamaica." On May 31, the rumors were confirmed. Slipping away from his captors in Petit Guavos with two or three others "at the hazard of their lives," Captain Elliot of the *Pembroke* stole a canoe and made his escape over three hundred miles of open water back to Jamaica to inform Beeston of the imminent threat. "The French had recruits of men and men of war from France and Martinique," the governor learned from the "weather-beaten" Englishman. "They had taken the *Faulcon* . . . [and] had drawn up . . . twenty sail of ships and vessels, and three thousand men, and were designed to take this island, and in order to it, monsieur Ducas the governor was coming with them: that Stapleton, Lynch, and others . . . that had deserted from us, had told him he would meet with but little difficulty . . . for the fortifications at Port-Royal were down since the earthquake, and two thousand men would take that place."[13]

Beeston responded with characteristic energy. The night of Elliot's arrival, he called an extraordinary meeting of the Council of War. Martial law was declared; the Assembly, then standing, was immediately dissolved; a proclamation was read throughout the plantations, stipulating that any slave who killed a Frenchman in the forthcoming assault would be freed as a reward (hundreds were subsequently recruited); all retired militia officers were called back to active duty; standing patrols of horse and foot were organized for Guanaboa Vale and Sixteen Mile Walk; the repairs being made to Fort Charles were brought to completion; two new batteries of culverin were set up at Port Royal, and barricades were thrown up in the streets. On June 6, further measures were taken. Knowing that he could not challenge the enemy at sea and that the 1,630 men at his disposal were not enough to guard the entire coastline, Beeston made a radical decision: to abandon the north, east, and west coasts to the enemy and concentrate his forces in the Jamaican heartland—the central southern shore. A civilian exodus ensued. While some of the more stubborn residents of the parishes to be abandoned chose to "trust . . . to the good nature of the French," the majority converged on Port Royal, Spanish Town, Carlisle Town, Old Harbour, and Withywood, bringing their "cattle, negroes, etc." along with them. The guns of Fort William at Port Morant were spiked and the round shot buried. Beeston had a fireship fitted out at the cost of £500. A sloop was dispatched to England begging the Lords of Trade for six men-of-war and at least 1,000 soldiers; salt provisions and flour were stockpiled. Fifty slaves were added to the crew of HMS *Advice,* and it and all the armed merchantmen then at Port Royal were anchored in line across the mouth of the bay, their broadsides facing the sea approaches. Small bands of militia were posted in the outlying parishes to report on enemy movements, while the majority were concentrated in the towns of the central southern shore, where breastworks were constructed by requisitioned slaves.[14]

On the morning of Sunday, June 17, the French fleet was spotted off Port Royal. Twenty-two sail strong and carrying 3,164 privateers and French colonists, it made for a daunting sight. Beeston, who heard the news at Spanish Town, feared that the French would attack Port Royal immediately.[15] The enemy, however, remained undecided. On board the flagship, the aging 55-gun *Téméraire*, a heated debate was in progress. While Governor du Casse advocated an immediate attack on Port Royal, his flag captain, Rear Admiral Rollon, disagreed. Once the fleet was committed to the roads, the sea breeze would ensure there would be no coming out again. Either victory would be secured or the entire French fleet would be lost. As it was apparent that the English had been forewarned, Rollon refused to take such responsibility; the fleet sailed east instead. Later that day, eight of their ships anchored off Port Morant. The other fourteen sailed into Cow Bay, "a bad" anchorage, according to Rollon's report, "full of lost anchors and isolated rocks" fifteen miles to the east of Port Royal.[16]

Eight hundred men were landed at Cow Bay. Led by Charles François Le Vasseur de Beauregard, one of Petit Guavos' leading privateers, and the much-feared Dutchman Laurens de Graff, "they fell to . . . plunder[ing]," Beeston recalled. They "burnt and destroyed all before them eastward, killed all the cattle . . . and fowls, drove flocks of sheep into houses and . . . fired them, burnt the canes, pulled up the . . . herbs, and cut down the . . . fruit-trees. Some of the straggling people that were left behind they tortured, particularly Charles Barber; and James Newcastle they murdered in cold blood after a day's quarter: Some women they suffered the negroes to violate, and some they dug out of their graves . . . there were never more inhuman barbarities committed by any Turks or infidels in the world; and what they could not carry away they destroyed." Meanwhile, forty-five small vessels were dispatched from the French fleet. Sailing round Point Morant to St. Mary's and St. George's, their crews disembarked and systematically plundered the parishes' largest plantations.[17]

On Thursday, June 23, a squall off Port Morant caused havoc among the eight French ships at anchor. The *Téméraire* and one other slipped their cables and were blown to the west. Finding it impossible to beat back up against the wind and current and running low on fresh water, Rear Admiral Rollon sailed westward to Bluefield's Bay instead. Sixty men were landed and soon afterward set upon by a militia detachment commanded by Major Bernart Andreis. One of Andreis's men was killed and two others were wounded. Having also sustained casualties, Rollon broke off the encounter. Signaling his men to board their ships, he upped anchor and set sail, leaving behind some freshly butchered beef and plundered cattle. The lost livestock were the least of du Casse's worries. With the wind against him and plagued by the deliberately contradictory advice offered by a succession of local "informants," he would be unable to rejoin the fleet until they were about to leave Jamaica.[18]

Beeston, meanwhile, remained at Spanish Town, content to wait for the enemy to make the first move. "We now expect them daily to attack us," he wrote to Sir John Trenchard, the secretary of state, on June 23,

and we shall do our best to defend ourselves. . . . Our people seem hearty yet, but time will weary them out . . . [and] I fear to think of the consequences to people who live well here but have nothing anywhere else. . . . I beg you to lay . . . our condition before the King and Council that relief may be sent to us and advice of its coming dispatched in good time; otherwise I doubt my ability to prevent the people from complying with the enemy in order to save . . . their property. . . . The relieving force must be speedy and . . . considerable, at least six men-of-war and a thousand or twelve hundred soldiers; else all will be lost, for the French will never leave us now till they conquer or we beat them off the coast. This is a matter of great moment, and I hope for your utmost favour herein.[19]

By the first week of July, with the French still anchored off Port Morant and Cow Bay, and landing parties continuing to ravage the countryside of St. David's, St. George's, St. Thomas's, and St. Mary's, English morale took a turn for the worse.[20] On July 2, Beeston sent another dispatch to England, once more begging for speedy relief. The next morning the Council ordered the arrest of a certain Captain Usher Tyrrell "for insubordination and conniving at desertion," and on July 5, "four or five armed Irish" with the garrison at Port Royal "contrived to run away to the" French. "The plot was betrayed by one of them," Beeston reported, "and the ringleader tried by court martial and executed."[21] Despite such events, the governor himself was decidedly more optimistic about Jamaica's long-term prospects than he had been in June. "I think that if they had any hopes of carrying the island," he informed the Lords of Trade in a letter written on July 7, "they would not be so barbarous, for they spare nothing alive, except mankind, and those they punish and torture. They burn and destroy all that will burn, fill the wells with dead cattle and do all the mischief they can."[22]

By mid-July the French had done all the damage they could in the eastern parishes. The plantations had been fired, the slaves and livestock that had been left behind by the English had either fled into the mountains or been killed or captured, the walls of Fort William had been torn down, and the carriages of the seventeen guns mounted on the walls had been burned. On July 16, Graff and Beauregard gave the order to reembark. The next morning part of the French fleet was seen off Port Royal and by that afternoon twenty sail had gathered. Among them was HMS *Falcon*, the English frigate captured by Rollon back in May. By late afternoon the French had sailed back to Cow Bay. The troops were landed and a line of bivouac fires, visible from the battlements of Fort Charles, were lit. Beeston, safely ensconced in Spanish Town, was unconcerned. "[They did this] to amuse us," the governor wrote, "[to give] us cause to think they designed to try to force the pass in St. Andrew's." That night the governor's suspicions were proved correct. Under cover of darkness, the French reembarked. Leaving their campfires burning to confuse the English, the entire fleet, with the exception of three of the largest ships, sailed westward toward Vere. On the morning of July 18, Beeston "concluded their design was to surprize Carlisle-Bay." Two troops of horse and part of the infantry regiment of St. Catherine's were ordered to make the thirty-six-mile march from Spanish Town to reinforce the two hundred militia under Colonel Thomas Sutton who were already stationed there. Part of the regiment of Clarendon Parish, then at Port Royal, was also dispatched, along with a section of the regiment of St. Dorothy's, at that time based in Old Harbour, less than twenty miles away from Carlisle Bay as the crow flies. Those on horseback arrived at ten o'clock that night. The infantry would not make it until the next morning.[23]

Beeston's instincts proved right yet again. At mid-afternoon on July 18, the French arrived at Carlisle Bay. Edward Daniel, the captain of a Royal African Company vessel named the *Mediterranean*, watched them approach. Having recently arrived in Jamaica from West Africa with a cargo of 470 slaves, Daniel had been driven into Carlisle Bay by the same contrary winds which were preventing Rollon and the *Téméraire* from rejoining the French fleet.[24] Seeing that there was no escape from the French fleet, Daniel disembarked and set fire to the *Mediterranean*. He and his forty-strong crew then marched inland with the slaves to reinforce Colonel Sutton, who had drawn up his militia, now numbering "two hundred and fifty men, besides blacks," behind an "ill-made" breastwork whose embrasures mounted twelve cannon. Beeston later criticized Sutton for the positioning of his men. "On the south was the sea," the governor explained, "on the west a large river, on the north a village of houses, and on the east they had left a wood standing." To make matters worse, Sutton had "made no provisions for the men." The planter was showing his shortcomings as a military commander. With his escape route barred by the wood, the village, and the Rio Minho, his men would be slaughtered should they be forced to retreat.[25]

The French landed before dawn on July 19. Rather than tackle the English defenders head-on, Beauregard and Graff's men, who numbered some 1,500, disembarked one and a half miles to the east of Sutton's position. After seeing off a small English scouting party, who fired upon them before falling back to the breastwork, the French advanced through a screen of woodland, Beauregard leading the privateers in the vanguard, while Graff commanded the main body of colonists bringing up the rear. Hidden in their approach, the privateers emerged from cover to charge "very hotly" against Sutton's left flank at about 10 o'clock that morning. "There was a hot fire on both sides for a time," one witness later recalled. The cannon, discharged on the first approach of the French, did some execution, and "many of the [English] officers and most of the men fought bravely and killed many of the enemy." Nevertheless "the French officers [continued] forcing their men on," and when Graff's men came to the aid of Beauregard's, the tide turned. Colonel Lionel Claybourne and Captain John Vassel of the St. Elizabeth Regiment and Lieutenant Colonel Smart and

Lieutenant William Dawkins of the Clarendon Regiment were killed along with several of their men. Many others were wounded. The survivors broke and fled to the west. Several were killed or taken prisoner during the pursuit: twenty-two casualties by English accounts; 360 according to the French. Four of the militia's colors and all one hundred and fifty of their horses, saddled and bridled nearby, were also captured. With their line of withdrawal blocked by the Rio Minho, the English retreat was on the verge of becoming a rout: several men were drowned attempting to cross, while a crush of panicked and defeated militia formed on the near bank. Just as all seemed lost, the infantry reinforcements that Beeston had ordered from Port Royal arrived. Despite being "weary, lame and exhausted" following their thirty-mile overnight march, the latecomers, led by Captain Rakestead, "warmly" charged the French right. The action was pursued "with such gallantry" that Rakestead and his men bought their comrades enough time to cross the Minho without suffering further casualties.[26]

Following the battle, both sides withdrew. The French set up camp at the mouth of the Rio Minho, while the English occupied several fortified great houses farther up the valley. For the next two days, aside from a few minor skirmishes between the lines, neither side attempted to advance. The French plundered the town of Withywood and burned the properties straddling the small strip of coastline that they had retained, while the thoughts of several of the senior English commanders turned to the possibility of defeat. With their own plantations under a day's march from the French lines, Thomas Sutton and his neighbor and fellow planter, Francis Blackmore, contacted the enemy seeking to secure their own property should the colony fall to the French. Both planters were later arrested by Beeston for their betrayal and suspended from the island Council.[27]

On July 22, the French made one final attack. Their assault fell against one of the English outposts, "a brick house of one Mr. Hubbard," which had been occupied by Major Richard Lloyd and twenty-five militia. Lloyd, who it will be remembered was one of the chief protagonists of the Assembly of 1691, was well prepared. His men, cavalry troopers from the regiment of Port Royal, were "well-provided with arms, ammunition, water, and conveniences," and the fortified house was ideal for defense. The French attacked "smartly" but suffered heavy losses: several of their best officers were killed along with a number of their men. A few defenders also fell, but when a second militia detachment came to Lloyd's aid, the enemy were "beat[en] . . . off" and the English set about "plunder[ing] the dead." Expecting the French to renew their attack the following morning, Lloyd put fifty men into Hubbard's house on the night of July 22. The rest of the militia in the area, then numbering some 650, were positioned to ambush the enemy on their approach. The French, however, had had enough. English resistance was mounting; their leader, Governor du Casse, was still absent in the wind-bound *Téméraire*; and they had already lost as many as 350 killed or wounded. There seemed little possibility of conquering the entire island and therefore no reason to remain. An even more pressing cause for their departure was the spread of disease. While Beeston's estimate of French casualties in battle noted above seems exaggerated, their losses to sickness were undoubtedly higher: at least two hundred had succumbed on the *Envieux* and the *Téméraire* alone. Rear Admiral Rollon was among the dead, and by the time of the reverse at Hubbard's perhaps as many as seven hundred in total had perished. On July 24, the fleet set sail. Pausing briefly at Port Morant and Legoane to take on wood and water and to land their prisoners whom they could no longer afford to feed, the French departed Jamaica four days later and arrived at Petit Guavos on August 14.[28]

English losses had also been severe. "We have had . . . killed and wounded about a hundred men of all sorts, Christians, Jews, and negroes," Beeston recorded. "Fifty sugar works have been destroyed, besides many plantations in St. Thomas's, St. David's, and St. Mary's, and above a hundred burnt . . . in the parishes of Vere and St. George's."[29] According to Major Richard Lloyd, five rum distilleries, twenty-one cotton works, fifty-four indigo walks, and eleven provisions' plantations had also been put to the torch. Many of Jamaica's most prominent players, including former acting governor John White and the RAC agent Charles Penhallow, had lost property, while others, such as the Vassels and Dawkins, had had family members killed. Approximately 1,600 slaves, worth somewhere in the region of £40,000, had been captured and spirited back to Hispaniola. Another three hundred or so had taken advantage of the chaos to flee into the mountains and join the maroons.[30] Nevertheless, the repulse of the French had been a considerable achievement: the militia had acquitted themselves well as had the slaves forcibly pressed into service, at least fourteen of whom had earned their freedom by killing Frenchmen. The islanders' morale and sense of unity had received a considerable boost; Beeston had proved himself a capable leader, not afraid of taking risks; and fear of the French had waned. Perhaps the most significant consequence of the campaign was that the English government had been awakened to the very real risk of losing Jamaica. In early 1695 a fleet was dispatched carrying 1,800 regular troops assigned to garrison the island. Their transports were convoyed by no less than five frigates. Even following the Treaty of Ryswick, which brought the Nine Years' War to a close in 1697, the men-of-war were to remain. Jamaica would not be left unguarded again.[31]

Epilogue

THE PENULTIMATE PERIOD of the Nine Years' War saw the English take the offensive in the Caribbean. In late 1694 Beeston launched a retaliatory raid against Hispaniola. The meager forces the governor had managed to scrape together—three men-of-war, two barks, and a fireship—were unable to achieve anything significant. Having bombarded the coastal village of Esterre on October 11, and burned some privateers' huts on the beach at Cow Island, they returned home. Captain William Harman, the commander of the flagship HMS *Advice* died on October 16 of the wounds he had received.[1]

In mid-1695, the reinforcements sent out to the Caribbean from England were deployed in a second offensive against Hispaniola, organized in concert with the Spanish. After a voyage plagued by disease and infighting between the chief navy and army commanders, Commodore Robert Wilmot and Colonel Luke Lillington, the expeditionary force proceeded to the capital of Santo Domingo where a plan for a joint attack on French Hispaniola was arranged with the Spanish governor, Gil Correoso Catalán. On May 24, the combined army crossed the border into French territory. Having dispersed the heavily outnumbered defenders led by Laurens de Graff, the allies occupied Cap François on May 29, and the town of Port de Paix was besieged on June 25. The French defenders surrendered on July 15. The victors fell out over the spoils, thus bringing an end not only to the expedition but also to Beeston's hopes that the entire French colony would be conquered once and for all.[2]

The raids which had characterized Jamaica's involvement in the war prior to du Casse's invasion continued following the departure of Wilmot's fleet for England in September 1695. At the forefront of several minor actions was the former lieutenant of the *Guernsey*, Edward Moses. As commander of the 48-gun HMS *Reserve*, Moses launched a successful raid against Petit Guavos in March 1696. Having forced the French to destroy a 20-gun ship, he captured a sloop on his return to Jamaica. Later that year, Moses captured an 18-gun French privateer off Port Morant. In the action he had six men killed and twelve wounded and was shot through the shoulder and thigh.[3]

The final year of the war saw the arrival of a large French expeditionary force. Commanded by Admiral Bernard Jean-Louis de Saint Jean, Baron de Pointis, it consisted of twelve men-of-war, including an 84-gun flagship, the *Sceptre*, and a number of transports on board of which were 1,750 soldiers equipped with a large siege train. Pointis's aim was to secure a major prize before a peace treaty, then being negotiated back in Europe, could be concluded. Despite Governor du Casse's preference for an attack against Portobelo, Pointis chose the Spanish city of Cartagena as his principal objective. Considerably less formidable than it had once been, the city was captured on May 4, 1697, with the loss of only sixty men. Plunder worth nine million French crowns was extracted from the inhabitants before the French sailed away, leaving Cartagena to be reoccupied by the Spanish. The Treaty of Ryswick, signed that September in the Dutch Republic, brought an end to the Nine Years' War. By the terms agreed to, most of the territories captured during the conflict were returned to the countries that had occupied them prior to the outbreak of war.[4]

BY THE TIME HOSTILITIES broke out again between the English and the French in 1702, another old threat to the Jamaican plantocracy had remerged. The Windward Maroons, having "mightily increased in their numbers" through the steady arrival of a number of runaways, not least during the French invasion of 1694, had become "so bold [as] to come down armed and attack" and "destroy . . . one or two" isolated settlements in St. Thomas.[5] Beeston's temporary replacement as governor, the earthquake survivor and former colonel of the Port Royal militia Peter Beckford, "sent out 4 parties in pursuit of them." One, consisting of just twenty men, "came up with the . . . [Windwards'] main body of 300" in the Blue Mountains in September 1702. After an engagement of five or six hours, during which three of the militia were wounded and several of the maroons killed or captured, the surviving fugitives, having expended all their ammunition, fled deeper into the mountains. "They had . . . a Town and above 100 acres of land well planted with provisions," Beckford later informed the Lords of Trade. "This had been their nest . . . I believe for some years, but we have burnt their settlements, and I have ordered one of the parties to post themselves there, and the other three to pursue . . . they shall not rest till they are totally destroyed or reduced."[6]

Meanwhile, Cudjoe and the rest of the Coromantee escapees from Sutton's had established themselves in the wilds of the Cockpit Country. Merging with the remnants of previous groups to have rebelled, such as the survivors of Lobby's Rebellion in 1673, Cudjoe's band formed the nucleus of the group that would come to be known as the Leeward Maroons. They had endured a peripatetic existence throughout the 1690s. On the run from the militia and bounty hunters, Cudjoe had been forced to abandon several temporary strongholds. Nevertheless, the survivors endured and by the end of the decade, a strong, autocratic polity had emerged which would pose more of a threat to the island's plantocracy in the long term than their less-well-organized Windward peers. Governed by a mixture of strict military discipline and traditional Akan law, the Leeward Maroons combined their expertise of West African medicinal plants and crops with local knowledge picked up from earlier escapees and, perhaps, from the island's last surviving Tainos. Essentials that could not be acquired— principally arms, ammunition, and slave women—were captured in raids on the remote plantations of St. Elizabeth and Westmoreland Parishes (the latter having been established in 1703). Other goods could be acquired in the slave markets held throughout the island most Sundays. While the women, especially those seized as concubines, endured a lowly existence of domestic and agricultural drudgery, the men formed a proud warrior caste. Roaming their territory, hunting and fishing and honing their martial skills, they communicated over long distances with signal drums, conch shells, or cow horns. Around 1700 one of Cudjoe's many wives gave birth to a son. Also named Cudjoe, in time the child would go on to become the new leader of the Leeward Maroons. His exploits were to eclipse even those of his father.[7]

In 1703 Port Royal suffered a further setback. At about noon on January 9, a fire broke out in a wharfside warehouse. The flames spread rapidly in the densely packed streets. Gunpowder stores added to the blaze, while the American shingles with which a number of houses had recently been roofed proved highly flammable. Leaping from building to building, the conflagration engulfed the entire town. Dozens were burned to death. Only the forts were spared due to the efforts of their garrisons. In the aftermath, while the survivors were accommodated in the warships of Rear Admiral Whetstone, whose fleet was based at Port Royal to fight the French in the War of Spanish Succession, the Council met in an emergency session. Provisions were granted for the relief of the poor; orders were given to prosecute looters; boats and carts were impressed for porterage. Offers of help came in from neighboring colonies, while the Council debated whether to rebuild Port Royal or abandon it. On January 24, a bill was passed which prohibited the town's reconstruction. Kingston, which had thus far failed to grow as anticipated in the aftermath of the earthquake of 1692, was declared the chief seat of trade in Port Royal's stead.[8]

The old town refused to die. A number of residents opposed the bill. Led by the redoubtable Peter Beckford, they put in a counterproposal for its rebuilding. Citing the relative difficulty of access for shipping at Kingston, as well as its unhealthy location – "between a great swamp . . . of standing stinking water . . . and the Trade Winds [which] blew noisome smells from the ships, swamps and mangroves," they also raised the old fear that if Port Royal were abandoned, its seafaring inhabitants would desert the island and resettle with the French. In defiance of the Council's bill, several ex-residents started to rebuild.[9] By May, fifty houses, four or five taverns, and a butcher's shop had been constructed; by August some three hundred families were in residence. Port Royal continued to grow over the first decade of the eighteenth century and eventually the Council's bill prohibiting its reconstruction was overturned by an edict by Queen Anne.[10]

THOMAS SUTTON died on November 15, 1710. Although he had never fully recovered from the financial losses he incurred during the rebellion of 1690, since the French invasion of 1694 Sutton's tarnished reputation had improved somewhat. While he was never to rejoin the Council, he had been elected as one of Vere's two Assembly members in 1695 and was chosen as an Assembly member for Clarendon Parish and speaker of the Assembly in 1698. He was elected Assembly member for Port Royal in 1703 and again in 1706 and one of the streets of the new city of Kingston was named after him.[11] When he died at the age of seventy-two, Thomas Sutton was interred in the Parish Church at Vere. In his will, which he had composed three years before, Sutton left his plantation at Withywood and the fifty acres he owned at Yarmouth to his "beloved wife," Judith; the rest of his lands he bequeathed to his eldest son and heir, John, whom he desired to be educated in England. Sutton's daughters, Sarah and Anna, were left £100 each, while his daughter-in-law, Elizabeth Pennant, was granted £150. At his death, Sutton owned forty-seven slaves. It was a far cry from the days before the revolt when he had been the island's principal exponent of plantation slavery, with five hundred chattels subject to his will.[12]

IN THE SECOND and third decades of the eighteenth century, Port Royal suffered two further blows. On August 28, 1712, a severe hurricane damaged much of the shipping in the roads. Exactly ten years later, after two days and nights of "prodigious Lightnings and Thunder," an even more crippling hurricane swept the island for fourteen hours.[13] "The calamity wee are under is unexpressible," the governor, Nicholas Lawes, a former Council member under Inchiquin, informed the Lords of Trade the following month. "Many of our houses are blown down . . . most of the shiping in our harbours are destroyed and many hundreds of people particularly at the town of Port Royall have lost their lives by the fall of houses and inundation of the sea . . . the damage done to the Plantations throughout the whole country is inconceivable. H.M. fortifications has likewise suffered very much . . . The King's house and most of the publick buildings . . . are almost irrepairable." Roughly four hundred were killed in Port Royal alone, perhaps the most tragic deaths being those of two hundred slaves, newly arrived from Africa, who drowned when the Guineaman they were shackled on board of foundered in the storm.[14]

Meanwhile, in the Cockpit Country, Cudjoe's son and namesake had come of age. "A bold, skilful, and enterprising man," characterized by his ruthlessness and bent for realpolitik, Cudjoe inherited his father's mantle as the new leader of the Leeward Maroons in the mid-1720s. It was a complex time in the history of Anglo-Maroon relations. As all available land in the south of Jamaica had long since been allocated, new planters were beginning to exploit the fertile plains of the island's northern coast, a move which brought them into competition with both the Leeward and Windward Maroons. "Murders were daily committed, plantations [were] burnt and deserted" and soon all the residents were living "in dread both of the Rebels [and of] mutinies in their own Plantations." Throughout the mid and late 1720s bands of militia and armed bounty hunters and volunteers were dispatched into the mountains to hunt the rebels down.[15] The letters of the Duke of Portland, governor from 1721–1726; acting governor John Ayscough (1726–1728); and Governor Robert Hunter (1728–1734), make frequent references to the difficulties of such operations.[16] Nevertheless, some successes were achieved. In June 1729, Simon Booth, a civilian headhunter of some repute, "did kill one man and two women" in the Porus region on the border of Clarendon and Manchester Parishes. "[They] were marked TS, with a heart," an official report noted, "which was Sutton's work and [were] supposed to [have] be[en involved] in Sutton's rebellion . . . and out ever since." Booth also took several other captives, among them "an old negro woman of Colonel Sutton's, and out since that rebellion; besides seven children, the eldest not above seven years old."[17]

By 1730 the Windward and Leeward Maroons had become so powerful that the security of the island was seriously threatened. "[They] are grown to the height of insolence," Governor Hunter warned the Assembly that June. "[The] frontiers . . . are no longer in any sort of security, [and] must be deserted, and then the danger must spread and come nearer [to the main areas of white settlement]." A further cause for concern were the rumors of Spanish collusion. In return for military aid, it was said that the maroons were planning to turn over the colony to the governor of "Cracas" once the British had been expelled. By 1731 Governor Hunter was warning that the maroons' numbers had reached anything up to 10,000. Although it may have been an exaggeration, the figure is indicative of how serious the situation had become. London reacted swiftly to the news. Two regiments of regulars were dispatched to Jamaica from Gibraltar, their mission to bring an end to the maroon threat once and for all.[18]

The First Maroon War, as it was later called, proved much more difficult than the English government had anticipated. The Jamaican terrain was inhospitable; tropical illnesses decimated the ranks of the unseasoned regulars; and Cudjoe's and the Windward Maroons' use of hit and run tactics and their refusal to stand and fight unless assured of victory exasperated the redcoats and island militia alike. Additionally, the maroons were kept abreast of the enemies' movements via a network of informers among the plantation slaves, while their knowledge of their territory was only matched by their adversaries' ignorance. Although the regulars burned several abandoned settlements and killed and captured a few stragglers, in the opening years they failed to achieve a decisive breakthrough while also suffering frequent defeats themselves.[19]

In April 1734, with Jamaica once again under the leadership of acting governor John Ayscough following Hunter's death, the pro-government forces achieved their first victory of note. After a five-day battle with heavy casualties on both sides, the Windward Maroons' capital of Nanny Town, situated in the foothills of the Blue Mountains, was captured.[20] The surviving Windward Maroons split into two groups, one of which undertook an arduous cross-country trek across the spine of Jamaica to link up with Cudjoe's men in the Cockpit Country. The details of the two groups' meeting, recorded in an anonymous account held among the papers of eighteenth-century Jamaican historian Edward Long, provide a rare insight into Cudjoe's mindset. As well as insisting that he did not possess sufficient supplies to support the newcomers, Cudjoe reportedly blamed them for provoking the war with the whites by their "great indiscretion" previous to the arrival of the British regulars, "and told them it was a rule with him always not to provoke the white people unless forced to it." Cudjoe also showed the Windward Maroons "several graves where he said people were buried whom he had executed for murdering white men contrary to his orders and said the [Windward Maroons'] barbarous and unreasonable cruelty and insolence to the white people was the cause of their fitting out parties who would in time destroy them all."[21]

As the war dragged on, the whites considered suing for peace. In 1734, having been advised by the Board of Trade to pursue such a course, Governor Hunter sent a delegate named Bevil Granville into the mountains. When Granville eventually found a maroon with whom to negotiate, however, he was informed that they would never trust a white man. A second attempt made two years later proved equally unsuccessful, and it wasn't until 1738, under the governorship of Edward Trelawny (1738–1752), that Cudjoe agreed to come to terms. In February of the following year he met Colonel John Guthrie, a local militia commander said to be respected by the maroons for his honesty and skills as a woodsman, in a valley between the two sides' armed camps. After protracted negotiations, a fifteen-point treaty was signed on March 1, 1738.[22]

The terms ensured the liberty and freedom of Cudjoe and all his followers and granted them the possession of a swath of land totaling 1,500 acres. The maroons were also given hunting rights throughout the island as long as they kept at least three miles from all white settlements. They were granted permission to trade in white markets providing licenses were first obtained, and were given access to Jamaican law should their rights be infringed by a white resident. Cudjoe was given autonomy over all legal proceedings concerning his own people, apart from those guilty of murder, and two white ambassadors were permanently based in Cudjoe's capital of Accompong Town to act as intermediaries. To maintain the rights conceded them, the Leeward Maroons were required to aid the English in any future wars against external enemies and to return any runaway slaves who might seek shelter with them. On learning of this final clause, several of Cudjoe's followers plotted to overthrow their leader. They viewed the treaty as a shameful and unnecessary submission and a betrayal of those who would seek their freedom in the future. Learning of the scheme, Cudjoe had the four ringleaders arrested and sent to Spanish Town for trial. Two were condemned to death. The others were sentenced to transportation. As an act of good faith, Governor Trelawny

"Old Cudjoe making peace." Cudjoe was the son of an Akan warrior who led an insurrection out of Thomas Sutton's plantation in Clarendon in 1690, Jamaica's biggest slave revolt of the time. By the mid-eighteenth century, Cudjoe and his adherents were so well-entrenched in the Cockpit Country that the British were forced to negotiate. (Robert Charles Dallas, *The History of the Maroons*, 1803)

returned the four men to Cudjoe to do with as he wished. Cudjoe hung those who had been condemned to death and returned the other two, insisting that they be transported as initially prescribed. Trelawny, suitably impressed by his new ally's zeal, promptly complied.[23]

MEANWHILE, after the hurricane of 1722 Kingston eclipsed Port Royal as Jamaica's principal port and commercial center. After three major disasters in thirty years, even the most determined would-be residents were deterred from resettling at Cagway Point. By the mid-eighteenth century, while Kingston grew and prospered from the profits of the all-important sugar, rum, and slave trades (businesses worth some five times more than they had been in 1700), Port Royal entered a new phase in its history—as a Royal Navy base. The most celebrated event in this period came during the latter stages of the American War of Independence. Encouraged by the British defeat at Saratoga in 1777, the French sided with the Americans the following year. They were joined by the Spanish in 1778, and in 1779 the English declared war on the Dutch. As a result, the focus of the conflict switched from the North American mainland to the Caribbean, a region considered much more significant in economic terms. With the Royal Navy split between blockading the ports of New England and maintaining their presence in the West Indies, the French gained the upper hand. Between 1778 and 1782, with the aid of their Spanish allies, they captured the British colonies of Dominica, Grenada, Saint Vincent, Montserrat, Tobago, St. Kitts, and the Turks and Caicos. Jamaica was the next target on their list.

The first threat of invasion came in mid-1779. The arrival of the French admiral Charles-Hector Comte d'Estaing at Hispaniola with a fleet said to number 125 vessels led Rear Admiral Sir Peter Parker, then commander in chief of the Jamaica Station, to prepare for the worst. Troops and money were levied and repairs carried out to Port Royal's Fort Charles, then under the command of a promising twenty-year-old Royal Navy post captain by the name of Horatio Nelson. "We expect to have 500 [men] in [the] Fort," Nelson wrote on August 12, 1779. "[HMS] *Lion, Salisbury, Charon,* and *Janus,* [are moored] in a line from the Point to the outer shoal; *Ruby* and *Bristol* in the narrows going to Kingston, to rake any ships that may attack Fort Augusta; *Pomanan* and *Speke* Indiaman above Rock Fort, and *Lowestoffe* at the end of the dockwall."[24] Nevertheless, the invasion failed to materialize. The Comte d'Estaing sailed on to North America, where his career was blighted by the difficulties he encountered working alongside his "uncouth" revolutionary allies, while Nelson, having fallen ill with malaria, was nursed at Port Royal by a black "doctoress" named Cubah Cornwallis, before returning to Europe and greater things.

By 1782, following British defeat at the Battle of the Chesapeake the previous year, Jamaica was once more under threat. Aside from Barbados, St. Lucia, and Antigua, the island was the only Caribbean possession remaining in British hands, an anomaly that the Comte de Grasse, d'Estaing's replacement as commander in chief of French naval forces in the theater, and his Spanish ally, Francisco Saavedra de Sangronis, were determined to rectify. At Port Royal, all was hustle and bustle in anticipation of the French descent, but the British naval commander, Admiral Sir George Rodney, was determined to take the initiative. After learning that de Grasse had left Martinique with thirty-five ships of the line on April 7, Rodney set out to intercept them before they could join forces with their Spanish allies. Following an indecisive encounter on April 9, battle was joined three days later off a group of islets known as the Saints from which the ensuing encounter received its name. Aided by the aggressive tactics which characterized the Royal Navy of the time, and two recent technological advances—the use of the short-range yet high-calibre carronade, and the copper sheathing applied to his ships' hulls, Rodney won a decisive victory. By sunset four French ships of the line had been captured. Another had been destroyed and an estimated three thousand Frenchmen killed or wounded and five thousand others captured, including de Grasse himself. The French plan to invade Jamaica had been thwarted yet again. The colony would remain in British hands.[25]

FOLLOWING THE BRITISH defeat in the American War of Independence in 1783, Jamaica entered a period of economic decline. Sugar prices fell as the growth of Cuban exports added to an already glutted market, and plantation owners increasingly chose to live in England and leave their Jamaican affairs in the hands of locally based overseers. This latter trend led to a climate of short-termism: with little incentive to introduce costly improvements which would lower immediate returns, the overseers allowed buildings to fall into disrepair, new lands were seldom opened up to cultivation because of the large initial outlay required, and old fields became exhausted. Many overseers stole from their employers, and the slaves on estates owned by absentee landlords also suffered. Most damaging of all was the disastrous effect on triangular trade of the loss of the American colonies. The ships from New England, Rhode Island, Virginia, the Carolinas, and New York which had formerly supplied Jamaica with provisions and building materials were now prohibited from entering her ports by the Navigation Acts. Hopes that American shipping would be replaced by Canadian and Irish vessels proved wishful thinking; prices of provisions rose dramatically and the plantations became increasingly unviable as a result.[26]

The French Revolution of 1789 proved a mixed blessing for the Jamaican plantocracy. Whilst the ideologies of *liberté, égalité,* and *fraternité* inspired rebellion among the plantation slaves, the Haitian Revolution, which came about as an indirect result of events in Paris, led to a dramatic decline in the sugar production of the French Caribbean. The ensuing rise in sugar prices gave a new lease of life to the British colonies. Buoyed by the introduction of Bourbon cane, a new pest-resistant variety, Jamaican sugar production soared, and the island was once again declared Britain's "principal source of national opulence."[27]

The good times were not to last. In Britain, the idea that slavery was a fundamentally immoral practice was rapidly gaining ground. The principal orchestrator was Granville Sharp, an English clergyman's son who had an epiphany one day in 1765 when walking the streets of London and had since dedicated his life to the cause of abolition. Sharp's first success came in 1772 when Chief Justice Lord Mansfield declared slavery contrary to the laws of England, a judgment which meant that any slave who set foot in the British Isles was legally a free man. Elsewhere in the British Empire, however, the trade continued unabated.

Another important step toward abolition came in 1783 with the notorious case of the *Zong,* a slave ship owned by a Liverpool syndicate. In November 1781, when nearing their destination of Black River on the north coast of Jamaica, the crew of the *Zong* made a serious error of navigation. Having mistaken the Jamaican shoreline for that of Hispaniola, they had continued on a westerly course, only realizing their mistake two days later when they were some 300 miles leeward of Jamaica. Having already lost 62 of the 442 Africans loaded that August at Accra on the Gold Coast, and believing that the water supply remaining on the ship was insufficient to transport the remainder to Jamaica, the crew voted to throw half of the remaining Africans overboard. The decision was prompted by a loophole in the terms of the syndicate's insurance. If the slaves had been allowed to die on the ship, the *Zong*'s owners could not have claimed compensation. By jettisoning a portion of the "cargo" to save the remainder they were covered up to £30 per head. On November 29, 1781, fifty-four women and children were hurled into the ocean. Another seventy-eight fol-

In 1781, the crew of the slave ship *Zong* threw 132 slaves alive into the Caribbean as a way of reclaiming lost profit from the vessel's insurers. Publicized by the English abolitionists, the ensuing court case resulted in widespread condemnation of the trade. (*Engraving from an anti-slavery periodical, 1833*)

lowed in the next few days, while ten individuals, in a display of defiance, leaped into the water themselves.

Over the next few years the case of the *Zong* was thoroughly publicized by Granville Sharp. Public support for the abolitionist cause grew. London's Quakers threw their weight behind Sharp's efforts in 1783; four years later the Society for Effecting the Abolition of the Slave Trade was formed and Sharp won the backing of William Wilberforce, a wealthy independent MP for Hull, evangelical Christian, and personal friend of the British prime minister, William Pitt. The publication of Olaudah Equiano's *Interesting Narrative* in 1789 added further impetus to the cause. The Slave Trade Act, which regulated the number of slaves that could be transported in any vessel on the basis of a ratio of individuals per ton, was passed by Parliament in 1788. The act was made permanent in 1799, but progress toward actual abolition proved more difficult. The pro-slavery lobby remained powerful, and the anti-reform backlash in England which accompanied the opening of the French Revolutionary War further stilted the abolitionists' efforts. In 1791 Wilberforce's first parliamentary bill to abolish the trade was defeated; a second bill, brought the following year, which called for gradual abolition over a four-year period, passed through the House of Commons, but was held up by interminable delays and thereafter thoroughly diluted. In 1804 a third bill, this time calling for immediate abolition, was passed by the Commons only to be defeated in the House of Lords. Finally, the breakthrough was made in 1807. As tributes poured in for an emotional Wilberforce, the bill to abolish the slave trade was passed by 283 votes to 16.

Abolition did not bring an immediate end to slavery. Although unable to legally import further Africans, Jamaica's plantocracy continued to use slave labor. The creolization of the workforce, a trend long in progress, intensified as a result, but otherwise conditions on the plantations remained largely unchanged. Back in England, the push for empire-wide emancipation continued. In 1816 a series of bills requiring the compulsory registration of slaves were brought into effect. In 1823 the Anti-Slavery Society was founded and that May a resolution for gradual emancipation was passed. As a result, dispatches were sent to the sugar colonies to encourage the amelioration of the conditions under which slaves were held: the whip was to be forbidden in the field; flogging of women was banned outright; and slaves were to be allowed religious instruction. Although the more recently established crown colonies of Trinidad, Guiana, and St. Lucia were obliged to comply, Jamaica and the other older, more independent territories refused to instigate reform. The plantocracy resented what they saw as government interference, and some Assembly members even went as far as to suggest that they cede the island to the United States to ensure that their livelihoods remained unmolested.[28]

As word of these developments filtered down to the plantations, slave unrest grew. In 1823 a major rebellion occurred in Demerara, a British colony on the Caribbean coast of South America. Between 100 and 250 slaves out of an estimated 10,000 involved were killed. Twenty-seven others were executed after the revolt had been put down. A much larger rebellion followed in Jamaica eight years later. The so-called Baptist War, or Christmas Rebellion (1831–1832), was an eleven-day uprising by as many as 60,000 of Jamaica's 300,000 slaves. Led by a black Baptist preacher named Samuel Sharpe, the rebels aimed to implement a nonlethal general strike until their demands for "half the going wage rate" and greater freedom were met.

The strike got out of hand, however. Several plantations were put to the torch in the western parishes, more than £1 million worth of property damage was done, and several planters' homes were plundered. As the white population fled to the east, the militia attacked the main rebel strongholds. By the time the island was back under the government's control on January 4, 1832, 207 slaves and 14 whites had been killed. In the aftermath, an estimated 344 slaves were executed, among them the preacher Samuel Sharpe.[29]

By this stage, emancipation was considered inevitable in Westminster. With increasing competition from Cuba, Mauritius, and Brazil, the British colonies could only be maintained by the imposition of heavy import duties on foreign sugar. Leading newspapers openly supported emancipation, and public petitions raised as many as a million and a half signatures. In the Commons, debate no longer centered on whether or not the slaves should be freed, but rather on how slave labor would be replaced, how the social order of the sugar colonies would be maintained, and what compensation would be offered to the owners. A bill for partial emancipation was passed in 1834 and full freedom was granted four years later. Even so, the lot of the "emancipated" remained an unenviable one. Second-class citizens, they were harassed by the authorities, subject to taxes that favored their former oppressors, and denied political rights by loaded property qualifications. Although some black Jamaicans continued to work on the estates of their former masters, others were replaced by a combination of industrialization and "coolie" laborers, imported first from India and later from China, while a few managed to set up independent villages of small holdings on the least desirable land.[30]

By the 1860s conditions for Jamaica's black population had reached a new low. Unemployment was endemic; wages stood at 9 pence to 1 shilling per day; taxation was heavy; a series of floods and droughts had had a disastrous effect on recent crop yields with many sugar plantations being declared bankrupt as a result; and epidemics of cholera and smallpox had devastated the island's poorest communities. During the election of 1864, fewer than 2,000 black Jamaicans out of a population of 436,000 were eligible to vote. Despite outnumbering the island's whites by a ratio of thirty-two to one, the black population had no political control.

On October 11, 1865, two hundred black peasants led by the preacher Paul Bogle marched on the courthouse in Morant Bay in protest. When local militia opened fire on the crowd they killed seven. Eighteen more were killed in the riot that ensued and the courthouse and several neighboring buildings were burned to the ground. Over the next two days the protest spread across St. Thomas-in-the-East Parish. Houses were plundered, two white planters were killed, and several others forced to flee for their lives. The repression that followed was worse than anything seen in the days of slavery. Troops sent into the area killed 439. "We slaughtered all before us," one later recalled, "man or woman or child." Another 354 were arrested. Many, including Paul Bogle, were executed following improvised military trials. At least six hundred others were whipped and given lengthy prison sentences and over one thousand homes were burned.

The Morant Bay Rebellion proved a turning point in Jamaican history. Subsequently, the island moved slowly toward reform. In 1866 the legal system was remodeled along the lines of English common law, the much-hated militia was replaced by a constabulary force, and the Anglican Church was disestablished. Some of the money saved was invested in health care and social projects. In 1892 elementary education was made free for all and the total number of schools in the island reached nine hundred, twice the number there had been in 1866. At the turn of the twentieth century, black Jamaicans began to make an impact on island politics. Dr. Robert Love won a seat on the Council in 1906 and by the 1920s there were more black council members than white. The global depression that followed the Wall Street crash in 1929 saw major strikes break out in Westmoreland Parish in 1938 which led to the establishment of workers' unions. The consequent rise of Labour and Socialist parties would go on to produce several reform-minded prime ministers in the latter half of the twentieth century, and in 1962, following an eighteen-year period of "constitutional decolonization," Jamaica finally achieved its independence from Britain.[31]

IN MODERN-DAY JAMAICA, several reminders of the late seventeenth century remain. A string of archaeological dives on the site of the sunken city, conducted intermittently between the 1960s and the 1990s by a host of treasure hunters and state-backed operators alike, turned up a number of artifacts, many of which are on display in a museum housed in a restored Fort Charles. In Kingston, Beckford Street runs near Sutton Street. Other thoroughfares are named after Peter Heywood, William Beeston, and Nicholas Laws. In the Church of St. Dorothy in St. Dorothy's Parish is the grave of Colonel Thomas Fuller, the old councilor and planter who died a few weeks after Governor Inchiquin's arrival. Thomas Sutton's gravestone can be found in the parish church in Vere, while the tombstone of Judith de Lucena, wife of the merchant Moses de Lucena, stands in the Jewish graveyard in Hunt's Bay, three miles outside of Kingston on the Spanish Town road. In 2008, on an overgrown site on a bend in the Rio Minho in Clarendon Parish, the remains of a boiling house, mill house, and curing house once worked by the slaves belonging to Thomas Sutton were identified by two officers of the Jamaican National Heritage Trust, and on January 6, 2017, hundreds of descendants of Jamaica's maroons (as well as tourists) gathered under the ancient kindah tree at Accompong Town in the hills of the Cockpit Country to celebrate Cudjoe Day, some 279 years after he had secured his people's freedom.[32]

Notes

PROLOGUE

1. For descriptions of Port Royal, contemporary and seventeenth century, see Marx, *Port Royal: The Sunken City*, 5; Talty, *Empire of Blue Water*, 1–5; and Black, *Port Royal*. For details on Galdy, see Black, *Tales of Old Jamaica*, 27–32.

2. Ashley, *England in the Seventeenth Century*; Trevelyan, *England under the Stuarts*; Pincus, *1688*, 49–90; Jones, *The Anglo-Dutch Wars of the Seventeenth Century*; Zahedieh, *The Capital and the Colonies*, 2–16.

3. Dunn, *Sugar and Slaves*, 149–165; Cundall, *The Governors of Jamaica in the Seventeenth Century*, 118–135.

CHAPTER I: THE WEST INDIES FLEET

1. Pincus, *1688*, 83–87; Zahedieh, *The Capital and the Colonies*, 65–80; Waller, *1700*, 195–204; Rediker, *Between the Devil and the Deep Blue Sea*, 28–30.

2. Zahedieh, *The Capital and the Colonies*, 97–99; Waller, *1700*, 163–165; Davies, *The Royal African Company*, 97.

3. Zahedieh, *The Capital and the Colonies*, 2–16; Pincus, *1688*, 49–90; Jones, *The Anglo-Dutch Wars of the Seventeenth Century*.

4. *A List of all the ships now bound out from London to Barbadoes, Jamaica & the Leeward Islands*, PC 2/73, Folios 334–340, 345; Ship Arrivals Port Royal, June 1690, CO 142/13, folios 72–73; Zahedieh, *The Capital and the Colonies*, 238–279.

5. Rediker, *Between the Devil and the Deep Blue Sea*, 26–27, 31.

6. Vallance, *The Glorious Revolution*, 216–219; Childs, *The Williamite Wars in Ireland*, 13, 52; Ehrman, *The Navy in the War of William III*, 261–266; Childs, *The Nine Years' War and the British Army, 1688–97*, 109–114.

7. List of the West India Squadron, 23 October 1689, *Calendar of State Papers Colonial, America and West Indies, Volume 13, 1689–1692*; *Three Decks.org*, entry for HMS *Swan* (1673); HMS *Swan* pay book, ADM 33/143, folios 78–81; on Johnson see Governor Carlisle to Secretary Coventry, 4 December 1679, *Calendar of State Papers Colonial, America and West Indies, Volume 10* online at BHO; on life in the Royal Navy at the end of the seventeenth century see Ehrman, *The Navy in the War of William III*, 109–143.

8. HMS *Swan* pay book, ADM 33/143, folios 81, 86; HMS *Mary* log, entries for March 1690, ADM 56/65, folios 7–8.

9. On the O'Briens see O'Donoghue, *Historical Memoir of the O'Breins*. The spelling of the name varied, as was common at this time. Inchiquin's son James spelled his last name O'Bryan.

10. Routh, *Tangier*, 146–197.

11. On Inchiquin see Cundall, *The Governors of Jamaica in the Seventeenth Century*, 124; Childs, *The Williamite Wars in Ireland*, 13, 52; Tinniswood, *Pirates of Barbary*, 209– 218; *Calendar of State Papers Colonial, America and West Indies, Volume 13, 1689– 1692*, various entries from 11 September to 28 November 1689. For an insight into Inchiquin's financial affairs see his will, PROB 11/414, folios 157–159. Although it may seem strange that an Irishman with no experience of the New World should be chosen as the governor of Jamaica, one of England's wealthiest American colonies, to William III and the Lords of Trade Inchiquin seemed a perfectly suitable choice: the earl had more than proven his loyalty to England's new monarch; he had a solid military background, a must considering the likelihood of armed encounters in the Caribbean with the French or even a full-scale invasion of Jamaica. Inchiquin also had experience as an administrator, principally during his time as the governor of Tangiers, and considerable experience of running a colony. Although Ireland and Jamaica seem very different places to us today, their similarities would have seemed more obvious to an Englishman of the late seventeenth century. Despite its geographical proximity to England, Ireland was an alien land. Home to a barbaric, illiterate, tribal, and ungodly people whose precarious existence revolved around the ancient practices of cattle-raising, feasting, and raiding once ubiquitous across northern Europe, it seemed, in the view of William Blathwayt, chief bureaucrat of the plantations office and the first Whitehall official with a clear plan for strong royal authority in the transatlantic colonies, just as foreign a land as Jamaica. Both were in need of the strict application of the law to ensure they turned a healthy profit for the crown. Indeed, the very fact that Inchiquin had never set foot in the Americas may well have been yet another reason for his selection. The Jamaican elite were showing an ever-increasing desire for self-determination. To appoint one of their own to the role of governor may well have only served to accelerate the process. Inchiquin, on the other hand, had no vested interest and therefore no reasons to be disloyal to the crown. Furthermore, if events in the North American colonies, where news of the outbreak of the Glorious Revolution had led to armed insurrections and the deposition of several crown-appointed officials, were anything to go by, having a man with military experience on the spot could be very useful indeed. Given such assumptions, the choice of Inchiquin as the new governor seemed to William and Blathwayt alike to be a sound one indeed.

12. Clarke, *Proceedings and Reports of the Belfast Natural History and Philosophical Society, 157th – 161st Sessions*, 37–44; HMS *Swan* pay book, ADM 33/143, folios 86.

13. O'Malley, *Final Passages*, 139–170; F. J. Osborne, "James Castillo–Asiento Agent," *Jamaican Historical Review*, 8 (1971), 9–18.

14. *Calendar of State Papers Colonial, America and West Indies, Volume 13, 1689– 1692, List of the West India Squadron*, 23 October 1689; *A List of all the ships now bound out from London to Barbadoes, Jamaica & the Leeward Islands*, PC 2/73, fo-

lios 334– 340, 345; on the Duke of Bolton's Regiment see various entries in *Calendar of State Papers Colonial, America and West Indies, Volume 13, 1689–1692*, from 30 November 1689 to 14 October 1690, especially the letters from Inchiquin to the Lords of Trade, 6 July 1690, and Governor Kendall to William Blathwayt, 4 March 1690.

15. ADM 52/65, folios 3–4, HMS *Mary* Log; ADM 52/38, HMS *Guernsey* Log; Governor Kendall to the Earl of Shrewsbury, 4 April 1690, *Calendar of State Papers Colonial, America and West Indies: Volume 13, 1689–1692*, 243–255.

16. ADM 52/65, folio 4, HMS *Mary* Log; ADM 52/38, HMS *Guernsey* Log; Governor Kendall to the Earl of Shrewsbury, 4 April 1690, *Calendar of State Papers Colonial, America and West Indies: Volume 13, 1689–1692*, 243–255; ADM 33/143, folio 79, HMS *Swan* pay book.

17. ADM 52/65, folio 4, HMS *Mary* Log; ADM 52/38, HMS *Guernsey* Log; Governor Kendall to the Earl of Shrewsbury, 4 April 1690, *Calendar of State Papers Colonial, America and West Indies: Volume 13, 1689–1692*, 243–255; ADM 33/143, folio 79, HMS *Swan* pay book; Ship arrivals Port Royal, June 1690, CO 142/13, folios 72–73. On Madeira the drink see Zahedieh, *The Capital and the Colonies*, 255–256; Sloane, *A Voyage to the Islands*, volume I, xxviii. For a description of contemporary Madeira see Ovington, *A Voyage to Suratt, in the Year 1689*, 4–37.

18. ADM 52/65, folios 5–7, HMS *Mary* Log. On the routines of a transatlantic voyage see Phillips, *Journal of a Voyage* and John Taylor's account in Buisseret (ed.), *Jamaica in 1687*.

19. Ligon, *A True and Exact History of the Island of Barbadoes*, 24.

20. Ligon, *A True and Exact History of the Island of Barbadoes*, 25; Parker, *The Sugar Barons*, 22–30, 67–75; Dunn, *Sugar and Slaves*, 46–116.

21. Governor Kendall to the Earl of Shrewsbury, 27 June 1690, *Calendar of State Papers Colonial, America and West Indies: Volume 13, 1689–1692*, 218–227; Christopher Coddrington to Lords of Trade, 4 June 1690, *Calendar of State Papers Colonial, America and West Indies: Volume 13, 1689–1692*, 226–233.

22. Crouse, *French Struggle for the West Indies*, 146–161. For more on Hewetson see Marley, *Pirates of the Americas*, Volume I, 638–639.

23. Clarke, *Proceedings and Reports of the Belfast Natural History and Philosophical Society, 157th–161st Sessions*, 37–44; HMS *Swan* pay book, ADM 33/143, folio 79.

24. *Petition of John Earl of Clare to the King*, no date, Calendar of Treasury Papers, Volume I, 1556–1696, 333–337; *Agreement between St. Jago del Castillo and Captain Thomas Hewetson*, April 17 1690, *Calendar of State Papers Colonial, America and West Indies, Volume 13, 1689–1692*, 293–294.

25. Parker, *The Sugar Barons*; Blome, *A Description of the Island of Jamaica*; Buisseret (ed.), *Jamaica in 1687*.

26. Pawson, *Port Royal*, 109–164; Buisseret (ed.), *Jamaica in 1687*.

CHAPTER 2: AS HOT AS HELL, AND AS WICKED AS THE DEVIL

1. Venables, *The Narrative of General Venables . . . Relating to the Expedition to the West Indies*, 109.

2. Parker, *The Sugar Barons*, 88–103; Venables, *The Narrative of General Venables*

... *Relating to the Expedition to the West Indies*; Black, *History of Jamaica*, 34–40; Dunn, *Sugar and Slaves*, 152–153.

3. Dunn, *Sugar and Slaves*, 153–154; Parker, *The Sugar Barons*, 103–111, 132–136; Smith, *Colonists in Bondage*, 89–109, 136–206.

4. Parker, *The Sugar Barons*, 110, 133; Dunn, *Sugar and Slaves*, 153; Pawson, *Port Royal*, 25–28; Cundall, *The Governors of Jamaica in the Seventeenth Century*, 1–15.

5. Pawson, *Port Royal*, 7–22, 49–54.

6. Pawson, *Port Royal*, 28–36; Dunn, *Sugar and Slaves*, 154–156; Parker, *The Sugar Barons*, 133–141. Cundall, *The Governors of Jamaica in the Seventeenth Century*, 21–30.

7. Talty, *Empire of Blue Water* covers Morgan's career in depth.

8. Dunn, *Sugar and Slaves*, 153–162; Pawson, *Port Royal*, 57–105; Cundall, *The Governors of Jamaica in the Seventeenth Century*, 31–123.

9. Although no description of Inchiquin's arrival survives, John Taylor wrote a detailed text concerning the previous governor's inauguration. See Buisseret (ed.), *Jamaica in 1687*, 299–305. For details of recent arrivals at Port Royal from England see Ship Arrivals Port Royal, 1689–90, CO 142/13.

10. For details of the clothes worn in Port Royal see Dunn, *Sugar and Slaves*, 283–286; Buisseret (ed.), *Jamaica in 1687*, 266, 268, 288; Sloane, *A Voyage to the Islands*, volume I, xlvii; Pawson, *Port Royal*, 149–150.

11. On Francis Watson see Cundall, *Governors of Jamaica*, 117–123; Buisseret (ed.), *Jamaica in 1687*, 256; Sloane, *A Voyage to the Islands*, Volume I, lx and cxxxvii; and Saunders, *Lord Churchill's Coup*, 30.

12. On Ballard see *Survey of Jamaica 1670, St. Catherine's Parish*, Jamaican Family Search website; Sloane, *A Voyage to the Islands*, Volume I, cxxii, lxvii, cxii, and xcvii; Inchiquin to Lords of Trade, 31 August 1690, CO 138/7, folios 1–4. On Beckford see Rev. William May, *Jamaica: Description of the Principal Persons there*, in Vere L. Oliver, *Caribbeana*, 5–9, vol. 3; Pawson, *Port Royal*, 115. On Musgrave see Pawson, *Port Royal*, 117, 122. On White see Cundall, *Governors of Jamaica*, 131–139. On Freeman see Pawson, *Port Royal*, 125; *Sketch Pedigrees of some of the Early Settlers in Jamaica*, 29, 111, 113; Dunn, *Sugar and Slaves*, 175; *List of Marriages on Record in Jamaica Previous to 1680*, Add. MS: 21,931, British Museum, available online at Jamaican Family Search. On Walker see Sloane, *A Voyage to the Islands*, Volume I, xciv; Smyth Kelly to Blathwayt, 27 May 1789, Blathwayt Papers, vol. 22, folder 10, Jamaica. On Bernard see Dunn, *Sugar and Slaves*, 176; Hutton et al. (ed.), *The Philosophical Transactions of the Royal Society of London*, 625. On Bourden see De Jong, *The Life of John Bourden*. On Heywood see Pawson, *Port Royal*, 75–79.

13. Cadbury, "Quakers and the Earthquake at Port Royal, 1692," 20.

14. Buisseret (ed.), *Jamaica in 1687*, 299–305.

15. Pawson, *Port Royal*, 114.

16. Pawson, *Port Royal*, 116; on Thomas Churchill see *A Short Account of the Late State of Affairs in Jamaica*, July 1689, in *Calendar of State Papers Colonial America and West Indies, Volume 13*, 100–113.

17. Council Meeting Notes, 10 April 1690, CO 140/5, folio 107.

18. Council Meeting Notes, 10 April 1690, CO 140/5, folio 115.

19. Dunn, *Sugar and Slaves*, 209–210; Buisseret (ed.), *Jamaica in 1687*, 132–218; Sloane, *A Voyage to the Islands*, xvi–xvii; Pawson, *Port Royal*, 140–141.

20. Pawson, *Port Royal*, 116; Buisseret (ed.), *Jamaica in 1687*, 299–305.

21. Arbell, *The Portuguese Jews of Jamaica*, 18–19.

22. For descriptions of Port Royal at the end of the seventeenth century see Black, *Port Royal*, 24–25; Pawson, *Port Royal*, 109–131; Buisseret (ed.), *Jamaica in 1687*, 230– 242; Sloane, *A Voyage to the Islands*, Volume I, xlvii, lviii–lix.

23. Buisseret (ed.), *Jamaica in 1687*, 284.

24. *Council Minutes, Jamaica*, 14 October 1689, in *Calendar of State Papers Colonial, America and West Indies, Volume 13*, 153–171. Although in decline in England, where the last execution is thought to have been held in Exeter in 1684, prosecutions for witchcraft were still relatively commonplace in the Americas: February 1692 would see the opening of the infamous Salem witch trials in Massachusetts.

25. *Articles Exhibited Against Roger Elleston*, in *Council Minutes, Jamaica*, 26 July 1689, in *Calendar of State Papers Colonial, America and West Indies, Volume 13*, 100–113; William Chapman to Blathwayt, Jamaica, 12 May 1690, Blathwayt Papers, vol. 22, folder 6, Jamaica.

26. Sloane, *A Voyage to the Islands*, Volume I, xviii; Buisseret (ed.), *Jamaica in 1687*, 231; Pawson, *Port Royal*, 140–141.

27. Buisseret (ed.), *Jamaica in 1687*, 230–231, 239–240.

28. Pawson, *Port Royal*, 135.

29. Mair, *A Historical Study of Women in Jamaica*, 84–88; Dunn, *Sugar and Slaves*, 252– 255.

30. Buisseret (ed.), *Jamaica in 1687*, 267; Sloane, *A Voyage to the Islands*, Volume I, 106.

31. See the wills of William Turner, entered 19 July 1693, Thomas Gunn, entered 1692/3, and John Griffin, entered 25 July 1693, at *Port Royal Wills* website; Besse, *A Collection of the Sufferings of the People Called Quakers*, 389–390.

32. Dunn, *Sugar and Slaves*, 198, 248–249.

33. See the wills of John Willmaott and John Phillips at *Port Royal Wills* website; on Pike see Cadbury, "Quakers and the Earthquake at Port Royal, 1692." For the average cost of a slave see Davies, *The Royal African Company*, 312–315; and the records of slave auctions at Port Royal held in the National Archives, T70/644.

34. Smith, *Colonists in Bondage*, 43–86. For the quote see 68.

35. Dunn, *Sugar and Slaves*, 164–165, 269–270; Smith, *Colonists in Bondage*, 31, 34, 230; Buisseret (ed.), *Jamaica in 1687*, 266–267, 286–289.

36. Buisseret (ed.), *Jamaica in 1687*, 240.

37. Pawson, *Port Royal*, 161.

38. Black, *Port Royal*, 15–17.

39. See the inventory for Andrew Orgill, entered 1686, at *Port Royal Probate Inventories* website.

40. Smith, *Colonists in Bondage*, 175–187.

41. Dobson, *Scottish Emigration to Colonial America*, 75.

42. Smith, *Colonists in Bondage*, 188–197.

43. Coad, *A Memorandum of the Wonderful Providences of God*, 23.

44. Smith, *Colonists in Bondage*, 193–194.
45. Pawson, *Port Royal*, 141–148; Dunn, *Sugar and Slaves*, 181–182; Buisseret (ed.), *Jamaica in 1687*, 241.
46. Buisseret (ed.), *Jamaica in 1687*, 242.
47. Brooks, *Sir Hans Sloane*.
48. Ashcroft, "Tercentenary of the First English Book on Tropical Medicine, by Thomas Trapham of Jamaica," 475–477.
49. Dunn, *Sugar and Slaves*, 44, 104, 183–184, 186–187; Pawson, *Port Royal*, 13, 158, 159; Buisseret (ed.), *Jamaica in 1687*, 240.
50. Cadbury, "Quakers and the Earthquake at Port Royal, 1692"; Besse, *A Collection of the Sufferings of the People Called Quakers*, 389–390; also see the inventory for Thomas Gunn, entered 1692/3, at *Port Royal Probate Inventories* website.
51. Waller, *1700*, 265–274.
52. Black, *Tales of Old Jamaica*, 27–32.
53. Ship Arrivals Port Royal, CO 142/13, folios 85 and 95; Agnew, *Protestant Exiles from France*, 68.
54. Pawson, *Port Royal*, 85–105; Ship Arrivals Port Royal, CO 142/13; Pares, *Yankees and Creoles*, 37–91; Zahedieh, *The Capital and the Colonies*, 238–279; Zahedieh, *The Merchants of Port Royal*.
55. Pawson, *Port Royal*, 85–105; Ship Departures Port Royal, CO 142/13; Pares, *Yankees and Creoles*, 92–138; Zahedieh, *The Capital and the Colonies*, 184–237; Zahedieh, *The Merchants of Port Royal*.
56. Zahedieh, *The Merchants of Port Royal*; Hanson, *The Laws of Jamaica*, preface.
57. Zahedieh, *The Merchants of Port Royal*, 578–588.
58. Ten Broeck Runk, *The Ten Broeck Genealogy*, 10–29.
59. On the Norrises see the *Isaac Norris Letter Book* at the Historical Society of Pennsylvania. Also see Pares, *Yankees and Creoles*, 3–5, 8, 34, 38, 50, 66, 77, 86, 94.
60. T70/941, folio 27 & 28; Calendar of State Papers 2/3:522; 1702–3, 124, Jamaica Archives; Galante, *Port Royal – O Meio Circulante de uma Colônia Inglesa no Século XVII*; Port Royal Inventories, Volume 3, folio 428, Isaac Rodriguez de Lossa; Folio 405, Moises de Lucena, Port Royal, 6 January 1692/3. Also see Arbell, *The Portuguese Jews of Jamaica*; Buisseret (ed.), *Jamaica in 1687*, 238, 240, 250, 294; Dunn, *Sugar and Slaves*, 151, 183–184; Pawson, *Port Royal*, 129, 159.
61. Pawson, *Port Royal*, 156; Johnson, *Port Royal and the Slave Trade* (unpublished thesis), 77–78.
62. Johnson, *Port Royal and the Slave Trade*, 75–76; *Address of the Council and Assembly of Jamaica to the king James II*, Calendar of State Papers Colonial, America and West Indies, 12 July 1689, 100–113; Foster, *Jamaica: The Postal History*, 4.
63. Pawson, *Port Royal*, 135.
64. Zahedieh, *The Merchants of Port Royal*, 580–584.
65. Ship Arrivals Port Royal, CO 142/13, folio 136; Caliendo, *New York City Mayors*, Volume I, 64–65.
66. Ship Arrivals Port Royal, CO142/13, folios 87 and 102; Marley, *Pirates of the Americas*, Volume I, 127–129.
67. Ship Arrivals Port Royal, CO142/13, folios 67, 76, 83 and 90.
68. Ship Arrivals Port Royal, CO142/13, folios 70 and 102; *Will of Daniel Plow-*

man, PROB 11/540/267; *Jamaican Council Meetings Notes*, 21 May 1692, CO 140/5, folio 192.

69. Port Royal Inventories, Robert Scroope, entered February 1692/3, Vol. 3, folio 419; Ship Arrivals Port Royal, CO142/13, folios 95 and 100.

70. Ship Arrivals Port Royal, CO142/13, folio 101; Port Royal Inventories, Thomas Craddock, entered January 1684/5, Vol. 2, folio 78.

71. On Reginald Wilson see http://linleyfh.com/main.htm; Pawson, Port Royal, 62–63, 128, 155, 216; Royal African Company Slave Auction receipts, T70/644, folios 225–228; Wilson to Blathwayt, 18 August 1691, and 3 February 1692, Blathwayt Papers, Volume 26, folder 3.

72. Burnard, *Mastery, Slavery, and Desire*, 16–18.

73. Pares, *Yankees and Creoles*, 3–4.

74. Dunn, *Sugar and Slaves*, 185, 264, 277–280, 325–326.

75. Jamaican Council Minutes, 4 June 1690, CO 140/5, folios 53–54.

76. Buisseret (ed.), *Jamaica in 1687*, 248.

77. Buisseret (ed.), *Jamaica in 1687*, 243.

78. Dunn, *Sugar and Slaves*, 39, 44, 182–183, 267–269; Robertson, *Gone Is the Ancient Glory*, 36–64.

79. Council Meeting Notes, 11 May 1692, CO 140/5, folio 177.

80. Jamaican Council Minutes, 4 June 1690, CO 140/5, folios 53–54. For the reference to the leather chairs, see Jamaican Council Minutes, 11 July 1691, CO 140/5, folios 89–90.

81. Inchiquin to Lords of Trade, 6 July 1690, *Calendar of State Papers of Colonial America and West Indies*, Volume 13, 291–301.

82. Jamaican Council Minutes, 4 June 1690, CO 140/5, folios 53–54. For more on the *St. Jago* see Jamaican Council Minutes, 30 June 1690, and those of 5 July 1690, CO 140/5, folios 57–67.

83. Inchiquin to Lords of Trade, 31 August 1690, CO 138/7, folios 1–6; Sloane, *A Voyage to the Islands*, Volume I, cix; *Survey of Jamaica 1670, St. Catherine's Parish*, Jamaica Family Search Website.

84. Jamaican Council Minutes, 12 June 1690, CO 140/5, folios 55–57.

85. Buisseret, *Slaves Arriving in Jamaica, 1684–1692*, 86–87.

86. Dunn, *Sugar and Slaves*, 313–325.

87. *Address of the Council and Assembly of Jamaica to the king James II*, 12 July 1689, *Calendar of State Papers Colonial, America and West Indies*, Volume 13, 100–113.

88. Ship Arrivals Port Royal, CO142/13, folio 74.

89. Sales book of the *Hannah* slaver, T70/1217.

CHAPTER 3: BLACK IVORY

1. Sales book of the *Hannah* slaver, T70/1217; *Ship Arrivals Port Royal*, CO142/13, folio 74; Phillips, *A Journal of a Voyage*, 197; Davies, *The Royal African Company*, 221–224; Bosman, *A New and Accurate Description*, 471–493.

2. Out Letters (Customs) XII, 15, Entry Book: May 1689, 21–32, Calendar of Treasury Books, Volume 9, 1689–1692, available at British History Online; T70/50, folio 98, Royal African Company Out Letters.

3. Sales book of the *Hannah* slaver, T70/1217.

4. Davies, *The Royal African Company*, 221–224.

5. Sales book of the *Hannah* slaver, T70/1217; Phillips, *A Journal of a Voyage*, 195.

6. Sales book of the *Hannah* slaver, T70/1217; Phillips, *A Journal of a Voyage*, 197.

7. Law, *The English in West Africa*, Part 2, 402–404.

8. Ship Arrivals Port Royal, CO142/13, folio 74; Davies, *The Royal African Company*, 192–194.

9. *Will of Charles Danvers*, PROB 11/402; Rediker, *Between the Devil and the Deep Blue Sea*, 83–84, 120–121.

10. *Will of John Zebbett*, PROB 11/429.

11. Sales book of the *Hannah* slaver, T70/1217.

12. Rediker, *Between the Devil and the Deep Blue Sea*, 45–50, 83–87.

13. Sales book of the *Hannah* slaver, T70/1217.

14. Bosman, *A New and Accurate Description*, 485–486.

15. Sales book of the *Hannah* slaver, T70/1217.

16. Bosman, *A New and Accurate Description*, 490–493.

17. Sales book of the *Hannah* slaver, T70/1217.

18. Konadu, *The Akan Diaspora*, 58, 64, 68–69.

19. Bosman, *A New and Accurate Description*, 2–10.

20. Sales book of the *Hannah* slaver, T70/1217.

21. Phillips, *A Journal of a Voyage*, 206.

22. Konadu, *The Akan Diaspora*, 7–54, 103.

23. Konadu, *The Akan Diaspora*, 42, 64–86; Shumway, *The Fante and the Transatlantic Slave Trade*, 34–41.

24. Sales book of the *Hannah* slaver, T70/1217.

25. Bosman, *A New and Accurate Description*, 20–25; Shumway, *The Fante and the Transatlantic Slave Trade*, 62.

26. Sales book of the *Hannah* slaver, T70/1217.

27. Phillips, *A Journal of a Voyage*, 207.

28. Sales book of the *Hannah* slaver, T70/1217.

29. Bosman, *A New and Accurate Description*, 20–22.

30. Phillips, *A Journal of a Voyage*, 203.

31. T70/50, folio 97d. Quoted in Davies, *The Royal African Company*, 267.

32. Sales book of the *Hannah* slaver, T70/1217.

33. Davies, *The Royal African Company*, 223.

34. Sales book of the *Hannah* slaver, T70/1217; *Royal African Company Letter Book*, Letters from Africa, T70/12, folio 45; Davies, *The Royal African Company*, 239.

35. Davies, *The Royal African Company*, 240–244; Bosman, *A New and Accurate Description*, 45–54; Phillips, *A Journal of a Voyage*, 204–205; *Royal African Company Letter Book*, Letters from Africa, T70/12, folio 45.

36. Phillips, *A Journal of a Voyage*, 204–205.

37. Shumway, *The Fante and the Transatlantic Slave Trade*, 45–46; Davies, *The Royal African Company*, 267.

38. Konadu, *The Akan Diaspora*, 64.

39. Davies, *The Royal African Company*, 280–289; Bosman, *A New and Accurate Description*, 31, 52; Phillips, *Journal of a Voyage*, 195.

40. Sales book of the *Hannah* slaver, T70/1217.
41. Bosman, *A New and Accurate Description*, 312–322.
42. Law, *Ouidah: The Social History*, 29; Phillips, *Journal of a Voyage*, 228.
43. Sales book of the *Hannah* slaver, T70/1217.
44. Phillips, *Journal of a Voyage*, 210–214; Sales book of the *Hannah* slaver, T70/1217.
45. Phillips, *Journal of a Voyage*, 222.
46. Atkins, *A Voyage to Guinea*, 46.
47. Law, *Ouidah: The Social History*, 27.
48. Bosman, *A New and Accurate Description*, 264.
49. Phillips, *Journal of a Voyage*, 215.
50. Law, *Ouidah: The Social History*, 41–43.
51. Phillips, *Journal of a Voyage*, 215; *Royal African Company Letter Book*, Letters from Africa, T70/12, folio 45.
52. Law, *Ouidah: The Social History*, 25.
53. Law, *Ouidah: The Social History*, 18–20.
54. Konadu, *The Akan Diaspora*, 124–127.
55. Konadu, *The Akan Diaspora*, 126–127.
56. Konadu, *The Akan Diaspora*, 121.
57. Moore, *Biography of Mahommah G. Baquaqua*, 35–40.
58. Sales book of the *Hannah* slaver, T70/1217.
59. Phillips, *Journal of a Voyage*, 216–217.
60. Sales book of the *Hannah* slaver, T70/1217.
61. Atkins, *A Voyage to Guinea*, quoted in Sanders, *If a Pirate I Must Be*, 4–5.
62. Phillips, *Journal of a Voyage*, 218.
63. Bosman, *A New and Accurate Description*, 361.
64. Phillips, *Journal of a Voyage*, 218.
65. Sweet, *African Healing*, 29.
66. Bosman, *A New and Accurate Description*, 361.
67. Law, *Ouidah: The Social History*, 141.
68. Phillips, *Journal of a Voyage*, 218.
69. Bosman, *A New and Accurate Description*, 360–361.
70. Sales book of the *Hannah* slaver, T70/1217.
71. Phillips, *Journal of a Voyage*, 218.
72. Sales book of the *Hannah* slaver, T70/1217.
73. Law, *Ouidah: The Social History*, 46; Dunn, *Sugar and Slaves*, 236; Konadu, *The Akan Diaspora*, 101.
74. Konadu, *The Akan Diaspora*, 101.
75. Law, *Ouidah: The Social History*, 27–29.
76. Duncan, *Travels in Western Africa*, 298–299.
77. Phillips, *Journal of a Voyage*, 229.
78. Equiano, *The Interesting Narrative*, 46.
79. Barbot, *Barbot on Guinea*, 639.
80. Law, *Ouidah: The Social History*, 152.
81. Sales book of the *Hannah* slaver, T70/1217.
82. Davies, *The Royal African Company*, 291.
83. Phillips, *Journal of a Voyage*, 229.

84. Bosman, *A New and Accurate Description*, 365–366.
85. Smallwood, *Saltwater Slavery*, 42–43.
86. Taylor, *If We Must Die*, 180.
87. Davies, *The Royal African Company*, 291.
88. Equiano, *The Interesting Narrative*, 48.
89. T70/1211. Quoted in Davies, *The Royal African Company*, 291.
90. Sanders, *If a Pirate I Must Be*, 4.
91. Equiano, *The Interesting Narrative*, 51.
92. Pringle (ed.), *The History of Mary Prince*, 43.
93. Moore, *Biography of Mahommah G. Baquaqua*, 43–44.
94. Sales book of the *Hannah* slaver, T70/1217.
95. Rediker, *The Slave Ship*, 292; Davies, *The Royal African Company*, 292–294.
96. Phillips, *Journal of a Voyage*, 237.
97. Wills, *1688*, 237–241.
98. Wax, "A Philadelphia Surgeon on a Slaving Voyage to Africa, 1749–1751."
99. Equiano, *The Interesting Narrative*, 54.
100. Phillips, *Journal of a Voyage*, 221, 229.
101. T70/61, folio 159d. Quoted in Davies, *The Royal African Company*, 294.
102. Phillips, *Journal of a Voyage*, 230.
103. Sales book of the *Hannah* slaver, T70/1217; precis of letter from Edwin Stede, RAC agent at Barbados to London HQ, T70/17, folio 10.
104. Phillips, *Journal of a Voyage*, 232.
105. Sales book of the *Hannah* slaver, T70/1217; precis of letter from Edwin Stede, RAC agent at Barbados to London HQ, T70/17, folio 10.
106. Sales book of the *Hannah* slaver, T70/1217; precis of letter from Edwin Stede, RAC agent at Barbados to London HQ, T70/17, folio 10.
107. Sales book of the *Hannah* slaver, T70/1217; precis of letter from Edwin Stede, RAC agent at Barbados to London HQ, T70/17, folio 10.
108. Equiano, *The Interesting Narrative*, 54–55.
109. Dunn, *Sugar and Slaves*, 300–302.

CHAPTER 4: PLANTATION SLAVERY IN THE NEW WORLD

1. Galenson, *Traders, Planters and Slaves*, 72.
2. Ship Arrivals Port Royal, CO142/13, folio 74.
3. Davies, *The Royal African Company*, 295–296.
4. Sales book of the *Hannah* slaver, T70/1217.
5. Galenson, *Traders, Planters and Slaves*, 82–85.
6. Equiano, *The Interesting Narrative*, 54–55.
7. Burnard, *Mastery, Tyranny and Desire*, 134.
8. Equiano, *The Interesting Narrative*, 55.
9. *Hannah* Sales Receipts, T70/644, folios 1–4.
10. Davies, *The Royal African Company*, 296–297.
11. *Hannah* Sales Receipts, T70/644, folios 1–4.
12. Governor Coddrington to the Council of Trade and Plantations, 30 December 1701, *Calendar of State Papers Colonial, America and West Indies: Volume 19, 1701*, 696–729.
13. Phillips, *Journal of a Voyage*, 216; Behn, *Oroonoko*, 15.

14. Sloane, *A Voyage to the Islands*, Volume I, xlvii.

15. Craton, *Testing the Chains*, 25–26.

16. Palmer, *Human Cargoes*, 62–63.

17. *Hannah* Sales Receipts, T70/644, folios 1–4.

18. Sloane, *A Voyage to the Islands*, liii.

19. *Hannah* Sales Receipts, T70/644, folios 1–4.

20. Equiano, *The Interesting Narrative*, 55.

21. *Hannah* Sales Receipts, T70/644, folios 1–4; Davies, *The Royal African Company*, 294–296.

22. Davies, *The Royal African Company*, 334; Royal African Company Sales Receipts, Port Royal, T70/17 folio 10d; Penhallow and Ruding to RAC, 1 July 1690, T70/12, folios 84–85.

23. *Hannah* Sales Receipts, T70/644, folios 1–4.

24. Port Royal Inventories, Volume 3, Folio 485, Jeremiah Tilley, entered 21 November 1693; Vernon (ed.), *Cases Argued and Adjudged in the High Court of Chancery*, Volume II, Part I, 280–281; Mortimer (ed.), *Bristol Record Society's Publications, Volume XXVI, Minute Book of the Men's Meeting of the Society of Friends in Bristol*, 182–183.

25. On Banister see Parker, *Willoughbyland*, 248.

26. On Swimmer see *A Parcel of Ribbons* website, http://aparcelofribbons.co.uk/2012/11/the-swymmer-family-of-bristol/. On Rose see Craton, *A Jamaican Plantation*, 40; Beasley, *Christian Ritual*, 77.

27. Equiano, *The Interesting Narrative*, 56; Ligon, *A True and Exact History of Barbadoes*, 46.

28. Equiano, *The Interesting Narrative*, 57.

29. *Hannah* Sales Receipts, T70/644, folios 1–4.

30. Palmer, *Human Cargoes*, 61–62.

31. Inchiquin to Lords of Trade, 6 July 1690, *Calendar of State Papers of Colonial America and West Indies, Volume 13, 1689–1692*, 291–301.

32. Inchiquin to Lords of Trade, 6 July 1690, *Calendar of State Papers of Colonial America and West Indies, Volume 13, 1689–1692*, 291–301.

33. The flota was a convoy system employed from 1566 to 1790 by the Spanish to transport goods from Europe to its colonies in the New World. Due to the deficiencies of the Spanish merchant marine, the flota proved woefully inadequate, however, thus encouraging foreign ships to illegally intervene.

34. HMS *Swan* pay book, ADM 33/143, folios 78–81.

35. Inchiquin to Lords of Trade, 6 July 1690, *Calendar of State Papers of Colonial America and West Indies, Volume 13, 1689–1692*, 291–301.

36. Palmer, *Human Cargoes*, 64–73.

37. HMS *Swan* pay book, ADM 33/143, folio 82.

38. Dunn, *Sugar and Slaves*, 170–177.

39. On Sutton's holdings, see www.anthonymaitland.com. For the contemporary valuation see John Helyar letter, 7 August 1690, Helyar Papers, Jamaican letters, 17th Century, DD/WHh/1151–1153, Somerset Heritage Centre.

40. Inchiquin to Lords of Trade, 31 August 1690, CO 138/7, folios 1–6.

41. Delle (ed.), *Out of Many, One People*, 134–135; Jamaican National Heritage Trust, Archaeological Division. *Preliminary Archaeological Appraisal Report, Sut-*

ton Land Settlement, Clarendon. Kingston, May 2008; Craton, *A Jamaican Plantation,* 108.

42. Thomas Sutton's Will, PROB 11/520.

43. Inchiquin to Lords of Trade, 31 August 1690, CO 138/7, folios 1–6.

44. Jamaican National Heritage Trust, Archaeological Division. *Preliminary Archaeological Appraisal Report, Sutton Land Settlement, Clarendon.* Kingston, May 2008.

45. John Helyar letter, 7 August 1690, Helyar Papers, Jamaican letters, 17th Century, DD/WHh/1151–1153, Somerset Heritage Centre.

46. Dunn, *Sugar and Slaves,* 170–177.

47. www.anthonymaitland.com.

48. Schomburgk, *The History of Barbados,* 298.

49. Dunn, *Sugar and Slaves,* 176.

50. www.anthonymaitland.com. On the link between Sutton and Blackmore see Buisseret (ed.), *Jamaica in 1687,* 38.

51. Davies, *The Royal African Company,* 113–118; O'Malley, *Final Passages,* 85–113.

52. Port Royal Wills, Oliver Cransborough, volume 6, folio 62, entered 5 April 1689; CO33/14, folios 13, 39; www.slavevoyages.org, id 24313.

53. T70/12, folio 78.

54. O'Malley, *Final Passages,* 95.

55. Schomburgk, *The History of Barbados,* 298.

56. Petition of Thomas Sutton, September 1689, *Calendar of State Papers Colonial, America and West Indies, Volume 13, 1689–1692,* 137–153.

57. Buisseret (ed.), *Jamaica in 1687,* 37–38, 248–250.

58. *History of Clarendon,* pdf. http://www.nlj.gov.jm/historynotes/History%20of%20Clarendon.pdf.

59. Mair, *A Historical Study of Women in Jamaica,* 61; Palmer, *Human Cargoes,* 69.

60. Palmer, *Human Cargoes,* 69.

61. Dunn, *Sugar and Slaves,* 252.

62. Thomas Sutton's Will, PROB 11/520.

63. Dunn, *A Tale of Two Plantations,* 157.

64. Dunn, *A Tale of Two Plantations,* 434; Dunn, *Sugar and Slaves,* 303–306.

65. Ligon, *A True and Exact History of Barbadoes,* 51.

66. Dunn, *A Tale of Two Plantations,* 142–144.

67. Sloane, *A Voyage to the Islands,* lii.

68. Dunn, *A Tale of Two Plantations,* 143.

69. Sloane, *A Voyage to the Islands,* lii; Dunn, *A Tale of Two Plantations,* 325–326.

70. Sloane, *A Voyage to the Islands,* cxxii.

71. Sloane, *A Voyage to the Islands,* cxli.

72. Dunn, *Sugar and Slaves,* 198.

73. Ligon, *A True and Exact History of Barbadoes,* 54.

74. Dunn, *Sugar and Slaves,* 198.

75. Burnard, *Mastery, Tyranny, and Desire,* 232.

76. Mair, *A Historical Study of Women in Jamaica,* 87.

77. Burnard, *Mastery, Tyranny, and Desire*, 156.

78. Burnard, *Mastery, Tyranny, and Desire*, 228–240.

79. Inchiquin to Lords of Trade, 31 August 1690, CO 138/7, folios 1–6; John Helyar letter, 7 August 1690, Helyar Papers, Jamaican letters, 17th Century, DD/WHh/1151–1153, Somerset Heritage Centre.

80. Ligon, *A True and Exact History of Barbadoes*, 48.

81. Dunn, *A Tale of Two Plantations*, 143.

82. Inchiquin to Lords of Trade, 31 August 1690, CO 138/7, folios 1–6; John Helyar letter, 7 August 1690, Helyar Papers, Jamaican letters, 17th Century, DD/WHh/1151–1153, Somerset Heritage Centre.

83. Ligon, *A True and Exact History of Barbadoes*, 115; Buisseret (ed.), *Jamaica in 1687*, 286.

84. Craton, *A Jamaican Plantation*, 144–145.

85. Dunn, *Sugar and Slaves*, 164–165; Smith, *Colonists in Bondage*, 226–284.

86. Preston, *A Pirate of Exquisite Mind*, 53–55.

87. Preston, *A Pirate of Exquisite Mind*, 16–37.

88. Dunn, *A Tale of Two Plantations*, 151–152; John Helyar letter, 7 August 1690, Helyar Papers, Jamaican letters, 17th Century, DD/WHh/1151–1153, Somerset Heritage Centre; Ligon, *A True and Exact History of Barbadoes*, 114.

89. Ligon, *A True and Exact History of Barbadoes*, 114.

90. Wodrow, *The History of the Sufferings of the Church of Scotland*, Volume IV, 186–187.

91. Governor Kendall to Earl of Shrewsbury, 26 June 1690, *Calendar of State Papers Colonial, America and West Indies, Volume 13, 1689–1692*, 276–291.

92. Smith, *Colonists in Bondage*, 226–284.

93. Smith, *Colonists in Bondage*, 236.

94. Ligon, *A True and Exact History of Barbadoes*, 86–89; Dunn, *Sugar and Slaves*, 190–192.

95. Ligon, *A True and Exact History of Barbadoes*, 86–89; Dunn, *Sugar and Slaves*, 190–192.

96. Ligon, *A True and Exact History of Barbadoes*, 89–90.

97. Littleton, *Groans of the Plantations*, 19.

98. Dunn, *Sugar and Slaves*, 194–195; Littleton, *Groans of the Plantations*, 20; Ligon, *A True and Exact History of Barbadoes*, 90–91.

99. Dunn, *Sugar and Slaves*, 195–196; Ligon, *A True and Exact History of Barbadoes*, 91–93.

100. Dunn, *Sugar and Slaves*, 250–252.

101. Delle (ed.), *Out of Many, One People*, 77–101.

102. Buisseret (ed.), *Jamaica in 1687*, 268.

103. Sloane, *A Voyage to the Islands*, xlviii.

104. Delle (ed.), *Out of Many, One People*, 148.

105. Dunn, *Sugar and Slaves*, 251.

106. Sloane, *A Voyage to the Islands*, xlviii.

107. Delle (ed.), *Out of Many, One People*, 14.

108. Burnard, *Mastery, Tyranny, and Desire*, 253.

109. Dunn, *Sugar and Slaves*, 278; Dunn, *A Tale of Two Plantations*, 154.

110. Buisseret (ed.), *Jamaica in 1687*, 268.

111. Sloane, *A Voyage to the Islands*, xx.
112. Dunn, *Sugar and Slaves*, 240; Delle (ed.), *Out of Many, One People*, 164; Craton, *Testing the Chains*, 50.
113. Buisseret (ed.), *Jamaica in 1687*, 269.
114. Ligon, *A True and Exact History of Barbadoes*, 50.
115. Sloane, *A Voyage to the Islands*, xlviii–xlix.
116. Dunn, *Sugar and Slaves*, 250–251.
117. Buisseret (ed.), *Jamaica in 1687*, 272.
118. Speech of Nicolas Lejeune, St. Domingue, 1788. Quoted in Delle (ed.), *Mastery, Tyranny, and Desire*, 137.
119. Dunn, *A Tale of Two Plantations*, 149–150.
120. Sloane, *A Voyage to the Islands*, lvii.
121. Burnard, *Mastery, Tyranny, and Desire*, 104, 150.
122. Sloane, *A Voyage to the Islands*, lvii.
123. Burnard, *Mastery, Tyranny, and Desire*, 150.
124. Sloane, *A Voyage to the Islands*, lvii.
125. Buisseret (ed.), *Jamaica in 1687*, 278.
126. Pinckard, *Notes on the West Indies*, 343.
127. Dunn, *Sugar and Slaves*, 239, 245.
128. Craton, *Testing the Chains*, 52–57.
129. Burnard, *Mastery, Tyranny, and Desire*, 217–218.
130. Craton, *Testing the Chains*, 67.
131. Craton, *Testing the Chains*, 63–65.
132. Craton, *Testing the Chains*, 75–76; Price (ed.), *Maroon Societies*, 256–258.
133. Ligon, *A True and Exact History of Barbadoes*, 46.
134. Burnard, *Mastery, Tyranny, and Desire*, 173.
135. Konadu, *The Akan Diaspora*, 8, 44; Craton, *Testing the Chains*, 110; Burnard, *Mastery, Tyranny, and Desire*, 142.
136. Konadu, *The Akan Diaspora*, 140.
137. Trial of William Hunt's Quawcoo, December 11, 1736. Minutes of the Antiguan Council, January 12, 1737, CO9/10. Quoted in Craton, *Testing the Chains*, 123.
138. Price (ed.), *Maroon Societies*, 20.
139. Dunn, *A Tale of Two Plantations*, 172–180.
140. Price (ed.), *Maroon Societies*, 20, 179, 78–79, 94–95, 33.
141. Behn, *Oroonoko*, 16.
142. Craton, *Testing the Chains*, 77–78. See also footnote 24, 353–354; Price (ed.), *Maroon Societies*, 258.
143. Price (ed.), *Maroon Societies*, 24.
144. John Helyar letter, 7 August 1690, Helyar Papers, Jamaican letters, 17th Century, DD/WHh/1151–1153, Somerset Heritage Centre.
145. Craton, *Testing the Chains*, 76.
146. Quoted in Hilary Beckles, "Crop Fetes and Festivals in Caribbean Slavery," in Alvin O. Thompson (ed.), *In the Shadow of the Plantation*, 249.
147. Trial of William Hunt's Quawcoo, December 11, 1736. Minutes of the Antiguan Council, January 12, 1737, CO9/10. Quoted in Gaspar, *Bondmen and Rebels*, 250.

148. Inchiquin to Lords of Trade, 31 August 1690, CO 138/7, folios 1–6; John Helyar letter, 7 August 1690, Helyar Papers, Jamaican letters, 17th Century, DD/WHh/1151– 1153, Somerset Heritage Centre.

149. Inchiquin to Lords of Trade, 31 August 1690, CO 138/7, folios 1–6; John Helyar letter, 7 August 1690, Helyar Papers, Jamaican letters, 17th Century, DD/WHh/1151– 1153, Somerset Heritage Centre.

150. Inchiquin to Lords of Trade, 31 August 1690, CO 138/7, folios 1–6; John Helyar letter, 7 August 1690, Helyar Papers, Jamaican letters, 17th Century, DD/WHh/1151– 1153, Somerset Heritage Centre.

151. Inchiquin to Lords of Trade, 31 August 1690, CO 138/7, folios 1–6; John Helyar letter, 7 August 1690, Helyar Papers, Jamaican letters, 17th Century, DD/WHh/1151– 1153, Somerset Heritage Centre.

152. Inchiquin to Lords of Trade, 31 August 1690, CO 138/7, folios 1–6; John Helyar letter, 7 August 1690, Helyar Papers, Jamaican letters, 17th Century, DD/WHh/1151– 1153, Somerset Heritage Centre.

153. Long, *The History of Jamaica*, Volume II, 446–447.

154. Minutes of Council of Barbadoes, 24 January 1693, *Calendar of State Papers Colonial, America and West Indies, Volume 14, 1693–1696*, 5.

155. Craton, *Testing the Chains*, 122.

CHAPTER 5: NO PEACE BEYOND THE LINE

1. Little, *The Buccaneer's Realm*, 61–64; Sloane, *A Voyage to the Islands*, lxxxix.

2. Ritsema, *Pirates and Privateers*, 76–78; Marley, *Wars of the Americas*, Volume II, 298.

3. Pawson, *Port Royal*, 59.

4. Inchiquin to Lords of Trade, 6 July 1690, *Calendar of State Papers, Colonial America and West Indies, Volume 13, 1689–1692*, 291–301.

5. *Memorial of the Merchants Trading to Jamaica*, 26 July 1689, *Calendar of State Papers Colonial, America and West Indies, Volume 13, 1689–1692*, pages 100–113.

6. Entries for Jamaican Council Minutes, September to December 1689, *Calendar of State Papers Colonial, America and West Indies, Volume 13, 1689–1692*.

7. Francis Watson to Earl of Shrewsbury, 27 October 1689, *Calendar of State Papers Colonial, America and West Indies, Volume 13, 1689–1692*, 153–171.

8. Blathwayt to the Treasury Lords, 6 August 1690, MSSBL 328, Huntington Library; Council of Jamaica to Lords of Trade and Plantations, 7 May 1690, *Calendar of State Papers Colonial, America and West Indies, Volume 13, 1689–1692*, 255–263.

9. Minutes of Council of Jamaica, 24 June 1691, CO 140/5.

10. Minutes of Council of Jamaica, 12 December 1689, *Calendar of State Papers Colonial, America and West Indies, Volume 13, 1689–1692*, 186–199.

11. Order for Captain Spragg, 22 February 1690, *Calendar of State Papers Colonial, America and West Indies, Volume 13, 1689–1692*, 215–220.

12. Minutes of Council of Jamaica, 21 February 1690, CO 140/5.

13. Ship Arrivals, Port Royal, 14 January 1690, CO 142/13, folio 134.

14. Minutes of Council of Jamaica, 21 February 1690, CO 140/5.

15. Blathwayt to the Treasury Lords, 6 August 1690, MSSBL 328, Huntington Library.

16. Reginald Wilson to William Blathwayt, Port Royal, 10 May 1690, Blathwayt papers, vol. 26, folder 2.

17. Inchiquin to Lords of Trade, 6 July 1690, *Calendar of State Papers Colonial, America and West Indies, Volume 13, 1689–1692*, 291–301.

18. Inchiquin to Lords of Trade, 6 July 1690, *Calendar of State Papers Colonial, America and West Indies, Volume 13, 1689–1692*, 291–301.

19. Buisseret (ed.), *Jamaica in 1687*, 250, 252, 282–284; Dunn, *Sugar and Slaves*, 184, footnote 50.

20. Buisseret (ed.), *Jamaica in 1687*, 250.

21. Inchiquin to Lords of Trade, 31 August 1690, CO 138/7, folios 1–6.

22. Minutes of Council of Jamaica, 15 October 1690, CO 140/5, folio 70.

23. Minutes of Council of Jamaica, 15 October 1690, CO 140/5, folio 70.

24. McCrady, *The History of South Carolina*, 259; Stoney, *Plantations of the Carolina Low Country*, 19–20.

25. Sloane, *A Voyage to the Islands*, xxxii.

26. Will of Gabriel Pitt, PROB 11/409.

27. HMS *Swan* pay book, ADM 33/143.

28. Governor Lord Carlisle to Secretary Coventry, 4 December 1679, St. Jago de la Vega, *Calendar of State Papers Colonial, America and West Indies, Volume 10, 1677–1680*, 448–462.

29. Council of Jamaica to Lords of Trade, 18 June 1692, CO 140/5, folios 209–210; http://www.thepeerage.com/p1441.htm.

30. Beasley, *Christian Ritual*, 38; Buisseret (ed.), *Jamaica in 1687*, 248.

31. Ship Arrivals Port Royal, 4 December 1690, CO142/13, folio 81.

32. Council Meeting Minutes, 16 December 1690, CO140/5, folio 71.

33. Simon Musgrave to William Blathwayt, August 1691, Blathwayt papers, vol. 27, folder 1.

34. HMS *Swan* pay book, ADM 33/143.

35. Ship Arrivals Port Royal, 20 January 1691, CO142/13, folio 84.

36. Inchiquin's Will, PROB 11/414; Pawson, *Port Royal*, 154–155.

37. Ship Arrivals Port Royal, 6 February 1691, CO142/13, folio 84.

38. Council Meeting Minutes, 9 February 1691, CO140/5, folio 74.

39. Ship Arrivals, Port Royal, 23 February 1691, CO142/13, folios 84–85.

40. http://threedecks.org/index.php?display_type=show_ship&id=3249.

41. https://threedecks.org/index.php?display_type=show_ship&id=5665.

42. List of Ships under Captain Wright's Squadron, 1 March 1691, *Calendar of State Papers Colonial, America and West Indies, Volume 13, 1689–1692*, 393–402.

43. Inchiquin to Blathwayt, 3 April 1691, Port Royal, Blathwayt papers, vol. 22, folder 10.

44. Hardy, *A Chronological List of the Captains*, 11.

45. Council Meeting Minutes, 10 March 1691, CO140/5, folio 75.

46. Crouse, *French Struggle for the West Indies*, 199–201.

47. Ship Arrivals, Port Royal, CO142/13, folio 67.

48. Council Meeting Minutes, 2 March 1691, CO140/5, folio 95.

49. Ship Arrivals, Port Royal, CO142/13, folio 67; List of Ships under Captain Wright's Squadron, 1 March 1691; *Calendar of State Papers Colonial, America and West Indies, Volume 13, 1689–1692*, 393–402; HMS *Swan* pay book, ADM

33/143; Reginald Wilson to Blathwayt, 3 April 1691, Port Royal, quoted in Pawson, *Port Royal*, 69; Inchiquin to Blathwayt, 3 April 1691, Port Royal, Blathwayt Papers, vol. 22, folder 10; Peter Beckford to Blathwayt, 2 April 1691, Blathwayt papers, vol. 22, folder 4; Inchiquin to Blathwayt, 12 August 1691, Port Royal, Blathwayt papers, vol. 22, folder 10.

50. Inchiquin to Blathwayt, 3 April 1691, Port Royall, Blathwayt Papers, vol. 22, folder 10.

51. Council Meeting Minutes, CO140/5, folio 95–96.

52. HMS *Guernsey* Log, March 1691, ADM 52/38, folios 860–862.

53. HMS *Guernsey* Pay Roll, ADM 33/157.

54. HMS *Guernsey* log, 16 March 1691, ADM 52/38, folio 861; HMS *Guernsey* Pay Roll, ADM 33/157.

55. HMS *Swan* Pay Roll, ADM 33/143.

56. Inchiquin to Lords of Trade, 12 August 1691, CO 137/7, folios 16–21.

57. Council Meeting Minutes, 20 March 1691, CO140/5, folio 77.

58. HMS *Guernsey* Log, 25 March 1691, ADM 52/38, folio 862.

59. HMS *Guernsey* Log, 25 March 1691, ADM 52/38, folio 862; Dunn, *Sugar and Slaves*, 181.

60. HMS *Guernsey* Log, 25 March 1691, ADM 52/38, folio 862.

61. HMS *Guernsey* Log, 2 April 1691, ADM 52/38, folio 863.

62. Inchiquin to Blathwayt, 5 April 1691, Blathwayt papers, vol. 22, folder 10.

63. HMS *Guernsey* Log, 2–5 April 1691, ADM 52/38, folios 863–864.

64. HMS *Swan* Pay Roll, ADM 33/143.

65. HMS *Guernsey* Log, 9 April 1691, ADM 52/38, folio 864.

66. HMS *Guernsey* Log, 10–14 April 1691, ADM 52/38, folios 864–865.

67. Murray, *An Encyclopedia of Geography*, 1473.

68. HMS *Guernsey* Log, April 1691, ADM 52/38, folio 865.

69. HMS *Guernsey* Log, April 1691, ADM 52/38, folio 865; HMS *Swan* Pay Roll, ADM 33/143.

70. HMS *Guernsey* Log, May 1691, ADM 52/38, folio 867.

71. HMS *Guernsey* Log, May 1691, ADM 52/38, folio 867.

72. Crouse, *French Struggle for the West Indies*, 155.

73. HMS *Guernsey* Log, May 1691, ADM 52/38, folios 867–868.

74. Inchiquin to Blathwayt, 12 August 1691, Port Royal, Blathwayt papers, vol. 22, folder 10.

75. Helyar letter, July 1691, Helyar Papers, Jamaican letters, 17th Century, DD/WHh/1151–1153; Somerset Heritage Centre, Walter Ruding to RAC, 3 June 1691, T70/12, folio 46.

76. Council Meeting Minutes, 21 April 1692, CO140/5, folio 161.

77. Inchiquin to Blathwayt, 12 August 1691, Port Royal, Blathwayt papers, vol. 22, folder 10.

78. Simon Musgrave to Blathwayt, Port Royal, 31 January 1692, Blathwayt papers, vol. 27, folder 1.

79. Codrington to Blathwayt, 3 June 1691, *Calendar of State Papers Colonial, America and West Indies, Volume 13, 1689–1692*, 460–469; Codrington to Colonel Bayer, Antigua, 28 May 1691, 451–460.

80. Council Meeting Minutes, 29 May 1692, CO140/5.

81. HMS *Guernsey* Log, 8 June 1691, ADM 52/38.

CHAPTER 6: THE DECLINE AND FALL OF THE EARL OF INCHIQUIN

1. Buisseret, *Jamaica in 1687*, 251.
2. Inchiquin to Lords of Trade, 31 August 1690, CO 138/7, folios 1–6.
3. Inchiquin to Lords of Trade, 12 August 1691, CO 137/7, folios 16–21.
4. Inchiquin to Lords of Trade, 6 July 1690, *Calendar of State Papers Colonial, America and West Indies, Volume 13, 1689–1692*, 291–301.
5. Long, *History of Jamaica*, Volume I, 56.
6. Long, History of Jamaica, Volume I, 57.
7. Cundall, *Governors of Jamaica*, 118–123.
8. Council Meeting Minutes, 9 June 1691, CO140/5, folios 87–88.
9. Inchiquin to Lords of Trade, 12 August 1691, CO 137/7, folios 16–21.
10. Council Meeting Minutes, 9 February 1691, CO140/5, folio 74.
11. Cook, *Edmond Halley*, 53, 59, 74, 81. In 1682 Halley first observed the comet which would later be given his name.
12. Inchiquin to Lords of Trade, 12 August 1691, CO 137/7, folios 16–21.
13. http://www.antonymaitland.com/jamgenrl.htm; Marley, *Pirates of the Americas*, Volume I, 166.
14. Council Meeting Minutes, 16 December 1690, CO140/5, folio 71
15. Sloane, *A Voyage to the Islands*, lxxiv.
16. Inchiquin to Blathwayt, 12 August 1691, Blathwayt papers, vol. 22, folder 10.
17. Cundall, *Governors of Jamaica*, 124–130.
18. Robertson, *Gone Is the Ancient Glory*, 24–29, 59–62; Beasley, *Christian Ritual*, 38–53.
19. Robertson, *Gone is the Ancient Glory*, 59–62.
20. Clarke, *Proceedings and Reports of the Belfast Natural History and Philosophical Society, 157th–161st Sessions*, 37–44.
21. Long, *The History of Jamaica*, Volume I, 54.
22. Simon Musgrave to William Blathwayt, August 1691, Blathwayt papers, vol. 27, folder 1.
23. Council Meeting Minutes, 9 June 1691, CO140/5, folios 87–88.
24. Long, *The History of Jamaica*, Volume I, 54; Inchiquin to Lords of Trade, 12 August 1691, CO 137/7, folios 16–21.
25. Inchiquin to Lords of Trade, 12 August 1691, CO 137/7, folios 16–21.
26. Inchiquin to Lords of Trade, 12 August 1691, CO 137/7, folios 16–21.
27. *Account of the calling, proceedings and dissolution of the last Assembly of Jamaica*, Various Authors, 28 January 1692, reproduced in Council Meeting Minutes, 28 January 1692, CO140/5, folios 126–128.
28. Inchiquin to Lords of Trade, 12 August 1691, CO 137/7, folios 16–21.
29. Inchiquin to Lords of Trade, 12 August 1691, CO 137/7, folios 16–21; *Account of the calling, proceedings and dissolution of the last Assembly of Jamaica*, Various Authors, 28 January 1692, reproduced in Council Meeting Minutes, 28 January 1692, CO140/5, folios 126–128; Simon Musgrave to William Blathwayt, August 1691, Blathwayt papers, vol. 27, folder 1.
30. Inchiquin to Lords of Trade, 12 August 1691, CO 137/7, folios 16–21; *Ac-*

count of the calling, proceedings and dissolution of the last Assembly of Jamaica, Various Authors, 28 January 1692, reproduced in Council Meeting Minutes, 28 January 1692, CO140/5, folios 126–128; Simon Musgrave to William Blathwayt, August 1691, Blathwayt papers, vol. 27, folder 1.

31. Inchiquin to Lords of Trade, 12 August 1691, CO 137/7, folios 16–21; *Account of the calling, proceedings and dissolution of the last Assembly of Jamaica*, Various Authors, 28 January 1692, reproduced in Council Meeting Minutes, 28 January 1692, CO140/5, folios 126–128; Simon Musgrave to William Blathwayt, August 1691, Blathwayt papers, vol. 27, folder 1.

32. Francis Watson also dissolved the assembly. See Cundall, *Governors of Jamaica*, 124–130.

33. Simon Musgrave to Blathwayt, 18 August 1691, Blathwayt papers, vol.27, folder 1; 18 August 1691, Reginald Wilson to Blathwayt, Blathwayt papers, vol. 26, folder 3; 25/28 September 1691; Reginald Wilson to Blathwayt, Blathwayt papers, vol. 26, folder 3, Council Meeting Notes, 7 August 1691, CO140/5, folio 107; Brooks, *Quest for Blackbeard*, 214–215.

34. Ship Arrivals, Port Royal, CO142/13, 95–101.

35. Ship Arrivals, Port Royal, CO142/13, folio 95.

36. Earle, *Treasure Hunt*, 61, 78.

37. Ship Arrivals, Port Royal, CO142/13, folios 91, 95, and 99.

38. Port Royal Inventories, Robert Scroope, entered February 1692/3, vol. 3, fol. 419; Ship Arrivals Port Royal, CO142/13, folios 95 and 100.

39. Council Meeting Notes, 7 August 1691, CO140/5, folio 107; HMS *Guernsey* Log, entry for 23 August 1691, ADM 52/38; Gaines's ship is not to be mistaken for the *Seahorse* that had been in Port Royal in 1690 under Captain John How.

40. Marx, *The History of Underwater Exploration*, 18–23.

41. Phips was also rewarded with the governorship of Massachusetts. He arrived in 1692 at the time of the infamous Salem witch trials, a situation for which he proved ill suited. He died soon afterward.

42. Marx, *The History of Underwater Exploration*, 23–26. See also Earle, *The Wreck of the Almiranta*.

43. Marx, *The History of Underwater Exploration*, 8, 27.

44. Marx, *The History of Underwater Exploration*, 21.

45. Marx, *The History of Underwater Exploration*, 30–39.

46. Ship Arrivals, Port Royal, CO142/13, 95–101.

47. Simon Musgrave to Blathwayt, 18 August 1691, Blathwayt papers, vol. 27, folder 1; Reginald Wilson to Blathwayt, 18 August 1691, Blathwayt papers, vol. 26, folder 3.

48. HMS *Guernsey* Log, ADM 52/38, folio 865; HMS *Swan* Pay Roll, ADM 33/143.

49. Ship Departures, Port Royal, CO142/13, folio 143; Ship Arrivals, Port Royal, CO142/13, folio 92.

50. HMS *Guernsey* Log, 27 September 1691, ADM 52/38; Ship Departures, Port Royal, CO142/13, folio 143; Reginald Wilson to Blathwayt, 25–28 September 1691, Blathwayt papers, vol. 26, folder 3.

51. HMS *Guernsey* Log, 26–28 September 1691, ADM 52/38.

52. Beasley, *Christian Ritual*, 38.

53. Ship Arrivals, Port Royal, CO142/13, folios 97–98.

54. Ship Arrivals, Port Royal, CO142/13, folios 100–105.

55. RAC in-letter, Walter Ruding to RAC, 17 November 1691, T70/12, folio 47.

56. HMS *Guernsey* log, September to December 1691, ADM 52/38; HMS *Swan* Pay Roll, ADM 33/143.

57. *Philosophical Transactions*, Volume 17 (1693), 89.

58. Council Meeting Notes, December 1691 to May 1692, CO 140/5.

59. George Reeve to Lord Sydney, 3 February 1692, *Calendar of State Papers Colonial, America and West Indies, Volume 13, 1689–1692*, 597–605.

60. Sloane, *A Voyage to the Islands*, cxxxiv, cxli.

61. George Reeve to Lord Sydney, 3 February 1692, *Calendar of State Papers Colonial, America and West Indies, Volume 13, 1689–1692*, 597–605; Inchiquin's Will, PROB 11/414; Cundall, *The Governors of Jamaica*, 128.

62. Samuel Bernard to the Earl of Nottingham, 18 April 1692, *Calendar of State Papers Colonial, America and West Indies, Volume 13, 1689–1692*, 616–634.

63. Inchiquin's Will, PROB 11/414.

64. Reginald Wilson to Blathwayt, 28 April 1692, Blathwayt papers, vol. 26, folder 3; Musgrave to Blathwayt, 31 January 1692, Blathwayt papers, vol. 27, folder 1; George Reeve to Lord Sydney, 3 February 1692, *Calendar of State Papers Colonial, America and West Indies, Volume 13, 1689– 1692*, 597–605.

65. *Account of the calling, proceedings and dissolution of the last Assembly of Jamaica*, Various Authors, 28 January 1692, reproduced in Council Meeting Minutes, 28 January 1692, CO140/5, folios 126–128; Inchiquin to Lords of Trade, 12 August 1691, CO 137/7, folios 16–21; Inchiquin to Earl of Nottingham, 12 August 1691, CO 137/7, folios 16–21.

66. Cundall, *The Governors of Jamaica*, 131–139.

67. Council Meeting Minutes, 16, 18, 21 January 1692, CO 140/5.

68. Stern, *Portuguese Sephardim in the Americas*; Galante, *Port Royal*.

69. *The President and Council of Jamaica to Lords of Trade and Plantations*, 8 January 1692, *Calendar of State Papers Colonial, America and West Indies, Volume 13, 1689–1692*, 583–596.

70. Musgrave to Blathwayt, 2/3 February 1692, Blathwayt papers, vol. 27, folder 1.

71. Swetschinski and Schönduve, *De familie Lopes Suasso, financiers van Willem III*; Stern, *Portuguese Sephardim in the Americas*; Galante, *Port Royal*.

72. George Reeve to Lord Sydney, 3 February 1692, *Calendar of State Papers Colonial, America and West Indies, Volume 13, 1689–1692*, 597–605.

73. Council Meeting Minutes, 4 and 5 February 1692, CO 140/5.

74. Council Meeting Minutes, 2 March 1692, 6 April 1692, CO 140/5.

75. Council Meeting Minutes, April 1692, CO 140/5.

76. HMS *Guernsey* Log, 15 April 1692, ADM 52/38; Ship Arrivals, Port Royal, CO142/13, folio 105; Joseph Norris to Isaac Norris, 30 April 1692, Norris Letters, Historical Society of Pennsylvania.

77. Joseph Norris to Isaac Norris, 30 April 1692, Norris Letters, Historical Society of Pennsylvania.

78. HMS *Guernsey* Log, 30 April and 1 May 1692, ADM 52/38; Musgrave to

Blathwayt, 1 May 1692, Blathwayt Papers, vol. 27, folder 1.
79. *Philosophical Transactions*, 17 (1693), 89.
80. Buisseret (ed.), *Jamaica in 1687*, 118–120.

CHAPTER 7: A DISMAL CALAMITY

1. Pawson, *Port Royal*, 1–6; Sloane, *A Voyage to the Islands*, xlvii.
2. Sloane, *A Voyage to the Islands*, xlv–xlvii.
3. *Philosophical Transactions*, 17 (1693), 89.
4. Council Meeting Minutes, 28 May 1692, CO 140/5, folios 187–188; HMS *Guernsey* Log, May-June 1692, ADM 52/38.
5. Jamaican Council to Lords of Trade, 18 June 1692, CO 140/5, folios 209–210.
6. Ship Arrivals, Port Royal, CO 142/13, folios 102, 109; Ruding and Barnard to RAC, 25 April 1692, T70/12, folios 47–48;
7. HMS *Guernsey* Log, 20 May 1692, ADM 52/38.
8. Council Meeting Minutes, 7 June 1692, CO 140/5, folio 196.
9. Letter from Jamaica, 20 June 1692, in *Philosophical Transactions*, 17 (1693), 83.
10. Report of John Uffgress, reproduced in Marx, *Sunken City*, 21–22.
11. Cadbury, "Quakers and the Earthquake at Port Royal, 1692."
12. Account of Dr. Emmanuel Heath, reproduced in Philotheus, *A True and Particular History of Earthquakes*, 57–59.
13. Pawson, *Port Royal*, 165–168.
14. Letter from Jamaica, 20 June 1692, reproduced in *Philosophical Transactions*, 17 (1693), 83.
15. Account of Dr. Emmanuel Heath, reproduced in Philotheus, *A True and Particular History of Earthquakes*, 57–59.
16. Samuel Barnard to RAC, 17 June 1692, T70/12, folios 47–48; Edmund Edlyne to Blathwayt, Jamaica, 20 June 1692, in *Jamaican Historical Review* 8, 60–62.
17. Quoted in Renny, *A History of Jamaica*, 223.
18. Cadbury, "Quakers and the Earthquake at Port Royal, 1692."
19. Report of Anonymous Merchant, reproduced in Marx, *Sunken City*, 22.
20. Cadbury, "Quakers and the Earthquake at Port Royal, 1692."
21. *The Truest and Largest Account of the Late Earthquake in Jamaica*; Pawson, *Port Royal*, 165–168.
22. Account of Dr. Emmanuel Heath, reproduced in Philotheus, *A True and Particular History of Earthquakes*, 57–59.
23. Report of John Uffgress, reproduced in Marx, *Sunken City*, 21–22.
24. *Philosophical Transactions*, 415.
25. Cadbury, "Quakers and the Earthquake at Port Royal, 1692"; *Journal of the Institute of Jamaica*, Volume I, 147–150.
26. Smith, *A Natural History of Nevis*, 62–63.
27. Report of John Uffgress, reproduced in Marx, *Sunken City*, 21–22.
28. Account of Dr. Emmanuel Heath, reproduced in Philotheus, *A True and Particular History of Earthquakes*, 57–59.
29. Report of John Uffgress, reproduced in Marx, *Sunken City*, 21–22.

30. Barnard to RAC, 17 June 1692, T70/12, folios 47–48; Marx, *Sunken City*, 163–164.

31. Edmund Edlyne to Blathwayt, Jamaica, 20 June 1692, reproduced in *Jamaican Historical Review*, volume 8, 60–62; Council Meeting Minutes, 20 June 1692, CO 140/5; *Journal of the Institute of Jamaica*, Volume I, 147–150.

32. HMS *Swan* Pay Roll, ADM 33/143.

33. Accounts from *Philosophical Transactions*.

34. Account of Dr. Emmanuel Heath, reproduced in Philotheus, *A True and Particular History of Earthquakes*, 57–59.

35. Accounts from *Philosophical Transactions*.

36. HMS *Guernsey* Log, 7 June 1692, ADM 52/38.

37. Accounts from *Philosophical Transactions*.

38. *The Truest and Largest Account of the Late Earthquake in Jamaica*.

39. Cadbury, "Quakers and the Earthquake at Port Royal, 1692"; *Journal of the Institute of Jamaica*, Volume I, 147–150.

40. Accounts from *Philosophical Transactions*.

41. Account of Dr. Emmanuel Heath, reproduced in Philotheus, *A True and Particular History of Earthquakes*, 57–59.

42. *Account of the Late Earthquake in Jamaica*; *The Truest and Largest Account of the Late Earthquake in Jamaica*; Cadbury, "Quakers and the Earthquake at Port Royal, 1692."

43. Account of Dr. Emmanuel Heath, reproduced in Philotheus, *A True and Particular History of Earthquakes*, 57–59; Accounts from *Philosophical Transactions*, 412.

44. Report of John Uffgress, reproduced in Marx, *Sunken City*, 21–22.

45. Account of Dr. Emmanuel Heath, reproduced in Philotheus, *A True and Particular History of Earthquakes*, 57–59.

46. *The Truest and Largest Account of the Late Earthquake in Jamaica*.

47. Account of Dr. Emmanuel Heath, reproduced in Philotheus, *A True and Particular History of Earthquakes*, 57–59.

48. *The Truest and Largest Account of the Late Earthquake in Jamaica*; Account of Dr. Emmanuel Heath, reproduced in Philotheus, *A True and Particular History of Earthquakes*, 57–59.

49. *The Truest and Largest Account of the Late Earthquake in Jamaica*; Account of Dr. Emmanuel Heath, reproduced in Philotheus, *A True and Particular History of Earthquakes*, 57–59; Report of John Uffgress, reproduced in Marx, *Sunken City*, 21– 22; Accounts from *Philosophical Transactions*; Cadbury, "Quakers and the Earthquake at Port Royal, 1692"; J. A. Wale letter, 1692, quoted in Foster, *Jamaica: The Postal History*, 4; Edmund Edlyne to Blathwayt, Jamaica, 20 June 1692, reproduced in *Jamaican Historical Review*, 8 (1971), 60–62; *Journal of the Institute of Jamaica*, I, 147–150.

50. *The Truest and Largest Account of the Late Earthquake in Jamaica*.

51. *The Truest and Largest Account of the Late Earthquake in Jamaica*.

52. Cadbury, "Quakers and the Earthquake at Port Royal, 1692."

53. Account of Dr. Emmanuel Heath, reproduced in Philotheus, *A True and Particular History of Earthquakes*, 57–59.

54. Report of John Uffgress, reproduced in Marx, *Sunken City*, 21–22.

55. Account of Dr. Emmanuel Heath, reproduced in Philotheus, *A True and Particular History of Earthquakes*, 57–59; Report of John Uffgress, reproduced in Marx, *Sunken City*, 21–22; *The Truest and Largest Account of the Late Earthquake in Jamaica*.

56. Cadbury, "Quakers and the Earthquake at Port Royal, 1692."

57. Account of Dr. Emmanuel Heath, reproduced in Philotheus, *A True and Particular History of Earthquakes*, 57–59; Report of John Uffgress, reproduced in Marx, *Sunken City*, 21–22; *The Truest and Largest Account of the Late Earthquake in Jamaica*.

58. Cadbury, "Quakers and the Earthquake at Port Royal, 1692."

59. Barnett and Wright, *The Jews of Jamaica*, 6; Cadbury, "Quakers and the Earthquake at Port Royal, 1692."

60. Council Meeting Minutes, 14 June 1692, CO 140/5.

61. Council Meeting Minutes, June 1692, CO 140/5; HMS *Swan* Pay Roll, ADM 33/143.

62. Council Meeting Minutes, 21 June 1692, CO 140/5; HMS *Guernsey* Log, June 1692, ADM 52/38.

63. Reproduced in Pawson, *Port Royal*, 66.

64. Sloane, *A Voyage to the Islands*, 51.

65. Wale letter, 1692, quoted in Foster, *Jamaica: The Postal History*, 4.

66. Council Meeting Minutes, 28 June 1692, CO 140/5.

67. Cadbury, "Quakers and the Earthquake at Port Royal, 1692."

CHAPTER 8: INHUMAN BARBARITIES

1. Council Meeting Minutes, 28 June 1692, CO 140/5.

2. Cundall, *Governors of Jamaica*, 143–165.

3. Dunn, *Sugar and Slaves*, 296.

4. Beeston to Nottingham, 22 March 1693, *Calendar of State Papers Colonial, America and West Indies, Volume 14, 1693–1696*, 53–70.

5. Pawson, *Port Royal*, 168–170, 177.

6. HMS *Swan* Pay Roll, ADM 33/143; Council Meeting Minutes, 16 June 1692, CO 140/5, folios 196–198.

7. HMS *Swan* Pay Roll, ADM 33/143.

8. Admiralty to Neville, February 1694, NMM, ADM 1804/80.

9. *Deposition of Captain James Moodie*, 1701, reproduced at https://geesnmore. wordpress.com/charles-gee-bridget-neville/neville-family/.

10. Parker, *The Sugar Barons*, 97–111; Black, *History of Jamaica*, 51–52; Crouse, *French Struggle for the West Indies*, 190–196.

11. Beeston to Shrewsbury, 18 August 1694, *Calendar of State Papers Colonial, America and West Indies, Volume 14, 1693–1696*, 324–341.

12. Beeston to Lords of Trade, 6 November 1694, *Calendar of State Papers Colonial, America and West Indies, Volume 14, 1693–1696*, 390–399; Crouse, *French Struggle for the West Indies*, 191–192; Buisseret, "The French Invasion of Jamaica, 1694"; *A Narrative of Sir William Beeston of the Descent on Jamaica by the French*, in Lewis (ed.), *Interesting Tracts*, 249–259.

13. Lewis (ed.), *Interesting Tracts*, 249–259; Beeston to Shrewsbury, 18 August 1694, *Calendar of State Papers Colonial, America and West Indies, Volume 14, 1693–1696*, 324–341.

14. Lewis (ed.), *Interesting Tracts*, 249–259; Beeston to Shrewsbury, 18 August 1694, *Calendar of State Papers Colonial, America and West Indies, Volume 14, 1693–1696*, 324–341.

15. Lewis (ed.), *Interesting Tracts*, 249–259; Beeston to Shrewsbury, 18 August 1694, *Calendar of State Papers Colonial, America and West Indies, Volume 14, 1693–1696*, 324–341.

16. Buisseret, "The French Invasion of Jamaica, 1694."

17. Lewis (ed.), *Interesting Tracts*, 249–259; Beeston to Shrewsbury, 18 August 1694, *Calendar of State Papers Colonial, America and West Indies, Volume 14, 1693–1696*, 324–341; Buisseret, "The French Invasion of Jamaica, 1694."

18. Beeston to Trenchard, 23 June 1694, *Calendar of State Papers Colonial, America and West Indies, Volume 14, 1693–1696*, 291–301.

19. Beeston to Trenchard, 23 June 1694, *Calendar of State Papers Colonial, America and West Indies, Volume 14, 1693–1696*, 291–301.

20. Lewis (ed.), *Interesting Tracts*, 249–259; Beeston to Shrewsbury, 18 August 1694, *Calendar of State Papers Colonial, America and West Indies, Volume 14, 1693–1696*, 324–341; Buisseret, "The French Invasion of Jamaica, 1694."

21. Beeston to Trenchard, 2 July 1694, *Calendar of State Papers Colonial, America and West Indies, Volume 14, 1693–1696*, 301–305; Council Meeting Minutes, 3 July 1694, 301–305.

22. Beeston to Trenchard, 7 July 1694, *Calendar of State Papers Colonial, America and West Indies, Volume 14, 1693–1696*, 301–305.

23. Lewis (ed.), *Interesting Tracts*, 249–259; Beeston to Shrewsbury, 18 August 1694, *Calendar of State Papers Colonial, America and West Indies, Volume 14, 1693–1696*, 324–341; Buisseret, "The French Invasion of Jamaica, 1694."

24. Lewis (ed.), *Interesting Tracts*, 249–259; Beeston to Shrewsbury, 18 August 1694, *Calendar of State Papers Colonial, America and West Indies, Volume 14, 1693–1696*, 324–341; Buisseret, "The French Invasion of Jamaica, 1694." For details on the *Mediterranean*, see http://www.slavevoyages.org/voyage/14911/variables.

25. Lewis (ed.), *Interesting Tracts*, 249–259; Beeston to Shrewsbury, 18 August 1694, *Calendar of State Papers Colonial, America and West Indies, Volume 14, 1693–1696*, 324–341; Buisseret, "The French Invasion of Jamaica, 1694."

26. Lewis (ed.), *Interesting Tracts*, 249–259; Beeston to Shrewsbury, 18 August 1694, *Calendar of State Papers Colonial, America and West Indies, Volume 14, 1693–1696*, 324–341; Buisseret, "The French Invasion of Jamaica, 1694"; Beeston to Lords of Trade, 7 August 1694, *Calendar of State Papers Colonial, America and West Indies, Volume 14, 1693–1696*, 315–324.

27. Council Meeting Minutes, 2, 4, 5 August 1694, *Calendar of State Papers Colonial, America and West Indies, Volume 14, 1693–1696*, 315–324.

28. Lewis (ed.), *Interesting Tracts*, 249–259; Beeston to Shrewsbury, 18 August 1694, *Calendar of State Papers Colonial, America and West Indies, Volume 14, 1693–1696*, 324–341; Buisseret, "The French Invasion of Jamaica, 1694"; Beeston to Lords of Trade, 7 August 1694, *Calendar of State Papers Colonial, America and West Indies, Volume 14, 1693–1696*, 315–324.

29. Beeston to Shrewsbury, 18 August 1694, *Calendar of State Papers Colonial, America and West Indies, Volume 14, 1693–1696*, 324–341.

30. Richard Lloyd to the Council of Trade and Plantations, 23 May 1699, *Cal-*

endar of State Papers Colonial, America and West Indies, Volume 17, 1699 and Addenda 1621– 1698, 240–249.

31. Buisseret, "The French Invasion of Jamaica, 1694," 31–33; Parker, *The Sugar Barons*, 97–111; Black, *History of Jamaica*, 51–52; Crouse, *French Struggle for the West Indies*, 190–196.

EPILOGUE

1. Crouse, *French Struggle for the West Indies*, 196; Marley, *Wars of the Americas*, volume II, 210.
2. Crouse, *French Struggle for the West Indies*, 196–211.
3. Captain John Moses, 8 April 1696, ADM 106/492/119; Captain John Moses, 16 September 1696, ADM 106/492/245; Captain John Moses, 11 December 1696, ADM 106/492/301.
4. Crouse, *French Struggle for the West Indies*, 212–245.
5. Beckford to the Council of Trade and Plantations, 25 August 1702, *Calendar of State Papers Colonial, America and West Indies, Volume 20, 1702*, 548–566.
6. Beckford to the Council of Trade and Plantations, 22 September 1702, *Calendar of State Papers Colonial, America and West Indies, Volume 20, 1702*, 599–611; Craton, *Testing the Chains*, 79–80.
7. Price (ed.), *Maroon Societies*, 260–261; Craton, *Testing the Chains*, 77–85.
8. Black, *Port Royal*, 35–37; Pawson, *Port Royal*, 170.
9. Petition of Peter Beckford, 10 September 1703, *Calendar of State Papers Colonial, America and West Indies, Volume 21, 1702–1703*, 662–681.
10. Black, *Port Royal*, 35–37.
11. Dunn, *Sugar and Slaves*, 298.
12. Thomas Sutton's Will, PROB 11/520.
13. Black, *Port Royal*, 37–40.
14. Lawes to the Council of Trade and Plantations, 20 September 1722, *Calendar of State Papers Colonial, America and West Indies, Volume 33, 1722–1723*, 138–152; Atkins, *A Voyage to Guinea*, 238–242.
15. Price (ed.), *Maroon Societies*, 260–261; Craton, *Testing the Chains*, 77–85.
16. *Calendar of State Papers Colonial, America and West Indies, Volumes 33–40*.
17. Mair, *A Historical Study of Women in Jamaica*, 61.
18. Price (ed.), *Maroon Societies*, 263.
19. Craton, *Testing the Chains*, 81–85; Price (ed.), *Maroon Societies*, 263–266.
20. Price (ed.), *Maroon Societies*, 266.
21. Price (ed.), *Maroon Societies*, 269.
22. Craton, *Testing the Chains*, 87–91.
23. Price (ed.), *Maroon Societies*, 271–274.
24. Quoted in Black, *Port Royal*, 57–58.
25. Black, *Port Royal*, 41–62; Pawson, *Port Royal*, 173–200.
26. Parker, *The Sugar Barons*, 333–334.
27. Black, *History of Jamaica*, 87–92; Parker, *The Sugar Barons*, 345–350.
28. Parker, *The Sugar Barons*, 348–357; Black, *History of Jamaica*, 99–102.
29. Craton, *Testing the Chains*, 267–321.
30. Parker, *The Sugar Barons*, 348–357; Black, *History of Jamaica*, 99–113.
31. Craton, *Testing the Chains*, 323–334; Black, *History of Jamaica*, 114–134.
32. http://www.jamaicaobserver.com/news/January–6-come-again-_13322164.

Bibliography

MANUSCRIPT SOURCES

National Archives, Kew, London
    ADM 33 Admiralty Papers, Ships' Pay Books
    ADM 36 Admiralty Papers, Ships' Musters
    ADM 52 Admiralty Papers, Ships' Logs
    ADM 106 Admiralty Papers, Captains' In-Letters
    CO 138/6–7 Colonial Office Papers, In-Letters, Jamaica
    CO 140/5 Colonial Office Papers, Jamaican Council Notes
    CO 142/13 Colonial Office Papers, Ship Arrivals, Port Royal
    PC 2 Privy Council Papers
    PROB Last Wills and Testaments
    T70 Papers of the Royal African Company
National Maritime Museum, Greenwich, London
    ADM 1804 Admiralty Out Letters
Somerset Heritage Centre, Somerset, England
    DD/WHh/1151–1153 Helyar Papers. Jamaican letters, 17th
    Century
John D. Rockefeller Jr. Library, Colonial Williamsburg Foundation,
    Virginia.
    WBP #MS 1946.2 William Blathwayt Papers, 1631–1722
Historical Society of Pennsylvania
    Norris Family Papers Isaac Norris Letter-Book
Huntington Library, California
    MSSBL 328 William Blathwayt Letters

PUBLISHED PRIMARY SOURCES

Account of the Late Earthquake in Jamaica . . . London, 1692.
Atkins, John. *A Voyage to Guinea, Brasil, and the West Indies; In His
    Majesty's Ships, the Swallow and Weymouth.* London, 1735.

Barbot, Jean. *Barbot on Guinea: The Writings of Jean Barbot on West Africa, 1678–1712*. Charlottesville: University of Virginia/ Hakluyt Society, 1992.

Barnett, Richard D., and Wright, Philip. *The Jews of Jamaica: Tombstone Inscriptions, 1663–1880*. Jerusalem, 1997.

Behn, Aphra. *Oroonoko, or the Royal Slave: A True History*. London: Penguin, 2003.

Besse, Joseph. *A Collection of the Sufferings of People Called Quakers, Volume 2*. London: L. Hinde, 1753.

Blome, Richard. *A Description of the Island of Jamaica*. London, 1678.

Bosman, Willem. *A New and Accurate Description of the Coast of Guinea Divided into the Gold, the Slave, and the Ivory Coasts*. Delhi: Facsimile Publisher, 2015.

Bridges, Rev. George Wilson. *The Annals of Jamaica, Volume the First*. London: John Murray, 1828.

Buisseret, David (ed.). *Jamaica in 1687: The Taylor Manuscript at the National Library of Jamaica*. Kingston: University of the West Indies Press, 2010.

Chambers, Douglas B. (ed.). *Runaway Slaves in Jamaica (I): Eighteenth Century*. University of Southern Mississippi, February 2013.

Coad, John. *A Memorandum of the Wonderful Providences of God . . . during the time of the Duke of Monmouth's Rebellion and to the Revolution in 1688*. London: Longman, Brown, Green & Longman, 1849.

Concannon, T. A. L. (ed.). *Jamaican Historical Review, Port Royal, Volume VIII*. Old Woking: Gresham Press, 1971.

Donnan, Elizabeth (ed.). *Documents Illustrative of the History of the Slave Trade, Volume I, 1441–1700*. New York: Octagon Books, 1969.

Duncan, John. *Travels in Western Africa in 1845 & 1846: Comprising a Journey from Wyhdah, Through the Kingdom of Dahomey, to Adofoodia, in the Interior*. Volume II. London, 1847.

Equiano, Olaudah. *The Interesting Narrative of the Life of Olaudah Equiano, or Gustavus Vassa, the African*. London, 1794.

Hanson, Francis. *The Laws of Jamaica*. London: Charles Harper, 1683.

Hutton, Charles, George Shaw, and Richard Pearson (eds.). *The Philosophical Transactions of the Royal Society of London . . . Volume III, from 1683 to 1694*. London, 1809.

Journal of the Institute of Jamaica, Volume I. Kingston: The Institute, 1892.

Lewis, Lunan, and Jones (eds.). *Interesting Tracts, Relating to the Island of Jamaica: Consisting of Curious State-Papers, Councils of War, Letters, Petitions, Narratives &c, which throw great light on the history of that island, from its conquest down to the year 1702.* Santiago de la Vega, Jamaica: Lewis, Lunan and Jones, 1800.

Ligon, Richard. *A True and Exact History of the Island of Barbados.* London, 1673.

Lyttleton, Edward. *Groans of the Plantations.* London, 1689.

May, Rev. William. *Jamaica: Description of the Principal Persons there*, in Vere L. Oliver, *Caribbeana*, vol. 3, pp. 5–9. London, 1914.

Moore, Samuel. *Biography of Mahommah G. Baquaqua, A Native of Soogoo, in the Interior of Africa.* Detroit, 1854.

Mortimer, Russel (ed.). *Bristol Record Society's Publications, Volume 26, Minute Book of the Men's Meeting of the Society of Friends in Bristol.* Bristol Records Society, Bristol, 1971.

Ovington, John. *A Voyage to Suratt, in the Year, 1689: Giving a Large Account of that City . . . Likewise a Description of Madeira . . .* London, 1696.

Phillips, Thomas. *A Journal of a Voyage Made in the Hannibal of London, Ann. 1693, 1694, from England, to Cape Monseradoe, in Africa, and Thence along the Coast of Guiney . . .* Published in *A Collection of Voyages and Travels, Some Now First Printed from Original Manuscripts Others Now First Published in English. In Six Volumes.* Volume VI. Walthoe, 1732.

Philotheus. *A True and Particular History of Earthquakes, Containing A Relation of that Dreadful Earthquake which happen'd at Lima and Callao . . . also of that which Happen'd in Jamaica in 1692 . . .* London, 1748.

Pinckard, George. *Notes on the West Indies, Including Obsrvations Relative to the Creoles and Slaves of the Western Colonies, and the Indians of South America, Interspersed with Remarks upon the Seasoning or Yellow Fever of Hot Climates. Second Edition, with Additional Letters from Martinique, Jamaica, and St. Domingo.* Volume I. London: Baldwin, Cradock, and Joy, 1816.

Pringle, Thomas (ed.). *The History of Mary Prince a West Indian Slave Related by Herself: With a Supplement by the Editor to which is Added the Narrative of Asas-Asa, a Captured African.* London, 1831.

Sloane, Hans. *A Voyage to the Islands of Madera, Barbados, Nieves, S. Christophers and Jamaica . . . in Two Volumes.* London, 1707.

Stedman, Captain John G. *Expedition to Suriname, Being the Narrative of a five years expedition against the revolted negroes of Suriname in Guiana.* London: Folio Society, 1963.

The Truest and Largest Account of the Late Earthquake in Jamaica. London, 1693.

Venables, Robert. *The Narrative of General Venables with an Appendix of Papers Relating to the Expedition to the West Indies and the Conquest of Jamaica.* New York: Longmans, 1900.

Vernon, Thomas (ed.). *Cases Argued and Adjudged in the High Court of Chancery, Originally Published by Order of the Courts.* Volume II, Part I. London, 1806.

Ward, Edward. *A Trip to Jamaica with a True Character of the People and Island . . .* London, 1698.

PUBLISHED SECONDARY SOURCES

Agnew, David Carnegie A. *Protestant Exiles from France, Chiefly in the Reign of Louis XIV: Or, The Huguenot Refugees and Their Descendants in Great Britain and Ireland, Volume I.* Edinburgh: Turnbull & Spears, 1886.

Arbell, Mordechai. *The Portuguese Jews of Jamaica.* Kingston: Canoe Press, 2000.

Ashcroft, M. T. "Tercentenary of the First English Book on Tropical Medicine, by Thomas Trapham of Jamaica." *British Medical Journal,* 2 (25 August 1979), 475–477.

Ashley, Maurice. *England in the Seventeenth Century, 1603–1714.* London: Penguin, 1956

Beasley, Nicholas M. *Christian Ritual and the Creation of British Slave Societies, 1650–1780.* Athens: University of Georgia Press, 2009.

Black, Clinton V. *Tales of Old Jamaica.* London: Collins, 1966.

———. *The History of Jamaica.* Kingston: Longman Caribbean, 1983.

———. *Port Royal.* Kingston: Institute of Jamaica, 1996.

Brooks, Eric Saint John. *Sir Hans Sloane: The Great Collector and His Circle.* London, 1954.

Buisseret, David. "Slaves Arriving in Jamaica, 1684–1692." *Revue Française d'Histoire d'Outre-mer*, 54 (1977), 85–88.

———. *Historic Architecture of the Caribbean*. Kingston: Heinemann, 1980.

———. "The French Invasion of Jamaica, 1694." *Jamaica Journal*, 16 (1983), 31–33.

Burg, B. R. *Sodomy and the Pirate Tradition: English Sea Rovers in the Seventeenth Century Caribbean*. New York: New York University Press, 1984.

Burnard, Trevor. *Mastery, Tyranny, and Desire: Thomas Thistlewood and His Slaves in the Anglo-Jamaican World*. Chapel Hill: University of North Carolina Press, 2004.

Caliendo, Ralph J. *New York City Mayors: Part I: The Mayors of New York Before 1898*. New York: Xlibris, 2010.

Canny, Nicholas (ed.). *The Origins of Empire: British Overseas Enterprise to the Close of the Seventeenth Century*. Oxford: Oxford University Press, 1998.

Childs, John. *The Nine Years' War and the British Army, 1688–97*. Manchester: Manchester University Press, 1991.

———. *The Williamite Wars in Ireland, 1688–91*. London: Hambledon Continuum, 2007.

Clarke, R. S. J. (ed.). *Proceedings and Reports of the Belfast Natural History and Philosophical Society, 157th–161st Sessions*. Belfast, 1983.

Cook, Alan H. *Edmond Halley: Charting the Heavens and the Seas*. Oxford: Clarendon Press, 1998.

Cordingly, David. *Under the Black Flag: The Romance and the Reality of Life Among the Pirates*. San Diego: Harcourt Brace, 1997.

Craton, Michael. *Testing the Chains: Resistance to Slavery in the British West Indies*. Ithaca: Cornell University Press, 1982.

Craton, Michael, and James Walvin. *A Jamaican Plantation: The History of Worthy Park, 1670–1970*. London: W. H. Allen, 1970.

Crouse, Nellis M. *The French Struggle for the West Indies, 1665–1713*. New York: Octagon Books, 1966.

Cundall, Frank. *The Governors of Jamaica in the Seventeenth Century*. London: West India Committee, 1936.

Dallas, R. C. *The History of the Maroons, From Their Origin to the Establishment of their Chief Tribe at Sierra Leone: Including the*

Expedition to Cuba, for the Purpose of Procuring Spanish Chasseurs, and the State of the Island of Jamaica for the Last Ten Years; with a Succinct History of the Island Previous to that Period. Volume I. London: Longman and Rees, 1803.

Davies, K. G. *The Royal African Company.* New York: Octagon Books, 1975.

De Jong, Karsten. "The Life of John Bourden." *Irish Migrations Studies in Latin America*, 8, no 1 (August 2012).

Delle, James A. (ed.). *Out of Many, One People: The Historical Archaeology of Colonial Jamaica.* Tuscaloosa: University of Alabama Press, 2011.

Dobson, David. *Scottish Emigration to Colonial America, 1607–1785.* Athens: University of Georgia Press, 2004.

Dunn, Richard S. *Sugar and Slaves: The Rise of the Planter Class in the English West Indies, 1624–1713.* New York: Norton, 1973.

———. *A Tale of Two Plantations: Slave Life and Labor in Jamaica and Virginia.* Cambridge, Mass.: Harvard University Press, 2014.

Earle, Peter. *The Wreck of the Almiranta: Sir William Phips and the Hispaniola Treasure.* London: Macmillan, 1979.

———. *Treasure Hunt: Shipwreck, Diving, and the Quest for Treasure in an Age of Heroes.* New York: Thomas Dunne Books, 2007.

Ehrman, John. *The Navy in the War of William III, 1689–1697: Its State and Direction.* Cambridge: Cambridge University Press, 1953.

Foster, Thomas. *The Postal History of Jamaica, 1662–1860.* London: Robson Lowe, 1968.

Galenson, David W. *Traders, Planters, and Slaves: Market Behaviour in Early English America.* Cambridge: Cambridge University Press, 1986.

Gaspar, David Barry. *Bondmen and Rebels: A Study of Master-Slave Relations in Antigua.* Durham: Duke University Press, 1993.

Hardy, John. *A Chronological List of the Captains of his Majesty's Royal Navy; Commencing 1673, and Brought Down to 1783.* London, 1784.

Jones, J. R. *The Anglo-Dutch Wars of the Seventeenth Century.* London: Longman, 1996.

Konadu, Kwasi. *The Akan Diaspora in the Americas.* New York: Oxford University Press, 2010.

Law, Robin. *Ouidah: The Social History of a West African Slaving "Port,"* *1727–1892*. Athens: Ohio University Press, 2004.

———. *The English in West Africa, The Local Correspondence of the Royal African Company of England*. 3 volumes. Oxford: Oxford University Press, 1996, 2001, 2006.

Leslie, Charles. *A History of Jamaica, from the Earliest Accounts, to the Taking of Porto Bello by Vice-Admiral Vernon. In Thirteen Letters from a Gentleman to his Friend*. London: J. Hodges, 1740.

Little, Benerson. *The Buccaneer's Realm: Pirate Life on the Spanish Main, 1674–1688*. Washington, D.C.: Potomac Books, 2007.

Livingston, Noel B. *Sketch Pedigrees of some of the Early Settlers in Jamaica*. London, 1909.

Long, Edward. *The History of Jamaica . . . In Three Volumes*. London, 1774.

Marley, David. *Wars of the Americas: A Chronology of Armed Conflict in the New World, 1492 to the Present*. Santa Barbara: ABC-CLIO, 1998.

———. *Pirates of the Americas, Volume I: 1650–1685*. Santa Barbara: ABC-CLIO, 2010.

Marx, Robert F. *The History of Underwater Exploration*. New York: Dover, 1990.

———. *Port Royal: The Sunken City*. Southend-on-Sea: AquaPress, 2003.

Mathurin Mair, Lucille. *A Historical Study of Women in Jamaica, 1655–1844*. Kingston: University of the West Indies Press, 2006.

McCrady, Edward. *The History of South Carolina Under the Proprietary Government, 1670–1719*. Volume I. Berwyn Heights, Md: Heritage Books, 2008.

Murray, Hugh. *An Encyclopedia of Geography, Comprising a Complete Description of the Earth, Physical, Statistical, Civil, and Political*. London: Longman, Rees, Orme, Brown, Green, & Longman, 1834.

O'Donoghue, John. *Historical Memoir of the O'Breins; with Notes, Appendix and a Genealogical Table of their Several Branches*. Dublin: Hodges, Smith, & Co., 1860.

O'Malley, Gregory E. *Final Passages: The Intercolonial Slave Trade of British America, 1619–1807*. Chapel Hill: University of North Carolina Press, 2014.

Palmer, Colin A. *Human Cargoes: The British Slave Trade to Spanish America*. Urbana: University of Illinois Press, 1981.

Pares, Richard. *Yankees and Creoles: The Trade Between North America and the West Indies before the American Revolution*. Cambridge, Mass.: Harvard University Press, 1956.

Parker, Matthew. *The Sugar Barons: Family, Corruption, Empire and War in the West Indies.* New York: Walker, 2011.

————. *Willoughbyland: England's Lost Colony*. London: Windmill Books, 2015.

Pawson, Michael, and Buisseret, David. *Port Royal, Jamaica*. Kingston: University of the West Indies Press, 2000.

Peckham, Howard M. *The Colonial Wars, 1689–1762*. Chicago: University of Chicago Press, 1964.

Pincus, Steve. *1688: The First Modern Revolution*. New Haven: Yale University Press, 2009.

Preston, Diana and Michael. *A Pirate of Exquisite Mind: The Life of William Dampier, Explorer, Naturalist and Buccaneer*. London: Corgi, 2005.

Price, Richard. *Maroon Societies: Rebel Slave Communities in the Americas*. Baltimore: Johns Hopkins University Press, 1996.

Purkiss, Diane. *The English Civil War: A People's History*. London: Harper Perennial, 2007.

Rediker, Marcus. *Between the Devil and the Deep Blue Sea: Merchant Seamen, Pirates, and the Anglo-American Maritime World*. Cambridge: Cambridge University Press, 1996.

————. *The Slave Ship: A Human History*. New York: Penguin, 2007.

Renny, Robert. *An History of Jamaica: With Observations of the Climate, Scenery, Trade*. London: Cawthorn, 1807.

Ritsema, Alex. *Pirates and Privateers from the Low Countries, c. 1500–c. 1810*. The Netherlands: Deventer, 2008.

Robertson, James. *Gone Is the Ancient Glory: Spanish Town, Jamaica, 1534–2000*. Kingston: Ian Randle, 2005.

Routh, E. M. G. *Tangier: England's Lost Atlantic Outpost, 1664–1684*. London: John Murray, 1912.

Sanders, Richard. *If a Pirate I Must Be: The True Story of Bartholomew Roberts, King of the Caribbean*. London: Aurum, 2008.

Saunders Webb, Stephen. *Lord Churchill's Coup: The Anglo American Empire and the Glorious Revolution Reconsidered.* New York: Alfred A. Knopf, 1995.

Schama, Simon. *Rough Crossings: Britain, the Slaves and the American Revolution.* London: BBC Books, 2006.

Schomburgk, Robert H. *The History of Barbados: Comprising a Geographical and Statistical Description of the Island; A Sketch of the Historical Events Since the Settlement; and an Account of its Geology and Natural Productions.* London: Longman, Brown, Green, and Longman, 1848.

Shumway, Rebecca. *The Fante and the Transatlantic Slave Trade.* Rochester: University of Rochester Press, 2011.

Smallwood, Stephanie E. *Saltwater Slavery: Middle Passage from Africa to American Diaspora.* Cambridge, Mass.: Harvard University Press, 2007.

Smith, Abbot Emerson. *Colonists in Bondage: White Servitude and Convict Labour in America, 1607–1776.* Chapel Hill: University of North Carolina Press, 1947.

Smith, William. *A Natural History of Nevis, and the Rest of the English Leeward Charibee Islands in America.* Cambridge, 1745.

Stern, Malcolm H. "Portuguese Sephardim in the Americas." In Martin A. Cohen and Abraham J. Peck, eds., *Sephardim in the Americas: Studies in Culture and History.* Tuscaloosa: University of Alabama Press, 1993.

Stoney, Samuel Galliard. *Plantations of the Carolina Low Country.* New York: Dover, 1977.

Sweet, James H. *African Healing and the Intellectual History of the Atlantic World.* Chapel Hill: University of North Carolina Press, 2011.

Swetschinski, Daniël, and Schönduve, Loeki. *De Familie Lopes Suasso, Financiers van Willem III.* Zwolle: Waanders, 1988.

Talty, Stephen. *Empire of Blue Water: Henry Morgan and the Pirates Who Ruled the Caribbean Waves.* London: Pocket Books, 2007.

Taylor, Eric Robert. *If We Must Die: Shipboard Insurrections in the Era of the Atlantic Slave Trade.* Baton Rouge: Louisiana State University Press, 2006.

Ten Broeck Runk, Emma. *The Ten Broeck Genealogy: Being the Records and Annals of Dirck Wesselse Ten Broeck of Albany and His Descendants.* New York: De Vinne Press, 1897.

Thompson, Alvin O. (ed.). *In the Shadow of the Plantation: Caribbean History and Legacy.* Kingston: Ian Randle, 2002.

Tinniswood, Adrian. *By Permission of Heaven: The Story of the Great Fire of London.* London: Pimlico, 2003.

———. *The Verneys: A True Story of Love, War and Madness in Seventeenth Century England.* London: Vintage, 2008.

———. *Pirates of Barbary: Corsairs, Conquests and Captivity in the Seventeenth-Century Mediterranean.* Leicester: Charnwood, 2010.

Trevelyan, G. M. *England under the Stuarts.* London: Folio Society, 1996.

Vallance, Edward. *The Glorious Revolution, 1688: Britain's Fight for Liberty.* New York: Pegasus, 2008.

Waller, Maureen. *1700: Scenes from London Life.* London: Sceptre, 2000.

Wigfield, W. Mcd. *The Monmouth Rebels, 1685.* Gloucester: Alan Sutton, 1985.

Wills, John E. *1688: A Global History.* London: Granta Books, 2002.

Wodrow, Robert. *The History of the Sufferings of the Church of Scotland from the Restoration to the Revolution.* Volume IV. Glasgow: Blackie & Son, 1835.

Zahedieh, Nuala. "The Merchants of Port Royal, Jamaica, and the Spanish Contraband Trade, 1655–1692." *William and Mary Quarterly,* 43, no. 4 (October 1986): 570–593.

———. *The Capital and the Colonies: London and the Atlantic Economy, 1660–1700.* Cambridge: Cambridge University Press, 2012.

UNPUBLISHED PAPERS AND DISSERTATIONS

Brooks, Baylus C. *Quest for Blackbeard: The True Story of Edward Thache and His World.* University of Florida, 2016.

Clifford, Shelia Alicia. *An Analysis of the Port Royal Shipwreck and its Role in the Maritime History of Seventeenth-Century Port Royal, Jamaica: A Thesis.* Texas A&M University, May 1993.

Donachie, Madeleine J. *Ceramics at Port Royal, Jamaica, 1655–1692.* Texas A&M University, August 2001.

Galante, Luis Augusto Vicente. *Port Royal: O Meio Circulante de uma Colônia Inglesa no Século XVII.* Universidade de Brasilia, 2008.

Jamaican National Heritage Trust, Archaeological Division. *Preliminary Archaeological Appraisal Report, Sutton Land Settlement, Clarendon.* Kingston, May 2008.

Johnson, David A. *Port Royal, Jamaica, and the Slave Trade: A Thesis.* Texas A&M University, December 2000.

Matlock, Julie Yates. *The Process of Colonial Adaption: English Responses to the 1692 Earthquake at Port Royal, Jamaica.* Eastern Kentucky University, 2012.

Moore, Amanda. *Maroon Societies in Brazil, Jamaica and Mexico.* Syracuse University Honors Program, Spring 2005.

Parrish, David. *Jacobitism and the British Atlantic World in the Age of Anne.* University of Glasgow, October 2013.

Ramsden, Daisy K. *"Generally Fitt to be Trusted": Social Networks and the Moral Economies of Sugar Plantations in Early Anglo-Jamaica.* Dalhousie University, Halifax, Nova Scotia, July 2015.

Thornton, Diana Vida. *The Probate Inventories of Port Royal, Jamaica: A Thesis.* Texas A&M University, August 1992.

Wirtenburger, Kathryn. *The Jesuits in Jamaica.* Loyola University Chicago, 1942.

Online Resources

British History Online, *Calendar of State Papers Colonial, America and West Indies: Volumes 10, 11, 12, 13, 14, 20, 33.* http://www.british-history.ac.uk/search/series/cal-state-papers—colonial—america-west-indies.

Geesnmore, A Family History. https://geesnmore.wordpress.com/charles-gee-bridget-neville/neville-family/

History of Clarendon, National Library of Jamaica. http://www.nlj.gov.jm/history-notes/History%20of%20Clarendon.pdf

Jamaica Observer. http://www.jamaicaobserver.com

Jamaican Ancestors of Anthony Maitland. www.anthonymaitland.com

Jamaican Family Search. http://www.jamaicanfamilysearch.com

A Parcel of Ribbons: Eighteenth Century Jamaica Viewed through Family Stories and Documents. aparcelofribbons.co.uk

The Peerage. http://www.thepeerage.com/p1441.htm

Port Royal Wills and *Port Royal Probate Inventories.* Texas A&M University. http://nautarch.tamu.edu/portroyal/archives/wills.htm and http://nautarch.tamu.edu/portroyal/archives/invent.htm

Real Estate Transactions before 1692 Earthquake, City of Port Royal, Jamaica. University of Florida, Digital Collections. http://ufdc.ufl.edu/

Three Decks: Warships in the Age of Sail, https://threedecks.org/

Voyages: The Trans-Atlantic Slave Trade Database. http://www.slavevoyages.org/_Emory University.

Acknowledgments

While researching and writing this book, I received considerable help from others. Bruce H. Franklin, my publisher, offered encouragement and advice throughout, while the work of Noreen O'Connor-Abel, the copyeditor, and Tracy Dungan, the cartographer, have proved invaluable.

I also owe a debt of gratitude to the archivists at the National Archives in Kew, the Somerset Heritage Centre, and the Maritime Museum in Greenwich. Kaitlyn Pettengill, the digital services archivist at the Historical Society of Pennsylvania, Lisa Caprino, the reference services assistant at the Huntington Library in California, Audene Brooks of the Jamaica National Heritage Trust, and Marianne Martin, the visual resources librarian at the Colonial Williamsburg Foundation, were extremely helpful, while Kimberly Blackwin of the Jamaica Archives and Records Department went out of her way to suggest previously unanticipated lines of inquiry which considerably furthered my research.

I would also like to thank Anne Westmacott and Jane and David Hughes for reading through various drafts during the writing process, and Vanessa, my wife, and Emily, my daughter, for their patience and support. I dedicate this book to John Tridgell, a dear childhood friend whose untimely death earlier this year left a void in the lives of so many.

Index